The Last
FLANNELLED
FOOL

Also by Michael Simkins:

What's My Motivation
Fatty Batter
Detour de France

The Last
FLANNELLED
FOOL

My small part in English cricket's demise and its large part in mine

MICHAEL SIMKINS

EBURY
PRESS

5 7 9 10 8 6

This edition published 2011
First published in 2011 by Ebury Press, an imprint of Ebury Publishing
A Random House Group company

The Random House Group Limited Reg. No. 954009

Addresses for companies within the Random House Group can be found at
www.randomhouse.co.uk

A CIP catalogue record for this book is available from the British Library

The Random House Group Limited supports the Forest Stewardship
Council (FSC®), the leading international forest certification organisation.
Our books carrying the FSC label are printed on FSC® certified paper. FSC
is the only forest certification scheme endorsed by the leading environmental
organisations, including Greenpeace. Our paper procurement policy can be
found at www.randomhouse.co.uk/environment

Printed and bound by CPI Group (UK) Ltd, Croydon, CR0 4YY

ISBN 9780091927547

For Mike Nunn
who loved his cricket ...

Then ye returned to your trinkets; then ye contented
   your souls
With the flannelled fools at the wicket or the
   muddied oafs at the goals.

Rudyard Kipling
'The Islanders'

Acknowledgements

My thanks to everyone who has helped me, by accident or design, in the writing of this book, not least the wonderful writers on the game whose prose I mined: in particular, David Foot, David Frith, Gerald Brodribb, Stephen Chalke, Christopher Lee, John Barclay, Stephen Bates, Ian Jack, Alan Ross and the incomparable RC Robertson-Glasgow.

My special thanks to Andrew Goodfellow, James Gill, Mari Roberts, Liz Marvin, Rob Boddie, Peter Hayter, George Dobell, Duncan Steer, Andy Nash and, last but not least, my wife Julia. Certain names and locations have been changed. My apologies in advance to anyone who feels they should have got a referral to the third umpire.

I

Cork Suckers

'Mr Simkins?'

'Yes?'

'Would you follow me in and remove your trousers please?'

How often in my life have I fantasised about such a scenario as this? A smiling young woman in a nurse's outfit, beckoning me into a curtained-off area. Yet now I was actually here, the reality was very different. Be careful what you wish for, is the moral, I suppose.

I followed her into a small consulting room and sat down heavily on a table covered with a length of paper towel.

'I'll tell the consultant you're here. She's just having a look at the results of your scan. Won't be a moment.' She pulled the curtain behind her. I was alone.

I spent some minutes on the edge of the table, swinging my bare legs back and forth. God, were these things really mine? They looked much older. Like my dad's legs, in fact. And what about those gnarled, camel-like appendages on the end? Had they really carried me successfully back and forth across the cricket pitches of southern England for fifty-three years? Now any similarity to feet, either living or dead, was entirely coincidental.

What on earth had happened? How had they – and I – gotten so old? One famous theatrical impresario with a special interest in finely-turned calves had once described the lower half of my torso as possibly the finest example he'd ever witnessed in forty years of blundering unannounced into actors' dressing rooms on first nights. Now look at them. Sagging muscles, mottled skin, kneecaps the size of small grapefruit; and was it my imagination, or was that the first sign of varicose veins threading their way up the side of my left thigh?

This is how middle age occurs, I suppose. It creeps up on you while you're looking the other way. One moment you're fine, just the odd niggle here and there, nothing that can't be cured with a quick squirt of Ralgex. You still back yourself to cover those twenty-two precious yards before cover point can pick up and throw. No problem.

Then suddenly you find injuries and afflictions that once came and went in a matter of weeks are outstaying their welcome. You have to get up to pee in the middle of the night where once you could make it through till John Humphrys. You find yourself deciding to wait for the next bus rather than sprint for the one pulling away ahead of you. And you daren't stay up listening to the Test match coverage from overseas tours because you know if you don't get a full eight hours you'll be utterly unfit for purpose the next morning. Before you know it you look in the mirror and realise you've turned from Andrew Strauss into Johann Strauss.

I should have known this would happen. After all, the great Australian cricketer Bobby Simpson had discovered how a mere decade or so can change a man without him realising, and his story is a salutary lesson for anyone hoping to cheat Anno Domini. One of the great batsmen (and incidentally the only international cricketer with the nickname Simmo), he'd been called out from retirement in the 1970s by the Australian Cricket Board to take over a rookie national squad recently ripped and skinned by the defection of most of the best players to the Kerry Packer's World Series. It had been ten years since he'd last played.

Now aged forty-one, Simpson found his body could no longer stand the daily ordeal. In particular, somebody had made off with his legendary slip specialist's hands and replaced them with a pound of Palethorpe's pork sausages.

All these thoughts and more swirled through my brain as I sat waiting for the consultant. In only a few more weeks the 2010 cricket season would be beginning, and I had to get fit for the opening match. After all, the Harry Baldwin Occasionals were counting on me. As well as being the founder member and presiding genius, I had been their opening batsman for nearly three decades, and the notion of my not facing the first ball against the small Sussex innings of Burpham come 11 April was simply unimaginable. Whatever the injury that had caused me to be here today, sitting in my underpants at the Royal Free Hospital in Hampstead, I wasn't yet ready to throw in the cricketing towel. Anno Domini might have defeated the other Simmo, but I wasn't coming so easily.

The curtains swished back to reveal a careworn female doctor in her early thirties. She was carrying about a hundredweight of files in her hands, and even as she entered the cubicle an electronic pager hanging from her neck was already jittering into life. She dumped the files on a nearby chair and looked at me for the first time.

'Sorry to keep you, Mr Simkins. We're particularly busy just now. Let me have a quick look at your notes before I inspect your foot.'

While she riffled through my notes, I allowed myself to drift back into another doleful reverie. I should have seen this moment coming. It was brutally apparent, not only in the bedroom mirror but in everything around me. Even the conversation.

Take that incident of the young female stage manager, for instance. I'd long ago got used to the idea that there were some people on this earth too young to share the memorable moments of my own life – Neil Armstrong walking on the moon, or Sussex winning the John Player League – but only recently I'd been chatting to some young thing at a theatrical party, effortlessly dazzling her with my repartee and extensive repertoire of showbiz anecdotes, and then, just as I approached the punchline with one of my very best, the one about Tommy Cooper and the mayor of Blackpool, she'd uttered those fateful words:

'Sorry, Simmo, but who's Tommy Cooper?'

'Who's Tommy Cooper?' That sums up how decrepitude creeps up on you. You think everything is still just as it was, that nothing has changed, and then your body asks, 'Sorry, who's Tommy Cooper?'

'Mr Simkins?' The consultant was staring at me.

'Sorry, yes?'

'I said, just sit back and let's have a look at you. How on earth did you manage to damage your toes like this? Playing sport?'

Playing sport. If only. The tale of my bruised toes was more like something out of an episode of *Some Mothers Do 'Ave 'Em*. It had happened the previous weekend when I'd come down early in the morning to make a cup of tea. In my stupor I'd forgotten that we were having a new kitchen floor put in, and thus I ended up walking toe-ends first into a stack of loose planks. My subsequent expletives would have done justice to the England dressing room moments after Nasser Hussain had returned from being wrongly given out first ball in an Ashes decider.

The consultant inspected the joints in turn, kneading them

intimately. Her diagnosis was as crisp and unadorned as an innings by Paul Collingwood: unless I took things easily for the rest of the summer the problem could descend from acute into chronic. When I asked for a summary in layman's terms, she answered that the toes would hurt like buggery and were going to be a complete bastard to calm down.

'You see the thing is, at your age, a simple case of trauma can activate conditions that would otherwise be lying dormant. That's why we recommend people over fifty should wear slippers round the house. Have you got a pair you can use?'

Slippers. That final, dread emblem of everything elderly and past its sell-by date. And now it was being applied to me. Flaccid penises and winceyette pyjamas, and old dodderers shuffling along trying to move leaves out of their way with the aid of a walking stick with a rubber bung on the end. If the rest of my life was going to be spent wearing slippers, I might as well book into Dignitas now and have done with it.

'... So I'm afraid you'll be taking it easy for the whole of the summer, otherwise this could become a permanent problem.' The consultant was already gathering up her papers and glancing at her watch. 'Complete rest from strenuous physical activity. No jogging, hang-gliding or rock-climbing for at least five months. Still, I'm sure you can manage without that, can't you?' She offered up a watery smile. 'OK, you may get dressed now.'

It was just as I was leaving the room that she'd glanced down at her case notes again. Sex, Age, Religion, Smoker or Non-smoker ... the fancies and foibles of my life laid out in tiny ticks and crosses. Funny, if only I'd dressed a bit more hurriedly I might even have made it out of the cubicle. But, of course, I now have to sit down to put my socks back on – which is why I was still there when she delivered her coup de grâce.

'It says here you play cricket.'

'That's right. I run my own team. The Harry Baldwin Occasionals. We have our first match in a few weeks but I'll be taking it gently, don't worry. At my age it's time I fielded at slip in any case.'

Her mouth pursed into a tight, humourless smile.

'I'm afraid you won't be doing anything of the sort,' she said. 'Not if you don't want this to be your last season. Definitely no cricket. You'll have to do a spot of umpiring or something.'

'No cricket?' The room swam before my eyes.

'Absolutely not. Never mind. You'll just have to watch some instead. I'm sure that can't be too disagreeable. I'm a cricket widow myself.' Seconds later she was through the curtain and lost from view, leaving me to contemplate the wreckage of my summer.

When I got home, my wife Julia was on the floor doing some Ciffing behind the radiator covers. Cleaning surfaces with a leading proprietary cream cleaner is always her way of relaxing when she's got something on her mind. I knew she was anxious to hear my news.

'So? What's the prognosis? Are they broken?'

'Not exactly. But they might as well be.'

I relayed the consultant's diagnosis as best I could.

'Oh well,' said Julia. 'Does that mean we get our weekends back? You'd better tell your teammates in the Baldwins …'

Telling Julia was one thing. Breaking the news to the Harry Baldwin Occasionals was quite another.

Ironically, it had been Julia herself, a woman who didn't know her Mongoose from her Gray-Nicolls, who perhaps had best summed up the team I played for each weekend, and for whom the sport still meant so much. 'Meaningless encounters between groups of pathetic, middle-aged, sexually inadequate no-hopers' had been her affectionate pronouncement, not only on my own team, but also by extension the entire demi-monde of Sunday afternoon cricket and its panoply of spavined enthusiasts.

I'd started the team back in the 1980s, mainly in a reflex response to a general disaffection with a game that, at both social and professional levels, had seemed to me to be losing much of its quirkiness and eccentricity. Quirkiness and eccentricity were two nouns rarely used to describe the professional game these days, but they still perfectly summarised the group of old schoolfriends, out-of-work actors and assorted loafers who had coalesced into my own team as it now stood. I'd run the Baldwins as a personal fiefdom for much of the last two decades. Now aged fifty-three, my best days might be behind me, but still I liked to think of myself as the club's totemic opening batsman and guiding spirit.

Like endless teams of social cricketers the length and breadth of the country, a summer without a regular weekly game was unthinkable. For six days of each week we might be loving husbands, doting fathers and trusty breadwinners, but for a few precious hours each weekend cricket still surpassed all other considerations. Each of us gathered round the table of the upstairs bar in the Cork & Bottle in Westbourne Grove for our pre-season get-together had once dreamed as children of making a career in the professional game, and although we'd long been disabused of absurd notions, we still regarded the mere thought of being paid to play cricket 24/7 as the nearest thing to nirvana one could ever imagine.

Most of us had started with this tiny spluttering club back in our twenties when we could barely muster one reliable vehicle between us, but many were now grandparents with second homes and expensive divorce settlements to service. Yet, although the smell of expensive aftershave had long since given way to embrocation, we still wore that, dim, far-off look in our eyes at the prospect of once more hearing leather on willow.

Now today, on the first Sunday in March, just as every year, we were camped in the small, scrubby room in west London for our AGM, about to prepare for our forthcoming campaign. All the usual suspects were arrayed: the men with whom I'd spent the best years of my adult life, to the exclusion of all else – eschewing family parties, wedding invites, anniversaries – driving the length and breadth of the south-east in pursuit of the game we loved, revelling in each other's triumphs, consoling one another in defeat and, above all, reassuring ourselves that, however inept we might be, there'd always, *always* be next season.

I guess there's never a good time to break bad news. With our fixture secretary, Chris Buckle, still handing round the pristine sheets of A4 (opening match versus Burpham, near Arundel, 11 April), I interrupted and asked my confederates to brace themselves. I gave a brief résumé of my collision with both planks and consultant. Afterwards there was a silence.

'So you're out for the whole season?' said Chris, after a long pause.

I nodded. 'I'm afraid so, fellas. You're going to have to try and get on without me. I'm sorry if this is a shock but I've only just found out myself. I'm taking a year off.'

A second, longer pause followed while my teammates took in the full significance of my announcement. Our all-rounder, 48-year-old male nurse Steve Sarstedt, began idly knotting an empty crisp packet, while forensic-archaeologist-turned-forcing-middle-order batsman Phil Coleridge idly swilled some ice cubes round the top of his Coke glass. Les Sweeney, part-time barman and senior pro, reacted to this cricketing bombshell as he always does, namely by going for a leak. In truth, knackered bladders are an occupational hazard of social cricket among the over-50s. Never mind sightscreens and boundary markers, a functioning urinal within fifty yards of the wicket is our top priority these days in arranging the itinerary.

Finally Chris cleared his throat and offered up a suitable homily, one he must have honed throughout many years as chairman of his local Rotary Club.

'Oh well, not to worry, you weren't exactly troubling the scorers much last year, were you ...'

Nonetheless, there were all the usual commiserations. 'It won't be the same without you, Simmo,' said Phil. 'Would you like to do a spot of umpiring?' said Steve. By contrast, Les Sweeney showed just the sort of wily psychology that has brought him nearly four hundred career wickets during his time with the club: 'If you're not using your bat, any chance I could borrow it for the summer?'

But at each new entreaty I shook my head. Instead, I wished them well. This time next year I'd assuredly be up at 'em as if nothing had changed. In the meantime, *bon voyage*.

'So you're not even going to pay us a visit?'

I pursed my lips. 'I don't think so, fellas,' I said. 'Too painful. No point in me mooning about on the boundary, trying to pretend I'm still part of the action and offering to field whenever one of you gets caught short. In any case, you don't see injured professionals hanging about on the sidelines once they're crocked. They concentrate on their rehabilitation and return fitter and keener. Next season will come round soon enough. I don't want to become an object of pity in the dressing room.'

Les downed his pint. 'You should have thought of that back in 1985,' he said.

At the end of the meeting Chris Buckle found me in the street. The light was failing and it was beginning to spit with rain.

'Mike, are you sure you're OK?' he asked, putting a Rotarian arm on my shoulder.

'I'm fine,' I replied.

'But how are you going to get by without any cricket?' he continued. 'This is just not like you. There's a lot of summer ahead. I'm worried. What are you going to do with yourself?'

'I'm not going to be without any cricket,' I answered. 'On the contrary, I'm going to sample more than ever. I've decided to take the summer off and spend some time watching the professional game. It'll be just like the old days. I'm going to travel around, maybe go up north, revisit old haunts, catch a bit of whatever takes my fancy. Recharge my cricketing batteries. Check out some fixtures I've never managed to get round to. See if I can rediscover what it was that drew me to the sport in the first place. I'm looking forward to it, Chris, I really am.'

'Have you told Julia?'

'Absolutely, and what's more, she wants me to go. Couldn't be more encouraging.'

Suddenly and without warning, Chris enveloped me in a huge, endless, rib-cracking bear hug. Eventually he released me and stepped back. There were tears in his eyes. And mine as well.

'Well,' he said simply. 'Good luck. To both of you.'

Moments later his car roared away towards Bayswater. As he drove away I was reminded of novelist Susan Ertz's famous comment: 'Millions long for immortality who do not know what to do with themselves on a rainy Sunday afternoon.'

I pulled up my coat collar and set off for home.

2

Hims Ancient and Modern

'If I knew I was going to die today,' wrote mathematician GH Hardy, 'I think I should still want to hear the cricket scores.'

When was the precise moment I'd fallen out of love with the professional game? How could it be that eight little words, 'Please do not move behind the bowler's arm', sentiments that once would have seemed like the sweetest love poem, now conjured up all the allure of a wet weekend in Uttoxeter?

Who can say? You might as well ask when is the specific time that passionate lovemaking atrophies into sterile silence round the kitchen table, the only acknowledgement of a once raging inferno a mumbled request to pass the salt?

Any marriage guidance counsellor will tell you it's not a switch flicked, but an intricate and minutely incremental process. Sex once a night becomes once a week, then once a month, until before you know it you're both sitting watching *Have I Got Old News For You* and grumbling about who's got the zapper. By then it's too late to recall the frenzied passion that had first brought you together.

Yet passion it undoubtedly had been. Once a night and twice at weekends, I was a flannelled Barry White, with the professional game my first, my last, my everything, and a source of unending fascination whatever her mood and however attired, whether in the starched linen of the championship, the ornate splendour of Test cricket or the satin hot-pants of the International Cavaliers.

It gave me my first role models: Graham Roope and Colin Dredge; it offered me my first friends in the knot of loafers, deadbeats and assorted human detritus that sloshed around the windswept terraces of county cricket grounds, quietly following the domestic game through sun and rain, and it even supplied my first schoolboy crushes, many of whom are still alive and in senior commentary positions.

Looking back, my life then could be securely classified into two distinct eras: BC and AD – Before Cowdrey and After Denness. A moment of juvenile epiphany – watching Colin Milburn batting against the mighty West Indies on my parents' old black and white telly one evening in 1966 – was all it took. 'We applauded him all the way, for here was a man who could steal a West Indian heart,' said Garry Sobers afterwards of Milburn's heroic 94. And the heart of a fat, freckly nine-year-old newsagent's son from Brighton as well, Garry.

This brief exposure lit a blue touchpaper that flared for forty years. Soon I was watching cricket whenever I could, either on the box or at nearby Hove where I could gaze upon my heroes in person. In between times I began to follow the other county scores contained in the various newspapers on our shop counter. Even when my dad's newsagent and tobacconist bowed to inevitable economic pressure and began displaying girlie mags, my gaze rarely strayed beyond John Thicknesse or Crawford White.

As with any sporting obsession, it was the best of times, it was the worst of times. Nobody would pretend that watching county cricket was unalloyed pleasure. There were some terrible days as well, of course there were – freezing to death on splintered benches, huddling under brollies, sitting on piles of damp news-paper surrounded by discarded fruit pie wrappers, listening to fellow enthusiasts slowly boring themselves – and you – to obliv-ion, waiting for pitch inspections that never arrived and players' autographs that never materialised. I particularly recall one day of watching Leicestershire's Barry Dudleston and Mick Norman put on about thirty in an entire two-hour session against a trundling Sussex attack, an ordeal of such unutterable bleakness that suicide seemed an attractive option.

But even those moments seemed to be part of some ancient tribal ritual, one in which we could all share and which tied us ever closer to the timeless rhythms of the game. We were suppli-cants of the true faith, one that could not be experienced unless you gave yourself wholly over to its embrace. And faith was what mattered – faith that the sun would come out, that Dudleston would get an edge, that the old bloke in the next row would stop jawing on about his all-time Leicestershire XI and keel over with a heart attack.

Those of us gathered in the pews of the popular seating may not be the high priests of the sport – they were the ones on the TV or out on the field of play, or sitting in inebriated splendour on committee-room balconies – but we were at the very least handmaidens, each with our own small part to play in the preser-vation of time-honoured rituals, and with our own religious icons too: tartan Thermos flasks, cartons of orange drink and Ginsters pasties. We even possessed our own prayer book, in the guise of our trusty and indispensible *Playfair Cricket Annual*.

Even during the winter months my passion remained unabated. Dark frosty nights would find me with my radio under the bedclothes, twiddling away for all I was worth, following my flannelled superheroes as they did battle for justice in far-off countries of which I knew little except what I'd gleaned through the effusive prose of Alan Whicker.

If anything the game's enchantment was only heightened at dead of night. I spent entire weeks suffocating in the dark with my ear pressed to the tiny speaker, trying to follow events at Brisbane or Port of Spain through a jumble of static and competing foreign stations as the fragile reception slewed back and forth across the airwaves. There was something deeply magical about listening to the subtle blend of Brian Johnston mixed with snatches of Keith Fordyce and late-night chat shows in German.

Even that wasn't sufficient. After all, there were still those periods of the year, mostly late autumn and early spring, when there was no cricket to follow. What to do? My solution was a sinister foretaste of the brain-numbing cyberculture that engulfs today's computer-obsessed youth. I began playing my own Test series, first with dice and a pencil, then later with the aid of my prized Owzthat set, its tiny metal rollers perfectly replicating the deeds of my heroes in miniature.

It was the perfect fantasy world, one I could take with me wherever I went. But in order not to besmirch the clean, clear definitions of my real-life heroes, I devised a parallel world of imaginary cricketers, mirror images of the real things, whose destinies I could control with a flick of the wrist. These facsimile protagonists soon became as important as the real thing. By the age of twelve I had not only a full set of Test-playing nations but seventeen domestic counties as well: in total amounting to over two hundred imaginary cricketers. My virtual world reached its apogee in 1970 when, in an attempt to replicate the MCC tour to Australia (captain, Ray Illingworth of Leicestershire), I simultaneously took my own imaginary Owzthat MCC tour (captain, Eric Smith of Essex) on an identical itinerary: five tests, plus games against the various states, and even opening with a facsimile curtain-raiser against what I called 'Sir Robert Bateman's Governors XI'.

I had no idea of who Sir Robert Bateman might be, nor why he had been knighted, nor of whom he was governor, but never mind: the match seemed to add authenticity and verisimilitude, and that was all I required. Having completed my series (England winning 5–0), while following avidly the real thing (England winning 2–0), I filled in the long wearisome weeks before the start of the new domestic season by writing in fountain pen a 170-page book about my imaginary tour, having purloined one of my dad's old accounting ledgers for the purpose.

The result was *OFF TO AUSTRALIA*, with lavish colour illustrations in crayon. I still have the book now, admittedly with the spine falling apart and the pictures now heavily smudged by being badly stored inside mouldering banana boxes in the attic. Forty years on it seems incredible that I should have devoted such immense time and energy to such a pointless and exhaustive literary project. Yet I obviously enjoyed doing it. On the final page, I summed up Eric Smith's successful tour thus:

> *So we look back at the end of a good, exciting tour. England have proved they can muster up a very strong side if they choose, and it is a great shame, but frankly, Australia have not got enough good players.*

Reading it now, it's obvious that even then I'd spent too many hours reading EW Swanton.

By now I was straying further afield than merely Hove – to places such as Eastbourne, Hastings and Tunbridge Wells – and I made my first trip up to Lord's, when my brother's best friend, John Muxlow, took me to the home of cricket to see my beloved

Sussex play Lancashire in the 1970 Gillette Cup final. The crushing disappointment of seeing my local heroes so summarily swept aside in this sporting Valhalla was one of my first brutal lessons in life. Nice guys didn't always finish first. I cried myself to sleep that evening.

With each passing season my devotion grew stronger. In 1971 I watched my first three-day match in its entirety from first ball to last without missing a single delivery. I also began to read voraciously about the history of the professional game: *The Cricketer* magazine, of course, and its more sober-suited and egalitarian rival, *Cricket Monthly* – but also old books, biographies and tour diaries, each chronicling deeds and careers now half buried in the hurly-burly of the modern game. The roots of the sport proved both rich and nourishing to my adolescent sensibilities, and soon the names of Hobbs, Hammond and Hutton were as familiar to me as Barrington and Knott.

Most exotic of all was *The Book of Cricket* by CB Fry. Originally published in 1899 in sixteen weekly parts, the compendium edition was as big as a tea tray and could break your foot if you dropped it. Inside its shiny, yellowing pages were nearly two hundred prints depicting giants of the Victorian game. The towering figure of WG Grace on page 1, of course (his photograph was titled simply 'Jupiter'); Sussex's own local legend Prince Ranjitsinhji, or little Alfred Shaw, the most economic bowler in history, who'd started life as a crow-scarer. With their buckskin boots, raffish straw hats and straining cummerbunds, they more resembled explorers trying to locate the source of the Orinoco than county cricketers. To a teenager with a taste for high drama, it seemed all wonderfully romantic.

While I was still growing up, my obsession retained a juvenile charm about it, yet once the hormones kicked in, I realised the high price I was paying for my sporting myopia. With my schoolboy contemporaries running as hard they could towards sex, drugs and rock and roll, I was still firmly stuck in Sussex, rugs and sausage rolls. Nothing sums up my sexual and cultural dwarfism more than an encounter I had with a girl called Melissa in my mid-teens. She had bright pink hair, wore Kickers and smoked roll-ups, and danced at parties without any apparent self-consciousness, while I had an acrylic sweater with a pattern along the top and a side parting that made me look like a junior member of the current Conservative cabinet.

It took me all night to pluck up courage to join her on the dance floor, yet never has a chat-up technique been more stillborn.

Me: (jigging beside her) 'Who do you most admire?'

Melissa: (without looking up) 'Thin Lizzy. You?'

Me: 'I'm rather partial to Derbyshire's Fred Swarbrook.'

Eventually my obsession with cricket gave way, albeit temporarily, to one with acting, and for my two years spent at RADA my obsession had to jostle for space with iambic pentameters and ballet tights. Yet even now I found solace from restoration comedy and dialect classes by popping along to St John's Wood for a couple of hours. I still made it to the odd Test match as well, but it was essentially in the quieter atmosphere of domestic cricket that I found the perfect antidote for the mad, competitive world of acting. Few were the professional setbacks in this notoriously overcrowded profession that couldn't be improved by a couple of hours watching Vincent van der Bijl bowling to Nigel Briers in the sunshine of a metropolitan evening.

Once I'd graduated and began working, my ardour found fresh expression. The odd, unpredictable life of a jobbing actor proved an ideal occupation for the cricket lover, allowing me to act by night and watch cricket by day. I was also working at many of those exotic, holy places that until then I'd only dreamt about: Harrogate, Guildford, Kidderminster. One evening while performing pantomime at York Theatre Royal I even spotted Yorkshire's totemic middle-order batsman Phil Sharpe watching me from the stalls. It was, needless to say, a moment of unbearable sweetness.

And what things I saw during my time travelling. Basharat Hassan thumping sixes into the river Severn at Worcester; Mike Procter bombarding the beer tents in Sunday League matches at Cheltenham College, or Derek Underwood weaving his magic down at Canterbury. While working there in rep, I'd also managed to attend the great Sir Frank Woolley's memorial service at the nearby cathedral, where many of the old cricketers I'd only previously read about tottered in like living waxworks.

The main address that Saturday morning was provided by the mighty Swanton himself. Ray Illingworth once said of him, 'He was so snooty he wouldn't even travel in the same car as his chauffeur', and looking up at him now in the pulpit, illuminated by a shaft of watery autumn sunlight reflected through some high-up stained glass, he really did seem like God's cricketing representative on earth.

During my twenties and thirties the experiences continued thick and fast, at places as widespread as Colchester and Weston-super-Mare. I once even stood next to West Indies and Essex fast bowler Keith Boyce at a urinal in Leigh Delamere services.

In the summer of 1979 it appeared as if I might have found my perfect partner. With Canada pitched against mighty Pakistan in a qualifying match of the Cricket World Cup, I persuaded a Canadian actress with whom I was in rep at Leeds, and whose company I craved, to go with me on a hot date to Headingley to see her national team in action.

Indeed, for an improbable hour or two it looked like both Canada and I were in for an unlikely result. When Imran Khan's first ball of the match was confidently put away for a boundary by opener Glenroy Sealey, Melody became convinced this was the cricketing equivalent of a first-pitch home run in her beloved baseball.

'Wow, a home run first up,' she cooed when the ball smacked against the advertising hoardings just by where we were sitting. She even gave my arm a squeeze. By the time Canada had hoisted the hundred for the loss of only two wickets, so enveloped in the unfolding drama had she become that I was already contemplating which hotel we might check into at close of play.

Alas, it was to be the high point of our relationship, both cricketing and romantic. Canada eventually went down by eight wickets, and by the time Clive Lloyd hoisted the trophy aloft three weeks later, Melody was going out with another actor in the company, who had a sports car, his own flat in Belsize Park and noticeably bigger parts. Nonetheless I take some comfort from the fact Melody has remained in the UK and still watches cricket to this day. I still see her occasionally at The Oval.

I was back at the Headingley ground two years later to witness two days of 'Botham's Test' and later the same autumn stumbled upon the world's first ever floodlit cricket match at nearby Scarborough, a hastily arranged and highly disorganised affair between the local club side and a 'Rest of the World' XI at the town's dilapidated football stadium. Dennis Lillee wore three sweaters that night and opened the bowling with an apple. And in 1993 I found myself at Manchester to witness for myself the ball of the century.

Curiously, my sojourn at Old Trafford remains the only day's cricket I've ever witnessed in person at Manchester – yet fortune had decreed that I should be there, albeit in among a party of deep-sea fishermen from Fleetwood. The main source of their entertainment that day was a chubby, bleach-haired leg-spinner with a stud in his ear, whose name nobody knew and who was fielding directly in front of us at deep midwicket.

Eventually he was summoned up to bowl his first delivery in Test cricket in England. The rest, as they say, is history, or, more specifically, two decades of humiliation and misery for all cricket-loving poms. I'll never forget the silence all around me that followed Mike Gatting thirty seconds later as he made his bewildered way back to the pavilion. Moreover, the smell of fish that had previously clung to me had been replaced by something far worse. The smell of fear. It took two long decades and Shane Warne's retirement from the international arena to evaporate.

By now I was playing myself every Sunday, initially with various theatre-based teams and latterly with my own outfit – the Harry Baldwins, its name taken from one of the more rotund participants in CB Fry's famous book. Thus for the next two decades the professional game provided a perfect yin to my participatory yang.

It might have gone on like this forever: playing every Sunday, watching every other day and working in between. But it was all beginning to change. Within weeks of England's high-water mark, the moment when Michael Vaughan lifted the famous old urn at The Oval in that giddy, glorious, improbable summer of 2005, Murdoch moved in with his monetary chainsaw. Things were never to be the same again.

The loss of the transmission rights for terrestrial stations, first the BBC and latterly Channel 4, was a shock of seismic proportions, and I suspected its absence might have had a lot to do with my recent disaffection with the game. Sky took over the coverage at the end of that summer, and it's hard to enjoy the party when after years of having your glass permanently topped up you're suddenly being asked to stump up eye-watering sums to consume the same stuff at a pay bar. Like Richie Benaud, I'd always considered myself a dedicated free-to-air man, and when Channel 4 lost its franchise to Sky at the end of 2005 I'd decided not to go with it. In neither sex nor cricket have I ever had to pay for my fun, and I was blowed, so to speak, if I was going to start forking out now.

My self-imposed exile may have been tough, but in truth it had also come as something of a blessed relief. Even Channel 4's modish coverage had proved too rich a sauce for my simple palate. I'd been weaned on televised cricket on the BBC back in the 1970s and 1980s when all that was needed for a rewarding life was a couple of cameras and Peter West. All these skittering graphics, Hawk-Eye, Hot-Spot, ball charts, endless inane prattle and tumbling computer graphics was like being force-fed chocolate liqueurs having only ever known beef tea. The result could only ever be chronic cultural indigestion.

Where, for instance, were the simple things in life: like Jack Bannister or Tony Lewis? Life didn't seem the same without his grinning ventriloquist doll face, jaw clacking happily away as if Ray Alan had his arm up the back of his shirt. I felt the absence of Peter West's fumbling incompetence even more keenly, playing miniature facsimiles of the choicest batting strokes with the stem of his pipe as he posed another impenetrable question to a tired and emotional Denis Compton.

And most of all, I missed Jim Laker: the man whose laconic style and deadpan delivery summed up the voice of television coverage to an entire generation, the pundit who turned moroseness into an art form, the old pro who during the Gillette Cup semi-final from Taunton once coined the sublime phrase, 'That's a fittin' endin' to Dennin's innins.'

In his pomp, entire sessions of live TV coverage could pass without my beloved Jim uttering a single word by way of comment or observation. Some days when he was at the mike I used to get up and slap the side of my parents' TV set with the palm of my hand in the belief that the sound had failed. But no – by putting my ear to the tiny speaker in the front fascia I could tell all was still well. I could hear him breathing.

That generation of commentators had grown up in a world where understatement was the cornerstone of civilised behaviour. You only had to look at the footage of Laker's legendary spell against Australia at Old Trafford in 1956 and then compare it to Freddie Flintoff's unalloyed celebrations to see how much things have changed. Compared to the orgy of bottom-slapping and cheek-kissing that's unleashed nowadays, Laker's celebration of each new scalp has all the joie de vivre of a man who's just completed his income tax returns. A casual brush of calloused fingers through Brylcreemed hair, a desultory handshake with any teammate who could be bothered to walk over to congratulate him, and that trademark lopsided grin of his, one that I'm convinced was later cannibalised to spectacular effect by the actor who played Blakey in *On The Buses*. 'That's made my day, that has, Miller … '

I still enjoyed playing, of course, perhaps more than ever, but meanwhile the news from the professional game wasn't good. Ball tampering, allegations of match fixing and generally yobbish behaviour both on the field and off were all debasing the currency of the international game, while the intricate workings of the domestic version was being ruined by meddlesome tinkering. In any case, there was so much cricket on offer that you could barely clear your plate before being offered yet more to gag down. Endless identical contests, no sooner completed than forgotten, and competed for by players who looked utterly shagged.

My 1979 Wisden, bought in an era when my passion had been at its fullest flood, ran to 1,159 pages. Thirty years on the publication was a third heavier. The gentle fabric of the game, too, was tearing like tissue paper. Cavalry twill trousers and ancient Hush Puppies had given way to sharp suits and gleaming Rolexes, and where once the sport had been run by wise old ex-players and devoted amateurs with a keen sense of tradition and of the fragile nuances of the sport, they'd been replaced by shadowy businessmen with dodgy moustaches and a great deal too much hair gel for their own good.

The nadir had surely been Texas oil magnate Allen Stanford. Ian Botham's rictus grin at the launch of Stanford's cricketing super-circus, when Botham was forced to open suitcases full of dollar notes for the waiting news cameras as if caught in some nightmare version of *Deal Or No Deal*, said everything about how the wholesome-faced beauty I'd once adored was transforming itself into a tired old slapper. No wonder I'd sought refuge in the timeless charms of the Baldwins versus Upper Dicker.

Worst of all, the quaint, archaic progress of the domestic game had been thrown into a food blender. Two divisions, central contracts; now you needed not so much a *Playfair Annual* as a pocket calculator and a degree in international employment law to understand what was going off out there. When Mike Atherton said, 'County cricket in its present form fulfils no useful purpose whatsoever. Very few people turn up to watch, it doesn't prepare people for a higher level of cricket and it doesn't attract television deals or sponsorship', he wasn't so much putting the knife in as performing a sensitive post-mortem.

And what of the players themselves? At the last few games I'd watched in person I'd hardly recognised anyone on either side, a problem seemingly shared by their captains. Sussex stalwart Ken Suttle had once played 429 consecutive games for his county without missing a single match, longevity that would not only be impossible in the game nowadays but positively ridiculed. Only recently I'd watched a match between Kent and Worcestershire in which Yasir Arafat had bowled to Mohammad Ali, and I'd only been mildly surprised when informed they weren't the originals.

In truth I still dropped in at the odd Test match from time to time, but now it was usually courtesy of a spare ticket or, in the case of my swankier acquaintances, as part of a private hospitality box. And very lovely it had been too – after all, who but the most dedicated curmudgeon wouldn't enjoy watching Sachin Tendulkar and Jacques Kallis from the finest vantage point, and surrounded on all sides by bacon baps and free champagne. But it was the older, subtler textures of the domestic game that I'd mislaid or forsaken along the way. And it was these I most craved.

Curiously, it had been my wife Julia who'd suggested my pilgrimage.

'I think you should definitely go,' she'd said out of the blue, a few days after my hospital appointment.

'Why? You've never wanted me to before.'

'You've had a face like a slapped arse ever since this foot problem flared up,' she explained. 'I know you're going to suffer from not being able to play for the Baldwins, and I know you've offered to help around the house and stuff, but you're not exactly Barry Bucknell, are you? I'm not sure the infrastructure can take much more of it. So I was thinking – even if you can't actually play, that's no reason why you shouldn't watch some. Think of it – you'll be in the fresh air, you can travel around, you'll be spending time meeting lots of old duffers like yourself talking about the Duckworth-Lewis method and why creams are superior to whites and all that old guff you've tried to interest me in over the years. Lord's is only down the road, isn't it? And The Oval – you used to love going there. They're still only a tube ride away, and you've got two perfectly good feet. One perfectly good foot.'

'You really mean it?'

'Of course. Travel. Go to some nice places. Revisit some old haunts. Maybe even go up north. Why not? Take your flip-flops with you and get some nice warm sunshine on those poor old toes of yours. It'll do you good.'

I finally read the message not from her words but from her face. The firm but pleading expression which told me that a fit and healthy Simmo would be a treat for her to have in the house all summer, but in my current hobbling, maudlin, stone-kicking, self-pitying state she'd rather have me out from under her feet. And a small generous part of her heart could hear the quiet howl of my restless, middle-age wanderlust. She knew that the only real cure for her man's heart was walkabout.

Perhaps the summer of 2010 would be – quite literally – just what the doctor ordered.

Cricket fans – sports fans in general, it's fair to say – are notoriously superstitious. Nothing happens by accident. I'll only make runs if I'm wearing my lucky blue underpants. Jimmy Anderson will take a wicket if I take the recycling out before making myself a cup of tea, while if I put my right cricket sock on before my left, Les Sweeney will actually be able to land the ball on the cut strip. That's why we wear a look of perpetual anxiety. Even the most prosaic domestic ritual becomes pregnant with karmic significance, and the slightest divergence can spark a batting collapse or provoke a disastrous mid-pitch mix-up.

With the opening day of the season fast approaching, the resolve for my odyssey, one that had been inked in pen in our desk diary for weeks and had seemed such a liberating idea, began to weaken. I'm not by nature a plucky traveller, and now I began to fret. What if? What if my car broke down? What if there were roadworks on the Harrogate bypass? What if I missed a crucial career-changing job interview through being up at Aigburth watching Lancashire versus Hants, or returned from Trent Bridge only to find Julia had run off with a sound recordist? Worse of all, what if I went searching for my old flame and greatest love, only to find she'd turned into a wrinkled old hag?

I needed a sign.

And then on Sunday 4 April, the weekend before the start of the domestic season, Julia returned home from a shopping trip, dragging a huge canvas bag of plants behind her. 'I couldn't resist it,' she said. 'I've been to that new florist at the top of our road. They've got a 10 per cent sale. And you'll never guess!'

'What?'

'Well, I was in there having a nose round the back and I overhead the owner saying that she's John Emburey's daughter. Isn't he a famous cricketer?'

John Emburey! One of my greatest heroes, a player I'd seen countless times for Middlesex and England. I hurried up the road, my spirits dancing. A quick look at the owner's profile through the glass confirmed the rumour – put her in synthetic white flares and a 1980s figure-hugging shirt and it could be the great man himself, bowling England to glory down under. A few minutes' chit-chat with the proprietor confirmed it. What's more, she assured me that Embers occasionally did deliveries himself if they were short-staffed.

As if that wasn't sufficient celestial encouragement, there was the name of the shop itself. Achillea. Even my second-form grammar-school Latin was equal to this. Of course: Achillea, a plant that heals wounds.

Julia was right. My relationship with the game I once craved in all her carnal lipstick-slashed glory had been dulled by too much stale custom. It was spring. Regeneration and renewal was all around. Surrey were playing Derbyshire in five days' time. Perhaps my gammy foot was not a crisis at all, but an opportunity.

I hurried home with a spring in my half-step. Julia had unpacked all her purchases and was on her knees and cleaning the oven. I handed her a magnificent bouquet of exotic blooms gift-wrapped in raffia and pearly white paper and stood back.

'What's made you so happy?' she asked. 'It's the first time you've cracked your face in a month. Have you made your decision?'

I framed my lips and tongue into an impression of David Lloyd's trademark Accrington drawl.

'Start the car!' I yelled.

3

We Can't Go On Like This

Whenever anyone asks me – which admittedly isn't often – which single day I recall with most fondness of all the hundreds, possibly thousands, I've spent watching the best-loved game, one occasion always springs to mind as a contender.

Forty-odd years on, I can still summon up that faint, shivery frisson of … what? So many emotions are blended into those few hours, it's difficult to disentangle the component parts: a moment in time in which sporting obsession and wide-eyed wonder blended in one glorious spiritual confection, combining romance, hope, ambition, independence and burgeoning sexuality.

It was 22 August 1972. I was fifteen. It was the summer holidays. Donny Osmond's 'Puppy Love' had just been displaced as the UK pop number 1 in favour of Alice Cooper singing 'School's Out', and with remarkable (and unique) timing, I'd just had my first chaste kiss with girl called Eileen.

1972 was also an Ashes summer, with England competing against Australia in a pulsating five-match series that was even now boiling up to a thrilling climax at The Oval. Best of all, my parents had agreed I could travel unchaperoned from Brighton, where we lived, to south London to attend the game in person – a mind-boggling distance of fifty miles. What's more, my best mate Andy King was coming with me.

I'd watched every delivery throughout the summer on the

box with Andy. A natural Darbishire to my lumbering Jennings, he and I had become inseparable after discovering we shared both a love of the game and an astonishing ineptitude for playing it. But our real bond had been forged earlier that summer after Andy's dad returned from a business trip to Singapore with a battery-operated bowling machine.

Made in Taiwan, of low-grade pink plastic and looking much like the children's game Mousetrap, it consisted of a rotating plastic paddle controlled by feeble springs, which every ten seconds or so swatted a succession of tiny ping pong balls a distance of about three feet (considerably less if there was a draught).

'All the thrills of the real thing' proclaimed the blurb on the box cover. The illustration on the front box may have shown cricketers Fu Man Barrington and Mao Tse Dexter, but nonetheless it seemed impossibly sophisticated to our juvenile eyes.

No matter that the batteries barely lasted fifty swats per pair, or that the bat with which you were supposed to hit the fragile missiles had a plastic welt on the handle sharp enough to remove your fingers if held for more than a couple of minutes – it was still an automatic bowling machine, and throughout that long hot summer we'd mirrored the real-time series in the attic bedroom of Andy's parents house in Hove, complete with piping adolescent facsimiles of live commentaries from John Arlott and Richie Benaud.

Our replica series had been abandoned only when, in attempting to swing one of these piffling missiles towards his mum's wardrobe (Simkins' half century brought up in 51 minutes, 78 balls, two sets of Eveready SP2s), I toppled over and landed with my full weight on his parents' double bed, snapping all four legs simultaneously. After this the game was confiscated, the bedroom door firmly locked and the idea of funding our trip to see the real thing in London mooted, if only to protect their furnishings from further destruction.

For me, that day in London was what I imagine most teenagers must experience at their first visit to Glastonbury – heat, crowds, liberty, overpriced drinks and overflowing toilets.

Of events on the field I recall little. The exoticism of being in the capital without parental supervision obliterated all else. After-wards we found ourselves on a murderously muggy evening sitting in Kennington Park, a dilapidated area of grass opposite the entrance to Oval tube station. I can't even recall how or why we ended up there, but inevitably it would have had much to do with our reluctance to accept that our day of sublime adolescent free-dom was nearly over and soon we must catch the train home.

We sat there for an hour or more, surrounded by the pungent aromas of cannabis and dog shite, while all round us the commuter traffic of London roared and growled. For a provin-cial boy who still polished his shoes and whose concept of juve-nile insubordination was leaving his greens uneaten on the side of the plate, our brief sojourn here told us everything about the big city: mad, bad and dangerous to know. We left it sunburned, exhausted and very, very happy.

It was on the station concourse back at London Bridge while waiting to catch the train home that Andy had first noticed it: a tall soundproof glass cubicle, looking for all the world as if some-one had tried to convert a telephone box into an automatic photo booth. '*Calibre Auto-Recordings*' proclaimed a sign above the door. '*Make your own record. Preserve your voice for posterity! Instant collection! Amaze Your Friends! Take your audio memories home with you.*' The cost would clean us out of every last penny provided by our anxious parents for use in case of emergency. We opened the door and shouldered our way in.

The moment we inserted our precious funds in the slot a vinyl disc no bigger than a saucer flopped down on to a battered turntable and began to revolve. We inclined our lips towards a Bakelite microphone, its mouthpiece smelling of rancid onions and stale tobacco smoke, and waited instructions. A moment later a cumbersome stylus clattered down on to the edge of the record and a green light illuminated above our heads. '*Speak Now*' it flashed.

But how best to use our precious ninety seconds of fame? Sing a chorus of 'Puppy Love'? Tap out the opening bars of the BBC cricket theme, 'Soul Limbo', with our Biros on the metal console? We had to think fast; already five of our precious seconds had elapsed, the needle engraving our nervous coughs and whispered mutterings on to the vulcanite.

In the end we settled upon impersonating our broadcasting heroes by attempting to recreate a brief summary of the day's play in the style of Arlott and Benaud. Long before the two minutes were up we were even boring ourselves, and having allowed our feeble impressions to mutate into grotesque parodies, collapsed into raucous laughter. I still have the disc somewhere, and whenever I want to conjure up the memory of that day, all I have to do is to play it and I'm immediately back there, hearing again our hoarse adolescent voices against the distant rumble of a London station at rush hour.

Whether or not this summer would provide anything quite so piquant was impossible to say, but at least I was starting in the right place: in the shadow of the famous gasometer.

The cricket writer RC Robertson-Glasgow once observed, 'Essentially, The Oval is truer London than Lord's. The Oval, as it were, is Dickens; Lord's is Thackeray.' This unassuming old stadium, which had started life as a market garden, has always had an air of the true man-in-the-street about it, which is why, in contrast to its swanky neighbour across the Thames, it's such a jolly and thoroughly unstuffy place to watch the game.

It's also presumably why Philip Larkin chose to mention it in his paean to the millions of ordinary common or garden citizens who died in the trenches of the Great War. His poem, 'MCMXIV', details the thousands of Tommies waiting to go over the top to certain death at the hands of the machine gunners:

> *These long uneven lines*
> *Standing as patiently*
> *As if they were stretched outside*
> *The Oval or Villa Park.*

Larkin obviously knew his cricket and his London. You couldn't imagine the thousands of debenture holders up at St John's Wood being persuaded to go over the top unless there was a glass of Chablis and a voucher for a free golfing weekend waiting for them on the far side. But that's The Oval for you – with even its original turf, transported from nearby Tooting Common, it's as London as jellied eels and a pint of Pride.

What's more, it has stayed that way, despite numerous attempts to gentrify it. The Oval authorities might glance enviously at sleek new cricketing arenas such as the SWALEC Stadium in Glamorgan or the magnificent, if antiseptic, Rose Bowl in Southampton, with their elegant curves, ergonomic seating and spanking new transport links, but there's still something splendidly old-fashioned and slightly piecemeal to the place back home. The Oval resembles a cross between Lord's scruffier sibling and a luxury housing development in Bulgaria. Which is just how its patrons like it.

Nonetheless, The Oval's place in the development of the game is unequalled – for it was here, not at poncey Lord's, that the first Test in England (and only the second in history) was played, in 1882: and if that isn't enough sporting heritage for one venue, it also staged the first FA Cup Final. The Oval may wear its heritage lightly, but there's history in every brick and every blade of grass – even in the gasometer, which was built back in 1858.

Best of all, the ground's unglamorous atmosphere has given it one other unique advantage over its metropolitan rival, in that it's usually here rather than Lord's that our national side do their best work against the Aussies. The mere sign of an MCC 'egg and bacon' tie has usually been enough to send the most self-reliant English player reaching for the Sanatogen, but the atmosphere at Kennington is so relaxed it's inspired everyone from Jack Hobbs to Jonathan Trott to drop their shoulders and, in the current modish phraseology, 'express themselves'.

Thus there have been any number of memorable Ashes moments here, many of which have featured uncustomary England victories and almost all of which have entered cricketing mythology, including Len Hutton's record-breaking 364, Don Bradman's last-innings duck and the return of the urn in 1953 after an absence of nineteen years. More recently Messrs Vaughan and Strauss have both held the urn aloft within five short years of one another.

Perhaps because the ground has changed so little, it positively encourages a little gentle daydreaming. Sit in front of the famous old gasometer for long enough and, with the addition of a little too much sun and a little too much lager, it's still almost possible to imagine what it must have been like here back on the greatest occasion of all – that dank August afternoon in 1902 and the apogee of all Ashes contests.

The details of this sporting jewel have been well chronicled, but a bit like Geoff Hurst's goal or Olga Korbut's Olympic gymnastic display, a re-run through the archive is still guaranteed to thrill, however hackneyed the story has become and however many times it's trotted out.

The game itself, the fifth and final Test of that particular series, actually had little at stake. England had lost the urn earlier in the summer despite having what is still considered to be the finest side ever assembled, yet for this final match they pulled out all the stops. Led by the autocratic AC McLaren, and with such luminaries as Surrey's favourite son Tom Hayward and a whole host of stars from Fry's *Book of Cricket* (though sadly, not Fry himself), an England victory was considered the most likely option – and not a moment too soon if national pride was to be retrieved.

Consequently, in the best national tradition, England imploded on sight and found themselves in the fourth innings hopelessly adrift on 48–5, chasing 263 for victory. So parlous was the position that by the time Gloucestershire's dynamic all-rounder Gilbert Jessop strode out to bat at number seven, many of the more elderly members had already left the ground, so upset were they at the prospect of seeing their national side humiliated again.

What they missed as they hurried for their trams and buses was the most exciting hour or two in all Ashes history, at least until Edgbaston in 2005.

Somebody once said of this preternaturally aggressive player, 'If you can imagine Clive Lloyd as small, white and right-handed, then you've got Gilbert Jessop.' And much like Lloyd was later to accomplish on so many occasions, Jessop too seemed to turn an entire match with just a few minutes of concentrated brilliance. Whatever his mindset that afternoon, destiny was in his eyes. He reached his century in 75 minutes, with at least one of his boundaries being caught by his colleagues on the players' balcony, and when he was eventually out with the score at 187, he'd made one of the fastest centuries of all time.

Yet England was still nearly 80 short, and suddenly had another fresh mountain to climb. So emotionally charged were those final frenzied overs that virtually every ball has since become imbued with rumour and myth.

Whenever I consider the events of this improbable day, I find myself wondering how much of it was true. Was the tension really so unbearable that a spectator was seen to gnaw through the handle of his umbrella? And what about the most famous reported quote in all cricket history? Whether or not George Hirst actually said to his batting partner Wilfred Rhodes 'We'll get 'em in singles' is a matter of eternal dispute among cricketing cognoscenti (he later claimed he said nothing of the sort), but the fact is, the two batsmen did get 'em in singles, and as a result England won a pulsating, and wholly improbable, victory.

If I seem unduly obsessed by the desire to separate fact and fiction, the reason is simple. In my early twenties I came within minutes of meeting someone who had witnessed the innings and whom I knew would have been happy to share his memories. The crowd watching Jessop had included a little lad called Ben Travers, later to become the world-famous author of the Aldwych farces but who was then merely a cricket-mad 15-year-old living in London. Nearly eight decades later, the 94-year-old playwright came to see a Saturday matinee performance of a play I was appearing in at the Roundhouse in Camden Town, and what's more, the director had announced that the cast would be invited to have tea with this comedy colossus after curtain down.

I'd read somewhere of Travers's attendance all those years ago at The Oval, and on the Friday night before the performance I could hardly sleep for excitement. Just think – I was actually going to shake the hand of someone who had been there and seen it. Never mind questions about comic timing or how to get an exit round, I had a hundred questions of my own – and the first one was about the brolly chewer.

Alas. If you want to make God laugh, tell him your plans. An hour before curtain up, one of the cast members began projectile vomiting in the dressing room. Within half an hour the leading actress was in the next toilet cubicle, neither of them able to stray more than five metres without risking biological catastrophe. Travers arrived by private car at 2.15pm, was helped into his seat and sat there just long enough to be told along with about three hundred other disappointed theatregoing punters that the matinee had been cancelled due to collective food poisoning.

My only sight of him was from my dressing-room window, as he stood on the other side of a thin pane of glass, being helped into the back seat of a London taxi. I would have broken the window and clambered out after him in my costume if I'd been feeling up to it, but by then I was heading for the loo myself. Travers died soon afterwards, and my last, best chance to touch the hem of cricketing history disappeared with him.

'Every Spring is the only spring – a perpetual astonishment.' So wrote the author Ellis Peters. The first day of a new season is annual proof of her dictum. For anyone longing to hear bat on ball after months languishing indoors, it's hard to believe when you wake up on the opening day that you might be watching live cricket by lunchtime.

Being there to witness the very first delivery of the new season is a time-honoured ritual among fans. No matter that it's always a wide half volley outside the off stump accompanied by an extravagant shouldering of the bat. However predictable, that small, sacred event always provokes a grateful cheer from those blessed enough to be there in attendance. 'Thank God,' the cheers seem to say. 'We made it. We're still alive.'

The event teemed with extra significance in 2010, it being preceded by a brief ceremony in remembrance of Sir Alec Bedser, the great Surrey bowler who had died aged ninety-one, and whose great flat feet, indomitable physique and *Dixon of Dock Green* stoicism summed up the spirit of post-war English cricket: dogged and uncomplaining, even in pursuit of a hopeless cause. Perhaps it's no wonder that if you put his surname through spellchecker you come up with 'bedsore', for the great man had as much sex appeal as the average NHS ward. But boy could that man bowl. During my teenage years of voracious reading on the game's history, sometimes it seemed as if Bedser was the only decent fast bowler we had between the end of Larwood and the arrival of Trueman.

But anyone questioning his right to be mentioned in the same breath as these greats of the game need check only this one statistic: that he dismissed Don Bradman no fewer than six times in Test matches, more than anyone else. No further questions, m'lud.

If I was excited at the prospect of my forthcoming odyssey, it was nothing to the frenzy out on the streets. After weeks of speculation, Prime Minister Gordon Brown had dissolved Parliament, pitchforking the nation into three weeks of fevered election campaigning, in what was already predicted to be the closest contest for a generation. As I walked to my local Tube station I was assailed on every street corner by the face of David Cameron declaring, 'We can't go on like this'. Labour, too, had been busy: for anyone prepared to look up from their morning paper, Gordon's tailor's-dummy smile blazed out in teeth eight foot wide. It looked even less convincing than on the television.

At least events at The Oval retained a sense of sobriety. In fact, the brief ceremony to the great Surrey hero proved a suitably sombre and touching interlude. With the club flag flying at half-mast from the pavilion turret, the two sides, Surrey and Derbyshire, each sporting black armbands, lined up to face the stand that bears his name, and for a full minute both players and spectators stood together in mute tribute. It was a poignant reminder of the departing winter some had not survived.

Not that I saw any of it. What with finding my binoculars, digging out some hand-warmers, retrieving my knitted balaclava from the attic and heating up a flask of warming oxtail soup, by 10.45 I was still labouring up the escalator at Oval.

It was in every way a strange beginning to the season. Traditionally the opening day is for diehards only, staring blankly out from the stands as driving rain and wind strafes the sodden playing surface. But not today. The man ahead of me on the up escalator was wearing crocs, and at the tiny sweetshop by the station entrance there was a queue for ice creams. Just to complete the air of unreality, the girl who sold me my entrance ticket greeted me in a strong southern American drawl. 'You have a nice day now, y'hear?' she said as I rattled through the turnstiles. These were already odd times.

Within a few minutes I'd taken my seat. In particular I was pleased to see that Derbyshire had won the toss and were already prospering at 42–0, for in recent years the county has been struggling on from season to season amidst a barrage of calls for them to be subsumed or wound up. If they could win here, it would do their case for continued sovereignty much good, as well as providing them with their first championship victory in SE11 for forty-four years.

Not that Surrey was going to allow such a cataclysmic event to occur without a fight. At the pavilion end, the giant South African pace bowler André Nel was working up a lively pace against the Derbyshire captain, Australian Chris Rogers, while at the other end the attack was being carried by a young bowler named Linley, which presumably explains the constant calls to 'Come on, Viscount' from a nearby Surrey supporter.

Nel is everything you want from a quickie: fast, furious and looking as if he'd just love to headbutt both teams if only he could find permission somewhere in the ECCB rules and regulations. He once explained his incendiary temperament thus: 'Günther is a guy who lives in the mountains and doesn't get enough oxygen to the brain and it makes him go crazy. As soon as I get thrown the ball, it's like a little switch in my head, and Günther takes over,' he explained. If so, Günther was certainly enjoying his outing today after months locked in the basement.

What with the sunshine, the crowd and this lovely old ground with its implicit invitation to sit back and daydream, my spirits soared. I bought a lolly and noticed it actually trickling down the gap between forefinger and thumb within minutes of purchase. Normally on opening days you'd need to break it off with a screwdriver.

The only other occupant of my part of the ground was a Derbyshire supporter dressed from head to foot in his club's colours. With a leather skullcap pulled down over his head and an auburn beard spilling down his shirtfront towards an ample paunch, he could have earned a living as a lookalike for WG Grace or either of the Hairy Bikers. At least a third of his bottom crack was on full view to anyone sitting in rows B to P, a proportion that radically increased whenever he stood up, which was about twice an over.

Much of the reason for his movement was a young child, presumably his son (or grandson – it was impossible to tell), kneeling in front of him on the grass. The child was playing with a trio of string puppets, consisting of a witch, Donald Duck and Joe 90, all of whom were similarly kitted out in Derbyshire club colours.

The puppets proved strangely mesmerising. While his dad watched the cricket and worked his way steadily through a tin of shortbread, the child passed his time by continually draping his marionettes over the boundary boards, a noisy process rendered almost impossible by a stiff breeze that kept entwining the strings.

Every few minutes Joe 90 would be blown from his moorings, whereupon the child would reach over, retrieve his tiny chum and then try to untangle all the strings again prior to restoring him to his rightful position. Just as he'd get Joe 90 back into position, another gust would send either Donald or the witch sprawling on to the grass, and the whole lengthy procedure would begin afresh. In truth, I could have watched this all day and still considered my £15 well spent.

Inevitably it wasn't long before I got chatting to a nearby spectator, for if it's true that in England you're never alone as long as you want to talk about the weather, the cricketing equivalent is merely to request a look at a neighbour's scorecard. Hari Gupta was happy to oblige. He'd been here since before 10am. 'I love the game, I love everything about it,' he admitted as he rootled around in his haversack. So keen was he, he'd arrived in time to watch the players warming up.

'My friend, you can tell a lot by watching players warming up,' he assured me. 'This new team manager, Chris Adams, he had them running up and down the stands for nearly half an hour. I tell you, they'll do well this summer. Too much dead wood here last season. But now – ah-ha!' He cackled at the prospect. 'Imagine, running up and down the stands at 10am. Even Mark Ramprakash. This new regime means business, I tell you.'

Suddenly and without warning he lurched forward and grasped my hand. 'What I'm about to tell you is a most frightful story,' he muttered darkly. Even as he did so the sun went behind a cloud and a gust of wind swirled Joe 90 and Donald Duck into a new and complex carnal scenario. I felt like I'd been catapulted into an episode of *Tales of the Unexpected*.

Hari had been born in Uttar Pradesh. Nowadays he played for a local side in England, purveying slow medium pace with considerable success on Saturday afternoons. Or at least, he had until this last winter. At Christmas he'd returned to see his family in his homeland, when the taxi he was travelling in from the airport hit a herd of cows at 40mph.

'The driver, he had fallen asleep,' said Hari, shaking his head. 'Can you imagine what it is like to hit cattle at 40mph?'

I resisted the temptation to suggest it must have been offal, instead merely shaking my head in mute sympathy. 'Would you like to see what those animals did to me?' he continued. 'Prepare yourself, my friend.' Even as he spoke he was already pulling up the side of his sports shirt.

This sort of scenario – middle-aged men disrobing while telling me to prepare myself – has always held terrors for me, ever since a cricket-related incident back in my mid-twenties.

As Hari wrestled with his trouser belt, my mind flew back to August 1981.

At the time I'd been on a canal boat holiday on the river Severn with my girlfriend Abigail, and finding ourselves a few miles from a three-day championship match at nearby Cheltenham College, we'd hitchhiked the short distance from our mooring in Tewkesbury via a lift from a passing lorry.

We'd barely got up speed when our driver had started talking about how he'd just returned from a spell working in the United Arab Emirates, where he'd sustained himself throughout nearly three years in this alien culture by eating nothing but fried chicken.

What nobody had told him, he'd continued, was that in the UAE they inject their poultry with fast-acting growth hormones to maximise profit, and as a result he'd grown a pair of 36 DD breasts. With the lorry now doing a steady sixty along a dual carriageway and Abigail already fumbling for the passenger-door handle, he'd asked if we'd like to see them.

The incident remains the only time in my life that I've declined such an offer. But it was too late. One hand had already left the steering wheel and was even now unbuttoning his shirt, revealing a brace of bosoms that wouldn't have disgraced Jayne Mansfield.

I don't remember much more about the encounter, other than that we were eventually dropped, still alive and well, if somewhat breathless, on a roundabout a short distance from the ground. But of one thing I was sure – the episode had not only marred our day's cricket and subsequent cruise, but eventually given rise to feelings of sexual inadequacy on both our parts that led to the demise of the relationship some months later.

All this flashed before me now as Harry lifted up his shirt and pulled it high above his midriff. Good God. This was the last thing I wanted so early on in my odyssey. To my relief I found myself merely staring at a stitched zigzag that circuited his trunk like a huge zip.

'It gets worse,' he murmured. 'The passengers I was sharing the ride with, they were so incensed they beat up the driver in front of me. There I was, pouring with blood in the wreckage of this damned car, my life draining away, and all they could think of doing was getting out and kicking the driver. So you see, I am lucky to be alive. I consider myself a blessed man. My playing days are over, I have also taken early retirement, but at least I can watch all the cricket I like. Insha'Allah!

'And you know what?' he concluded as I returned his score-card with trembling fingers, 'I have been waiting all my life for this day. The moment when I could spend my days watching the game I love. And now I'm here there's nothing to watch. Look!' He produced from his trouser pocket a copy of the ubiquitous *Playfair* almanac, and began riffling through its coarse-grained pages until he found the fixture list.

'No county cricket here for the whole of June and July! Nearly nine weeks at the height of the summer, all of it given over to that bloody Twenty20.'

This was a theme I was to hear countless times throughout my travels. Admittedly from people in V-neck pullovers and sensible shoes rather than baseball caps and their jeans halfway down their knees, but still, Hari Gupta was merely the outrider for battalions of disgruntled cricket lovers I was to encounter the length and breadth of the country, each of whom viewed the 2010 itinerary with a blend of despair and fury.

I don't know quite why I decided to revisit nearby Kennington Park where my mate Andy and I had ended up after our day of teenage freedom back in 1972. Perhaps because I needed to walk off a burger I'd had as a snack, or perhaps because, delightful as the cricket was, I had no particular emotional investment in the outcome. Or maybe, as was so often to be the case this summer, I just wanted to reassure myself that my past was still alive and well.

Whatever the reason, I found my steps taking me out of the gates, on past the tube and back across the road for the first time in nearly forty years. Funny, I hadn't thought about this place for some time. Now, on a warm spring day, and with a leisurely afternoon before me, I found myself being drawn there.

Perhaps my memory of the park as a place of latent menace was aroused by some lingering trace of its infamous past. According to a notice board at the entrance, a gibbet used to stand in the south-east corner, from which highwaymen and diverse villains swung, to the general gaiety of the local community. The precise spot, last used in 1799, was marked by a modern wrought-iron fountain, which spluttered away noisily on this April afternoon, its drainage holes blocked by discarded juice cartons and fag ends.

Where now truanting teenagers did wheelies on chopper bikes and threw half-eaten McFlurries into the flowerbeds, the Methodist preacher John Wesley had once preached to a crowd upwards of 30,000, while later it had been the venue for what was described as a 'Monster Rally' by the Chartist movement during the turbulent times of 1848, when an entire social class attempted to secure a people's independent democracy. More recently, it was the starting point for the poll tax riots.

Most striking of all was a paragraph on the notice board suggesting an attraction left over from the Great Exhibition of 1853 was to be found here. 'Prince Albert Consort's Model Lodge', an example of futuristic housing for London's poor, had apparently been deconstructed brick by brick and moved to the park from Crystal Palace. The precise location was now obliterated on the accompanying park plan by the words '*Delroy Eats Pussy*' that had been oversprayed in black paint.

I set off enthusiastically. Eventually I spotted a beaten-up villa-cum-hut, with a gently sagging roof of lichen-encrusted slates, now in service as a café. The woman behind the counter seemed nonplussed by my enquiry as to whether this was Albert's lodge from the Great Exhibition.

'Oh, I don't think it can be love,' she replied. 'It's been here at least ten years. I'm so sorry.'

Having taken my order for a baked potato with double-deluxe cheese and bacon filling, she handed me a chunky plastic wafer, which, she explained, I should keep with me; it would start vibrating when the meal was ready for collection. I wandered back out into the sunshine and picked my way along a peeling balcony.

The only other occupant was a small, desiccated woman with permed white hair, blotchy skin and a frighteningly overshot jaw that made her resemble the bulldog in *Tom and Jerry*. She seemed immersed in her copy of the *Daily Mail*, but when I asked if I could share her table in the sun she assured me I could make myself at home, and even removed her handbag to allow me to shuffle alongside her. Her beige cardigan was neatly pressed despite having gravy stains on both sleeves, she had a faded nylon scarf round her neck, and her finger ends were delicately coloured with purple nail varnish.

'This is more like it,' I said.

She agreed it was. In between coughs she introduced herself as Helen and admitted that what with all the cold weather this was the first time she'd been able to leave her flat in weeks. When I asked if she knew the park well, she gave a rueful laugh and explained she'd known little else. Born in the flats opposite The

Oval ground, she still lived less than a thousand yards from where she was born.

Helen hadn't heard of the Chartists, nor of Wesley's equally famous congregation, but there was plenty she did know. 'Charlie Chaplin played in this park, how about that?' she said. 'He grew up just over there and used to bring his girlfriends here on a summer evening. And Bob Marley, he was here too, he played football over there while he was appearing in Brixton. Oh yes, this place has seen some stuff all right ... '

Closing her eyes, she turned her face to the sun. 'I've seen some stuff here myself,' she continued. 'I remember the Blitz. It was terrible. This whole area, well, they tried to wipe it from the face o' the earth. I'll never forget it.'

She had an alarming tale to tell. The park had suffered one of the worst civilian catastrophes of the entire war. 'There was a public shelter they'd dug just over there, and it took a direct hit. A hundred people were in there and they all copped it, poor buggers didn't stand a chance. Full of people it was, old folk, babies. They could only identify about fifty of the bodies, so we all had to wait to see who didn't come 'ome.'

I sat there trying to imagine the scene as she described it. Terrified civilians, collapsing walls, desperate attempts to pull loved ones clear from the rubble, and then the decision to bulldoze the whole thing into a mass grave and cover it with soil.

Helen seemed to catch my mood. 'Still, no use dwelling on it,' she said cheerfully. 'We had some good times an' all. Me and my mates, we'd go up to town on the bus to the Victoria Palace or the Palladium. I saw Liberace there twice, and Frankie Laine, we all stood along the back wall of the stalls. Kids today, all they know are drink, drugs, all getting off their faces – and they think that's happiness! We never had any of that, but we had

Johnnie Ray at the Palladium for two and six. I know which I'd prefer ... '

My plastic wafer jittered into life and began careering wildly across the table. By the time I'd collected my meal Helen had taken her cardie off and was scrutinising a photo of Gordon Brown announcing the date of the forthcoming General Election.

'Of course, it's going to be nothin' but the election now, is it?'

Had she made up her mind who to vote for, I wondered.

'Well I'm not voting for that bloody Brown,' she replied. Her principal objection to the incumbent PM turned out not to be his continuing support of the war in Afghanistan, nor the shocking state of the economy, but the fact that he resembled Hermann Goering.

'I mean, look at him,' she said, swivelling her newspaper round. 'I mean, every time I see him, I think he just looks like he's about to send the Luftwaffe over.'

Whether or not it was a coincidence, the opposite page had juxtaposed the PM with a picture of Goering himself, pinning medals on to a line of athletic-looking teenagers in serge shorts. But surely he couldn't be held personally responsible for how he looked? If that were the case, then flautist James Galway would surely have to be condemned in similar fashion for resembling the Yorkshire Ripper.

'I wouldn't mind if it were just him,' she continued, 'but I mean, look at this bloke.' She turned the page to reveal a photograph of the defence secretary Bob Ainsworth in conversation with some dust-smeared troops during a recent visit to Camp Bastion. 'Who does he remind you of?'

It was impossible to deny a likeness to Adolf Hitler.

'Well, there you are then. I mean, who'd have a toothbrush

moustache these days?' she said, warming to her theme. 'You're asking for trouble, aren't yer?'

In the distance I could hear the pavilion bell sounding to herald the start of the afternoon session. I gathered up my stuff and bade Helen goodbye. She shook my hand warmly. 'It's been lovely talking to yer,' she said. 'You take care of yourself and enjoy the cricket. Hope your team win.'

As I left the table I noticed a horse-racing supplement peeking out from underneath her paper. The Grand National was being run the following afternoon at Aintree and she'd circled the names of several runners and riders on a special race pull-out, which now fluttered about on the table next to her. Could she, as a parting gift, perhaps suggest a decent tip for the race?

'Well, now you're askin'. Helen thrust her jaw forward until it was nearly touching the tabletop. 'I mean, it could be anybody's, couldn't it. The thing to do is to choose an 'orse who's not in the betting but might get over. Hang on a moment, love, and I'll sort you something aht … ' She began tracing a delicate line with her finger down the list. 'Well, what about this one?' she declared finally. 'Black Apalachi. 14 to 1. Not bad odds neither.'

I assured her I'd put twenty quid on it as soon as I got back into The Oval.

'You do that, darling. Well, enjoy your cricket. What is it, one day, or the proper thing?'

'It's the proper thing,' I replied. 'The full four days.'

'Smashing,' she said with a grin, exposing a row of yellowing teeth. 'Well, the forecast's good for the weekend, so that's you taken care of, isn't it?'

'Yes, but don't tell my wife.'

'I wouldn't dream of it, dear.' She let out a final cackle and waved me off.

Helen, who could well have been sitting in this very park on that day forty-odd years ago when I sat here with Andy, seemed to me to represent a breed of Londoner who made The Oval and its environs such a lovely place in which to spend some time: unpretentious, old-fashioned, naturally suspicious of interlopers, and yet with an innate streak of goodness running through them. I imagined her as a young woman, dodging Goering's doodlebugs and going up west with her pals to watch Johnnie Ray at the Palladium. Perhaps her old dad had even been one of the spectators who'd sat in 1902 watching Jessop and Hirst. Who knows – he might even have been the phantom brolly chewer of old London town.

Just as I was hurrying off I heard a shout behind me.

'Hey, dearie!' Helen was waving her pen in the air. 'I never even asked your name.'

'It's Michael,' I called back.

'Nice to meet you, Michael. And don't forget, Black Apalachi. Twenty quid each way if I were you.'

'Thanks, I will.'

Two hours later, with the players now at tea and with the Australian Rogers already sniffing a double century, I completed my promise. It didn't take me long to find the Ladbrokes marquee, and minutes later I was back in my seat alongside Joe 90 and the witch, applauding the first centurion of the 2010 season and with a chit in my back pocket confirming my faith in Helen's intuition. As somebody who's always considered the best way of doubling my money is to fold it in half and put it back in my wallet, it seemed a fanciful way of spending precious funds – yet I dearly wanted Helen to be proved right.

As the afternoon faded into evening and the air regained its customary April chill, Rogers stroked his way to a sublime six-hour

178 not out. It was the sort of innings that any of the rose-tinted greats of the game would have been happy to claim as their own, although God help Andrew Strauss's men in the coming winter tour if Aussies such as Rogers can't even get into the national side. By the end of play, virtually the only other spectator was a fox that crawled out from under the covers to sun itself near the boundary edge. Its arrival seemed to sum up the day – one full of quaint surprises and chance encounters. If the rest of the summer would only be like this, I'd have few complaints. All I needed now was for Helen's prophecy in the Grand National to come up trumps, and I would consider myself, like Hari Gupta, a blessed man.

The following evening I collected the best part of a hundred quid. Black Apalachi had come in second at 14 to 1. And if Helen predicted that with nothing more to hand than a chewed-up pen, who knows what else she might be right about? The following morning I hurried down to my local bookmaker's and placed another twenty quid on Gordon Brown to lose his job come 15 May.

I should have ridden my luck. If only I'd put twenty more on Derbyshire to beat Surrey for the first time at The Oval since 1966, and another fifty on Derbyshire's new captain Chris Rogers to become the first player in the history of the county to score both a double hundred and a hundred in the same match, I wouldn't be having to write this book.

4

Tate and Guile

The actor Tom Courtenay once observed to me with his customary gloom, 'You don't choose the teams you support: they choose you'. In his case it was Hull FC, the town of his birth, which is probably why he wears such a melancholic look in virtually every role he plays.

But there's always someone worse off. In Tom Courtenay's case, it was me. My parents' decision to move to Brighton in the early 1960s condemned me to spend an entire lifetime supporting Sussex.

Sussex was my first love, and of all places in the cricketing world, the salty old county ground out at Eaton Road, among the suburban villas and 1930s apartment blocks, still exerts a special pull. Long after Test match cricket and all the furious commercial brouhaha of the modern game had dulled my palate, I could always find something spiritually soothing to suck on just by lolling in the deckchairs beneath the scudding clouds and wheeling seagulls and letting the old place enfold me in its comforting bosom.

Perhaps part of the ground's enduring charm is that it's so wrapped up in my own past. After all, I've wasted some of the best years of my life here, even if much has changed in the forty-plus years since I'd first paid homage as a chubby ten-year-old schoolboy.

When I was growing up Brighton in the 1960s, the town used to be a delightfully rackety old place, the sort of town to which raffish businessmen driving Triumph Heralds took their secretaries for dirty weekends, where headless torsos were regularly deposited in the left luggage office at the railway station and the local constabulary wore special white helmets during the summer. As Keith Waterhouse so perfectly put it, 'Brighton always looks as though it is a town helping police with their enquiries.'

Much of its charm has been obliterated in the intervening years, to be replaced by an all-pervading grunginess and a flourishing sexual hedonism that at times threatens to overpower its more delicate flavours. When the writer Samuel Rogers wrote in 1829 that Brighton was 'very gay and full of balls', he had no idea quite how prescient his comments were.

The adjoining borough of Hove, however, has clung to its air of affable snootiness despite all attempts to roughen it up. These geographical Siamese twins may have been merged into a city, but the latter has always remained the pious maiden aunt to the former's sex-crazed larrikin; and even now, sitting in the sun among slumbering colonels, you could almost forget you were barely a mile from the official drugs capital of the UK.

My favourite spot from which to watch county cricket as a kid was a now-demolished stand on the eastern side of the ground abutting the main scoreboard, and nicknamed by habitués 'the hen coop'. The title said it all. In other circumstances it would have done sterling service as a bus shelter in Chechnya. Its capacity was no more than thirty or forty, although this was a redundant statistic even in the mid-1960s as hardly anyone other than me ever ventured in there.

The seats gave you splinters, there were nails protruding that could reduce your school shorts to tatters within minutes, while even in high summer it formed an impromptu wind tunnel that could have powered most of East Sussex if only the technology had been in place. Yet I loved it.

It was from the hen coop that I watched my first delivery, ate my first pork pie, filled in my first scorecard and retrieved my first cricket ball whence it had been dumped by a withering pull from Leicestershire's Peter Marner.

I remember the dizzy sensation of fumbling for the ball between the rotting white benches, and upon clasping it in my greasy, fat-encrusted fingers, being seized with a thrill of pure visceral pleasure. Good God, I was actually holding the same orb that only twenty seconds previously had been rubbed on the crotch of Tony Buss's cricket whites.

Tony Buss: he was one of my first heroes. Even the surname suggested sexual awakening, being the old Sussex word for a kiss. In fact, there were two of them. Busses, that is. Tony and his younger brother Michael, who opened the batting and always played as if he could see Twenty20 on the horizon and thought he'd get in a bit of practice in case anyone perfected the art of cryogenics. Tony and Mike: Trolley and Motor, as they were known among the coop cognoscenti. You wait a hundred years for one and then two come along at once.

The only other regular occupant of my roost was an old man in his seventies or eighties with sprouting nostril hair, who was always surrounded by bags of sweets and crumpled newspapers. He sat in the very back corner, as if attempting to evade detection by the authorities, which, given the sort of spectator who frequents county cricket, might well have been the case.

Yet he knew his stuff. He'd seen all the greats, could compare Hammond with Hobbs, could rattle off details of virtually every match played here since the relief of Mafeking and, most wonderful of all, claimed to have once seen the great Prince Ranjitsinhji, Maharaja Jam Sahib of Nawanagar, the most illustrious and exotic batsman in Sussex's 170-year history. At least, that's what he told me.

I often recall the old bloke's reminiscences now, accompanied by hacking coughs and the crunch of barley sugars. 'Ranji batted as if he was on spring heels,' he told me. 'He was like a dancer. I was only a very young boy like you are now, but I never forgot it.'

His rheumy-eyed recollection seemed fantastical, particularly since Ranji's ancient moth-eaten blazer hung in the main pavilion like some cricketing Turin Shroud. Did I really talk to a man who'd actually seen him; or was it merely the malicious chatter of some bitter old geezer with too much time on his hands and an impressionable young juvenile to hand?

Of course, it would be no problem to find out. In this wonderful world of Google, when a cricket stat is never more than a double tap away, I could confirm or disprove his claim by the click of a mouse and a touch of mental arithmetic. But if it's all the same to you, I'd rather not. While the possibility remains that he might have been telling the truth, I can continue to feel part of a link back to something deep and timeless.

In any case, I had my own heroes, every bit as wondrous to my untutored eye. Not only the Busses, but the stick-thin, sepulchral figure of Alan Oakman, who resembled a cricketing undertaker silently measuring the batsman for a coffin at short leg; or little Kenny Suttle, who was so diminutive that when he ran between the wickets he resembled something out of a *Pixie and Dixie* cartoon.

Most of all there was wicket-keeper/batsman Jim Parks. Sanguine and sun-tanned, his face permanently creased into a broad smile, he seemed to me the embodiment of how the game should be played. A purveyor of stinging drives and jaunty footwork, I collected his autograph so many times he must have thought I was learning to forge his signature; and his autobiography, the unfortunately titled *Runs In The Sun* (my mum always said it sounded like something you suffered from on holiday), was the most cherished of my burgeoning collection of second-hand cricket books, especially when I discovered a letter sent from the author to the previous owner of the tome nestling amongst its pages.

In 1970 I watched on TV as he stood alone against the might of Lancashire in the Gillette Cup final while all around him folded; while at Eastbourne the same summer he delivered his own unique billet-doux to me by driving the ball to bring up his 150 against Essex straight into my sandwiches on the boundary edge.

But mostly my memories are a patchwork of wonderful 40s or 50s, usually seen after tea when I could escape from school, often with Sussex up against it, and always in even time. When he was summarily dispensed with at the end of 1972, much of the sparkle went out of cricket at Hove for a while, and when the following year I saw him keeping wicket for Somerset it was a surreal and disturbing image, a bit like discovering your dad dressed in women's clothing.

In subsequent decades I continued to follow Sussex from both near and afar. Governments may fall, politicians may be assassinated, Norman Lamont may have to extricate sterling from the European Exchange Rate Mechanism, but I could always rely on Sussex to spontaneously combust whenever they got the merest sniff of silverware. One of only three counties never to have won the championship in 170 years of trying, their timeless bungling seemed the one fixed point in a fast-changing world.

In 1981 pigs very nearly flew. Under the new leadership of the splendidly titled John Robert Troutbeck Barclay, Sussex seemed as if they might actually break the habit of a lifetime and win the competition. 'Trout', as he's still universally known, is one of those genuine, unthinking eccentrics who seem to have stepped straight from the pages of a *Boy's Own* annual. Enthusiastic to the extent where you suspect the poor chap might have an undiagnosed psychological condition, and so unconsciously and disarmingly toffish that you could charge visitors to London to visit him as a heritage attraction, Trout is also straight out of the Mike Brearley school of cricket: possessing little playing ability but a fiendish cricketing brain.

When Trout inherited the captaincy, he also inherited a side spearheaded by two genuinely fearsome overseas quickies, the magnificent Imran Khan and the lowering South African, Garth Le Roux. After a triumphantly successful season, it all boiled down, as in the best *Boy's Own* yarns, to a single over on a gloomy Midlands evening in the dying days of August. Sussex needed one more wicket against arch-rivals Nottinghamshire at Trent Bridge with a mere six balls of their match left. All that stood between them and glory was a hapless and terrified spinner called Mike Bore, an individual principally famous for hamster cheeks, a perpetually startled expression and a batting average of eight.

In his memoir on that season, even the unfailingly courteous Trout felt emboldened enough to describe Bore as a batsman of 'startling indistinction'. What is certain is that Bore arrived at the crease wearing a motorcycle crash helmet. The destiny of the entire championship would hang on the outcome of the next six deliveries.

Which, of course, is how the championship is supposed to be. This is what the whole thing is designed for, this is the game at its best – an entire summer, simmering away on the hob quietly while we all go off and do other things, eventually reducing down to a single delicious spoonful of the weather, the pitch, the light and the naked courage of a bloke resembling Harpo Marx facing one of the fastest and most romantic bowlers on the planet. Shere Khan bowling to sheer panic.

On the third ball Imran trapped Bore in front of all three. Back leg, on the shin. Extremely adjacent. Goodnight, nurse. Daddles the Duck. Stop the Car. Yet to Imran's stupefied disbelief (apparently in the dressing room afterwards he sat for nearly an hour simply parroting the single phrase, 'He was plumb'), the umpire gave Bore not out. The home crowd, partisan at the best of times and now positively rabid, roared their approval at Sussex's evident and palpable heartbreak. Bore survived, Notts went on to win the title by two points, and 170 years of south coast agony, stretching in a long unbroken thread from Ranji, through Gilligan, Tate, Dexter, Greig and Parks, continued its unbroken course.

As the team trooped up the steps at the end of the match, Barclay recalled how, for the first and only time in his life, he was nearly wrestled to the ground by a furious opposition supporter – in this case not a boozed-up yobbo in a cutaway T-shirt, but an elderly lady in sensible shoes and with huge gaps in her teeth, who delivered an impressive and anatomically accurate stream of obscenities at the Sussex skipper before eventually being led away by stewards.

In his charming memoir about that season, Barclay concluded with typically disarming grace, 'Sussex will win the championship one day. And the joy will be great when it comes.'

Maybe, but it didn't look likely to occur in his lifetime. Or mine for that matter. During the 1990s I saw far less cricket at Hove than before as acting and actresses took up a greater share of my time, but the reports weren't good as Sussex fell back into middle-table mediocrity. In any case my ties with the town were loosening. My dad died, we sold the sweetshop and my mum moved to Ipswich. But perhaps it was just as well: by the mid-1990s Sussex was as wretched a team as I'd ever endured, causing their beleaguered captain, Alan Wells, to observe that his side had rechristened themselves Mackintosh, 'because they were always getting pissed on'.

But then in 2000 something went very wrong. Now led by a combative and disenchanted northerner called Chris Adams, tradition and ancient rites among the old deckchairs and clacking knitting needles were unceremoniously junked in what remains one of the most shocking volte-faces in the entire history of the sport.

Adams was cut from very different cloth to the Parkses and the Busses of this world; there was nothing of the tang of oysters and Guinness about him. He was even nicknamed Grizzly because of his knuckle-scraping gait to the wicket that suggested a club-wielding caveman on the lookout for a handy dinosaur to clobber over the head.

Yet Adams was merely the puppet-master. The real agent of change was a small, cylindrical Pakistani leg spinner called Mushtaq Ahmed. His arrival transformed the club from Winnie the Pooh into Conan the Barbarian. In his first year he took so many wickets that Sussex gained promotion to the championship's newly-created first division. Followers of tradition gulped hard and spluttered into their pints up in Dexter's restaurant. This sort of thing would never do. Yet the following year it did.

If people ever ask me to recall the single most wonderful moment of my life, I always tell them (as long as Julia isn't within earshot) it was the moment in 2003 when Sussex finally won their first championship. The ground represented a geriatric version of *Dawn of the Dead* that afternoon. Spectators used to generations of under-achievement and failure sat pinching themselves or wandering round the ground in a daze with their arms outstretched. It was as if the cricketing Gods, having condemned the county to nearly two centuries of failure and humiliation, had now decided to redress the balance in one glorious moment.

Like about ten thousand other disbelieving souls, I'd hurried down specially to Hove to witness the realisation of the impossible dream. Yet even now, with a mere two additional batting points needed against Leicestershire and the whole of a late September afternoon in which to get them, there was a sense – almost a hope – that Sussex might yet concoct a king-sized cock-up and restore things to their natural order. When Sussex's batsman Murray Goodwin pulled a ball to the pavilion rails to bring up the vital third bonus point, the ground witnessed such scenes of mayhem as rarely seen since Armistice Day.

No sooner had the ball pinged off the boundary board in front of the pavilion than the entire Sussex playing staff, plus several that weren't, hurtled down from the dressing-room balcony and on to the field for a tribal war dance in which 170 years of pent-up frustration was finally vented. Meanwhile a crackly recording of a brass band playing the county's famous old anthem, 'Sussex by the Sea', filled the air over the loudspeakers. The disc sounded as if it had been recorded on a wax cylinder – which, in retrospect, it probably had been. After all, 170 years is a long time.

The song, originally written in 1907 by William Ward-Higgs, had been adopted by recruits to the Royal Sussex Regiment as they walked towards the guns on the Western Front during the Great War; in more recent years it had been purloined by the Sussex cricketing faithful. Until now it had been largely trotted out with a distinctly ironic tone, usually as an accompaniment to some new disappointment. But now we sang it as it had never been sung. The last night of the Proms was never this good.

Ironically, my own moment of ecstasy was cut short when a bony hand gripped mine just as I, too, was about to leap in the air. A disabled octogenarian colonel, who'd been sitting silently in the next seat to mine all through the afternoon session, had stumbled to his feet, upsetting a polystyrene tray of chips all over his lap in the process, and, oblivious of the rivulets of tomato sauce now running down his zip, had gripped my wrist.

'The first time I ever came to this ground was with my old dad,' he'd muttered in a quavering tenor as he fixed with me with his one good eye, 'and the first ball I ever saw, Maurice Tate hit it back over the ropes for six. I've waited my entire life for this moment. Now I can die happy.' We embraced like children.

Today I was travelling back to Brighton not only to pay homage to the ground that spawned me, and to Trout and Parks and Tate, but also to enjoy just the sort of typical day's county cricket I used to feast on as a child – a championship match under blue skies. As on that day of days five years ago, the opponents were Leicestershire. With luck all would be as I left it, right from my traditional approach through the Tate gates in Eaton Road, right through to a post-match supper at the Melrose, my favourite fish and chip shop on Hove prom.

In truth my pilgrimage today had other, more subtle attractions. For Leicestershire's squad included a player who holds a unique place in the history of the game. Not that anyone would know it – in fact, he'd almost certainly forgotten his achievement himself. But in any digest of the good, the bad and the gawd awful in the history of the game, the name of Leicestershire's AJ Harris will surely stand as tall any Bradman or Warne: possibly even more so. These colossi of the game may have scored thousands of runs or taken hatfuls of wickets. But even they never achieved the unique feat of AJ Harris.

Law 168 of the rulebook states that an incoming batsman may be timed out 'if he wilfully takes more than two minutes to come to the crease – the two minutes being from the moment a wicket falls until a new batsman steps on to the field of play.'

In practice such a dismissal is virtually impossible to effect unless there's a sudden bout of diarrhoea in the dressing room or someone's walked off with the key. So rarely is a batsman is given out by dint of pedestrian tardiness that in the entire history of the game from Hambledon to the advent of the Mongoose, only a handful has ever achieved this dubious honour. In fact, the list of players who've come a cropper in this most exotic of manners reads like something out of a script from *Dad's Army*.

The earliest known example occurred at Taunton in 1919, when one HJ Heygate, who was known to be crippled with rheumatism, staggered to the crease with the scores level to save his side despite having previously asserted he could hardly stand. Legend has it that since he'd only been persuaded at the last minute to make the ultimate sacrifice, he arrived at the crease with his pads strapped to a blue three-piece suit. Despite (or perhaps because) of this, the umpire pronounced him timed out and sent him back to the pavilion, a journey that took even longer. Cricket can be a cruel game.

Of subsequent examples, traffic delays, floods or faulty alarm clocks seem to be the principal culprits, and thus don't really count. But in 1931, Worcestershire's eleventh man, one JH Parsons, was so confident of his teammates' batting abilities that he trotted back to his digs to fetch his spectacles, only for the inevitable collapse to ensue the moment he'd left the dressing room. He returned only to find he'd been immortalised by being entered in the scorebook as 'Absent … 0'.

Perhaps the most spectacular example of tardiness at the crease is poor Abdul Aziz in the match between Karachi and a Services XI. Aged seventeen, he was hit above the heart in his first innings and pronounced dead on arrival at hospital. With an attention to detail that would surely have received a gold star from the late lamented Bill Frindall, the scorer dutifully recorded the details as:

1st innings. Abdul Aziz … Absent … hurt.

2nd innings. Abdul Aziz … Absent … dead.

And that's it. Three of only a handful of instances of a batsman being timed out in nearly two hundred years of non-stop cricket throughout the civilised world. The most recent is AJ Harris. The precise circumstances surrounding his superdawdle while playing for Nottinghamshire against Durham UCCE in 2003 remain shrouded in mystery. A groin strain? A difficult conversation on the dressing room payphone? The history books are vague. Yet whatever the cause, he remains one of an elite band of brothers, and although it was against all the odds that he might replicate it today, I wanted to be there just in case.

I reached Brighton soon after 9.30, and was pleased to see a bus already outside the terminus with its engine running, waiting for the short trip to the ground. The town may have lost much of its quirky charm in recent decades, yet one or two eccentricities remained, not least the fact the entire fleet of municipal buses are named after famous former residents. Only in Brighton can you travel to work in Dusty Springfield and return in Max Miller.

There are plenty of Sussex cricketers commemorated in the fleet (though, oddly, neither Buss), including Maurice Tate (number 56), Ranji (644) and John Langridge (651). In the wake of the Mushtaq's exploits in recent years, there's been a sustained and vociferous online campaign on Facebook to have one of the vehicles named after him.

This morning I was thrilled to see number 51, Ron Cunningham, waiting for me. While few in the town will raise more than an eyebrow at the bus's eponym, in his alter ego as local escapologist and amateur stuntman the Great Omani, Ron Cunningham was one of Brighton's most popular figures and a key character in my childhood story.

I'd first witnessed him, when I was still a small boy, being transported along the seafront strapped to a bed of nails on the roof rack of a Ford Popular to appear in a local carnival. Over subsequent years I can't think of a single charity bash or local fundraiser in which Omani hadn't made an appearance, either setting fire to his hat, walking barefoot across hot coals or, in his most famous exploit, standing on his head on the very edge of Telscombe Cliffs. He died in 2007, his last request being that his coffin be fitted with a trapdoor.

Mind you, even the great man himself would have struggled to wrestle free from the mayhem that was the town centre this morning. It was still rush hour, and since my last visit here some bright spark in the transport department had designed a special taxi filter with a right turn into the station forecourt. Consequently not only Ron Cunningham but also Ivy Compton-Burnett and Jimmy Edwards were being hemmed in by a line of stationary vehicles for minutes on end.

I reached the main entrance to Eaton Road just before 10am. Anybody arriving for a day's cricket here is likely to make their approach by way of the aforementioned Tate gates, a wrought-iron testimonial to a player whose memory is forever associated with the ground, and whose genial spectre still prevails above all others.

His story would make the perfect sporting biopic, if only you could get a decent screenwriter and persuade the hero's uncanny lookalike Tom Cruise to smear his hair down like Little Lord Fauntleroy and accept the title role.

Picture the scene prior to the opening credits – a Test match at the height of the Edwardian era in 1902, a crucial Ashes decider, with both sides crammed full of giants of the game. And there, down at fine leg, celebrating his thirty-fifth birthday, is Fred Tate, Maurice's dad, playing his first Test match as a reward for a long and stolid career at county level.

Everyone is thrilled old Fred has finally got his chance on the grand stage, and with his reputation for rock-solid reliability, forged over many years of playing for Sussex, he's the perfect debutant. With Australia holed at 10–3 in their second innings and the whole of England now scenting blood, Australia captain Joe Darling skies a delivery from Len Braund high into the air. The England captain AC Maclaren has posted Tate precisely for such a mishit, and with the ball swirling in the sky, the scoreboard operators are already changing the scoreboard to 10–4. Meanwhile twenty thousand frenzied spectators rise to their feet. Thank God, there's Fred beneath it. He's never let anyone down.

But he drops it. It goes straight through his fingers with a sickening crunch of leather on bone. Australia goes on to win the match, and the Ashes, and Fred Tate is branded forever as the most hapless bungler in the history of Anglo-Australian contests.

So much so, in fact, that when the Old Trafford turf was relaid in 2008, the very spot where he dropped the catch was carefully removed and can still be seen in front of the pavilion at Whalley Range cricket club. Well over a century on, it's still known as Tate's spot. Now that's true notoriety.

Needless to say, Poor Fred knew he'd blown it, and at the conclusion of the match, with the triumphant Aussies already breaking open the crates of beer in the adjoining dressing room, he sat there, mute, inconsolable, in a dark corner of the dressing room, his life and his career broken in one moment of inexplicable ineptitude.

'Never mind,' he allegedly said, as he wearily gathered his kit and walked off into sporting oblivion. 'I've got a little kid at home who'll make it up for me.' His son, Maurice, was eight at the time.

Maurice did more than that. He turned out to be one of the greatest – possibly the greatest – fast-medium bowlers in all history. Sussex born and bred, he played throughout his career for the county, taking over 2,300 wickets and blasting high-octane runs in the middle order with what was the living definition of the word gusto. More than that, he played thirty-nine Test matches for his country, bagging 155 dismissals (including one with his very first delivery) and almost single-handedly winning an entire Ashes series Down Under in 1924/25 with 38 wickets off over 600 balls bowled.

But it's for the way he played the game that Tate is forever remembered by the Sussex faithful. The epitome of the word cheerful, there doesn't seem to be a single photograph of him (and thankfully there are lots at Hove) in which he's not smiling broadly like one of those automated laughing sailor boys you get in slot-machine arcades – usually with a trilby or panama, a pipe clamped to his mouth, and two huge rosy cheeks sufficiently radiant to fry your breakfast egg on.

Sunny and wholehearted, the story goes that he was habitually followed to Hove each morning of a match by a posse of small boys, each of whom knew from long experience he would help get into the ground free of charge.

'Are *all* these boys yours, Maurice?'

'Yes.'

Never mind Trueman and Leeds or Botham and Taunton. If ever a cricketer epitomised the spirit of the county for which he played, Maurice was your man.

By 10.20 I was in the pavilion with a muffin and an up-to-date scorecard. It may be just another working day elsewhere, but Sussex has a healthy membership, mainly due to Hove being one of the retirement capitals of the south coast, and today business was already brisk, the rectangular tables crammed with spry couples tucking into breakfast and cups of scalding coffee and discussing the likely events of the day ahead. It felt good to be back.

With the five-minute bell ringing out, I caught up with the previous day's events by getting into conversation with an old codger at an adjoining table. The match was already intriguingly balanced. Yesterday, the first day of the four, had been one of those glorious days of championship cricket that makes you wonder why anybody ever thought the one-day version was even necessary.

According to my new friend Albert, the tone for the extraordinary events had been set before a ball had even been bowled, when Leicestershire's new captain, Matthew Hoggard, had spectacularly thrown up on the boundary rope during pre-match practice.

The incident was described to me in graphic detail by Albert even as he tucked into a huge plate of bacon and eggs, and to judge by the look of glee on his face, that event in itself had been enough to justify the entrance fee. But Hoggard's digestive pyrotechnics had merely been the hors d'oeuvre, with no fewer than seventeen wickets falling in the day, the visitors being skittled out for just 117 and Sussex then wobbling themselves to 112–6.

Late in the afternoon the home side had rallied with an unbroken eighth wicket partnership of 52 between evergreen batsman Murray Goodwin (the very player whose pull shot off Leicestershire's Phillip DeFreitas five years ago had given me my proudest moment) and the club's ebullient overseas pro, Pakistani all-rounder Rana Naved-ul-Hasan.

In many ways Rana is the living embodiment of old Maurice. An individual of seemingly inexhaustible cheer, he has the perpetual air of a bloke who's just stumbled by chance on a game of beach cricket while on holiday and can hardly believe his luck. Much as Tate must once have done, he bowls fast medium with furious bonhomie and, also like Tate, loves nothing more than coming in six or seven down just when the opposition think they've done their job and breaking their hearts by bladdering frenzied centuries off them.

His career was nearly ended a couple of years ago when he clattered into some boundary boards at Chester-le-Street and nearly took his shoulder off in the process, but back in harness this season, he'd taken 4 for 49 in eleven overs the previous morning, and by close of play had helped add fifty for the eighth wicket with the bat.

Long before Albert had finished his exhaustive report of the previous day's events, a huge cheer from outside heralded Rana's re-emergence from the clubhouse to continue his innings. The

Sussex faithful, used to long years of mishap and heartbreak, love nothing more than a wholehearted trier, and his appearance with Goodwin was an occasion to be celebrated. You can usually gauge how Rana is going to perform by the extent of his grin as he enters the field, and today it looked as if someone had wedged in a slice of honeydew melon sideways. Look out, Leicestershire, it seemed to say.

So it proved. I'd been meaning to spend the morning ambling round the ground and paying my respects to the old place – perhaps stopping off at the site of the hen coop (now an unprepossessing prefabricated sponsors' box with all the allure of a Wickes' window display), or perhaps the club's battered old mobile bookshop, run with rueful wisdom by Neil Beck, one of the few men I know who still smokes a pipe without looking faintly ashamed about it; or maybe even just sitting in the lower tier of the pavilion near Brenda, the woman whose job it is to run on with spare balls in case of emergency and whose breezy and never-ending stream of chatter is one of the perennial joys of watching cricket in these parts.

But there was no time for such rheumy-eyed nostalgia, for the on-field action was unputdownable. During the first ninety minutes of the session I watched spellbound from the top tier of the pavilion as Goodwin and Rana barrelled their way to a glorious eighth wicket partnership of 164 in a manner that suggested they'd had a bet beforehand to see who could cause the most mayhem.

Delivery after delivery was belted to oblivion by the two men. It was absolutely thrilling stuff, just as long as you weren't from Ashby-de-la-Zouch or Lutterworth. But few here were. April in uncertain weather and when your captain and leading bowler is *hors de combat* is no incentive to drive two-hundred miles. Carnage was on the menu today, and the only celebrants were the ruddy-faced topers in the pavilion, swilling down pre-lunch pints of Harveys and cheering the seemingly endless series of boundaries.

Rana may have begun the day 24 runs behind his senior partner, but he, like Tate, is not a bloke to hang about, and after one of the most emphatic assaults I can recall he reached his century first, including nine fours and with two huge sixes clattered off Leicestershire's spinner Claude Henderson. Under his barrage, the visitors' bowling attack wilted like a bouquet of tulips left overnight without water. Poor AJ Harris ran in pluckily from the Cromwell Road end during a lively spell, but in truth he came in for more than his fair share of punishment, ending with one for 79 at well above four an over.

When Rana was eventually out, having hammered a century in only 113 balls, he departed to the sort of standing ovation I could only dream of. But even then Leicestershire's misery wasn't over. Tail-ender Monty Panesar, a player who evokes a lusty cheer from friend and foe alike if he as much bends to tie up his bootlaces, is genuinely regarded as one of the more inept batsmen on the county scene; yet even he found occupation relatively easy against the shell-shocked bowling attack, and hung about for well over an hour for 14. By the time Harris and his compatriots had left the field at the conclusion of the Sussex innings, they were facing a first innings deficit of 278.

I spent the interval between innings back in the pavilion, soaking up the chatter of overexcited pensioners and enjoying the odd, 1930s aroma of treated wood, shepherd's pie and stale beer that always seems to hang around. Ranji's blazer was still in the display case at the far end, and snaps of the rubicund Tate beamed at me from the wall above the bar.

Several times during the break I glimpsed young Harris making his way back and forth along the walkway from the pavilion players' dining room to the dressing room. I smiled hopefully as he passed in the hope of striking up a conversation and finding out the truth behind his unique claim to cricketing fame, but he palpably had other things on his mind, not least how he and his teammates were going to claw back that first innings deficit. Of one thing I was certain: unless Leicestershire suffered a shocking collapse or Harris was the current incumbent night watchman, my chances of seeing him even bat today, let alone being timed out, had almost evaporated.

I spent the remainder of the afternoon in a deckchair at the Cromwell Road end, doing what I always used to do here – eating, dozing, earwigging and watching the odd over. With its gaily-coloured deckchairs and capacious wooden benches positioned on a shallow grassy slope allowing an elevated view of the action, it must be one of the nicest places in the world from which to watch cricket. It's also directly in front of the practice nets and beneath the players' balcony, thus allowing you to pass the time by watching your heroes demonstrating their skills up close, or catching fragments of desultory and largely footling chit-chat carried on the breeze. The doyen of all English batsmen Jack Hobbs liked the spot so much he bought a flat just across the road once his playing days were over, and most afternoons could be seen staring down at the action with a cup of tea.

Because of its situation, the spot is also a meeting point for general cricketing pontificators to congregate. The actor Michael Jayston discussing his latest haul of wickets for Rottingdean cricket club is an habitué, as is former star bowler-turned-travel agent John Snow, offering trenchant observations for the sharp of hearing on both the state of play and the overall health of the tourist industry.

Today was one of those deliciously somnambulant interludes when dreams and reality mingle in a sort of fitful semi-conscious-ness, like one of those blissful times after rabid sex, if my memory serves me. Lulled by the warm sunshine, the drone of conver-sation and some soporific batting, I found myself drifting off to sleep – yet whenever I opened my eyes the players were still flitting back and forth before me, and all around me my fellow-spectators were talking the same inconsequential drivel. After all, we'd already had more than enough bang for our buck for one day.

The visitors went to work repairing the damage with all the dash of a chain gang preparing to break stones in some Siberian archipelago. Stark survival was the order of the day, particularly after their opening batsman Will Jefferson was dropped at third slip off the first ball, once more off the ubiquitous Rana.

Jefferson is one of those oddities of nature who is simply about a foot taller than anyone else you're ever likely to meet, and in whose hands the mightiest cricket bat looks like a child's toy. Thirty years ago he'd surely have been invited by Roy Castle to appear on *Record Breakers*. Like so many players whose early career trajectory doesn't quite achieve the required orbit, he'd recently moved from Essex to Leicestershire in order to revive his profile, and on the evidence of today he looked a useful acquisition.

Much of the interest surrounding his participation today was merely the hope of seeing him bat alongside number four, James Taylor. 'Tich' Taylor may have been voted young player of the year the previous season by the Cricket Writers' Club and thought by cognoscenti to be the most gifted young bat-man in the country, but he's also only five feet six, a full sixteen inches shorter than his compatriot. Watching two batsmen scurrying twenty-two yards at high speed when one can accomplish it in three steps to the other's twenty is the sort of spectacle that diehard cricket watchers simply love to sample, if only as a reminder of little Kenny Suttle and lanky Tony Greig, who entertained spectators from a previous generation in similar fashion. But it was not to be. Indeed, when Jefferson was finally out for 44 with Taylor still to come in, there was almost a sense of disappointment in the crowd that one of the game's great comic moments had been denied us.

By 5pm the visitors had chipped away at the deficit, mainly thanks to a bugger of an innings by their totemic batsman Paul Nixon, who hung about for an unbeaten 68. With half an hour to go the scoreboard was showing 200 for only three wickets down and the evening was turning chilly. Both the burger vans and the mobile bookshop had closed up for the day, and what remained of the crowd were now safely cocooned in the warm fug of the members' bar, watching the closing overs through the large picture windows.

The match would most likely end sometime tomorrow; probably, though by no means certainly, in Sussex's favour – but never mind, this had been a wonderful day of county cricket, fast moving, unpredictable, full of character and characters and offering over 400 runs and six wickets. My chance to see Harris become the first player in cricket history to be timed out twice would, of course, have been the cherry on the cake, but who was complaining? In any case, there was still plenty of time left elsewhere in the summer. Perhaps I'd drop him a reminder of my attendance next time our paths looked likely to cross.

It had been a grand day, one of recollections and fresh memories to store away for my twilight years. I was feeling chilly and in need of a good meal, yet something in me decided to make a final circuit of the perimeter. As I passed the top end of the ground my nostrils pricked at the familiar if piquant blend of chemicals and belching exhaust fumes that always signifies an ice-cream van.

Odd. Who would want an ice cream at this time of night in April with the street lights already twinkling and the evening almost upon us? But one spectator, at least, had made full use of the facility.

There, entirely alone, sitting languidly in a deck chair, surveying the final overs, his tongue flicking at a large whipped cone with a luxurious flake stuck suggestively in the top, was MCC president and former Sussex skipper John Robert Troutbeck Barclay. The boyish looks may have become more grizzled than in his salad days, the flop of hair a trifle thinner, the waistline a trifle fuller, but there was no mistaking him: sitting quietly in a fetching biscuit-coloured sports jacket and chinos, and looking the definition of both absorption and contentment.

'One day Sussex will win the title. And what joy will be had,' he'd once written. Since that far-off day in 1981 Sussex had not only finally claimed their first title, but had managed it twice more in the following three years. No wonder he looked happy.

A few minutes later I passed through the old Tate gates for the last time, erected to this gloriously uncomplicated cricketer who lit up the stage here for three decades. As I approached them the departing spectator behind me began whistling 'Sussex By The Sea'. It was a moment of pleasing symmetry. Tate would have liked it.

As a sport, cricket has more than its fair share of tales of once great stars declining into penury and anonymity (it must be the only game that has an entire book, David Frith's excellent *By His*

Own Hand, devoted to players who've committed suicide), and Tate's subsequent story, though far less dire than some, is typically melancholy. Having given his entire life to the club and by the summer of 1937 now forty-two years old, he was summoned to the committee room midway through the season by the chairman, one Brigadier d'Arcy Brownlow, to be tartly informed not only that he wouldn't be required next year, but that he needn't even bother with the rest of the current one. He later described the encounter as the unhappiest day of his life, explaining, 'it was not so much what was done as the way that they did it'. Once he'd hung up his stout boots and his even stouter heart, Maurice eventually took up as a publican in that most typical of Sussex villages, Wadhurst, as landlord of the Greyhound, where he died of a heart attack aged only sixty-one.

He's buried in the local churchyard. Not that you'd have known it until recently. The gravestone lay lopsided and overgrown in the churchyard and was so neglected that even the resident vicar of the church had no idea – until an investigation by Stephen Bates of the *Guardian* – who the incumbent was. Thankfully a campaign is now afoot to have his last resting place suitably renovated. Indeed, one horror-struck cricketing fanatic even drove down from London, upon reading in the press of the grave's shoddy state, and spruced up the site himself with a pair of secateurs and some cyclamen bushes purchased at a nearby garden centre.

But the moral is obvious. You might be a world-beater, but you're a long time dead and reputations are soon forgotten. Gather ye rosebuds while ye may.

Speaking of which ... At the far end of Selbourne Road I could see the sea, a bluey-grey line in the twilight. Somewhere down on the seafront was a plate of haddock and chips and a large wally with my name on it. After which, a trip back to the station on the top deck of ... who knows? Number 649, Adam Faith? Or maybe 688, Elsie and Doris Waters? Perhaps, if my luck was in, even number 56, Maurice himself. Now that really would be a fittin' endin'.

'Safe journey home, sir,' said the steward from his little booth as I passed through the gates. 'Hope to see you here again.'

'I hope so too,' I replied.

5

Bat and Bawl

When asked if he would ever watch a game of Twenty20 on the TV, the veteran Australian batsman Arthur Morris replied, 'I might. But not if I'm going to miss *The Bold and the Beautiful*.' Quite so. Yet these two seemingly unconnected branches of showbusiness have much more in common than you might think – non-stop action, explosive twists and turns, joy, triumph and heartbreak, as well as enough drama in a single helping to fill an entire edition of the *News of the World*.

I'd never watched a T20 match in full, but with the help of Sky TV and a comfy barside chair, that was about to be put right. Today I was planning to catch all forty action-packed overs of this bastard love child of WG Grace and Kerry Katona live from Bridgetown in Barbados. And with our old enemy pitched against us, what a game it promised to be.

It was Sunday morning, 16 May, and somewhere on the other side of the Atlantic, Paul Collingwood was dreaming of lifting the T20 World Cup. Strange times. Not just because with the domestic season well under way the England national side were still playing halfway round the world, but also because we'd actually reached the final. Having invented this newfangled form of the game in the first place, we finally seemed to be getting the hang of it, with only Australia standing between us and glory.

I'd been looking forward to the experience for some days, for it had been a melancholy old time in the Simkins household. That redoubtable force of nature, Julia's mother Wyn, a woman whose display of synchronised Indian club-swinging to the tune of 'Teddy Bears' Picnic' had once been the talk of Grimsby docks, had recently moved into a care home in Humberside, and this morning Julia was due to go up by train to visit her in her new abode.

Wyn had two great loves in life: Scrabble, and amateur oper-atics. The first she still played with some skill – indeed, she was unbeaten amongst the residents of the Havenbrook care home, even if she'd recently had to rely on the name of some species of the antelope family only found on the Namibian foothills to save her on a triple-worder.

Strange, a woman who, by her own admission, could no longer recall if she was 'on foot or 'ossback', could still come up with a gemsbok.

In many ways Wyn was still her old battling self, yet despite these occasional glorious flashes, the once-incandescent light was undoubtedly dimming, and Julia and I had spent the previous week compiling photographs and snaps of four decades of her operatic life to present to her today, as both as a gift and aide-memoire.

During her four decades with Gainsborough Operatic Society, Wyn had graduated from her first stumbling steps as third hula-hula girl from the right in their production of *South Pacific* (1955) into such leading roles as Ottilie in *The White Horse Inn*, Netty in *Carousel* and, her favourite, Margot the tavern keeper in *The Vagabond King*. Merely to view the yellowing press cuttings and curling snaps of these long-forgotten productions was to feel a profound sense of the passage of time.

A bit like blancoed pads and batting gloves with green spikes, these productions were the last vestiges of a way of life now gone forever. There she was in each successive show, whether in ball gowns, wimples or grass skirts, the same old Wyn: waist slightly thickening with each year, but the same imperious features, left hand coiled into the hip with the fingers splayed gently back out, always Wyn's trademark pose and her imagined means of how to suggest sophistication in a single gesture.

That am-dram world had once been an integral part of the weft and warp of small town life, yet it was disappearing faster than newspaper coverage of the county championship. *The Land of Smiles, Chu Chin Chow*, and *Rose Marie*, that tale of musical love among the Canadian Mounties.

'When I'm calling you-oo-oo-oooo, oo-oo-oo-oo' – that phrase hadn't been heard in public since Geoff Boycott last ran out one of his opening partners. A bit like three-day cricket, the three-act operetta was a thing of the past. Now it was all power plays and Andrew Lloyd Webber sitting on a plywood throne with a crown perched drunkenly on his head.

I took Julia to the station in the car on the Sunday morning, with the precious photo album perched carefully on her lap, almost as if it were Wyn's very ashes themselves. In three hours she'd be at the Havenbrook, surrounded by cups of instant coffee and the distant wail of residents pleading to be helped to the toilet. My destination offered similar vignettes, for in addition to the T20 final I was hoping to watch a game of typical rustic Sunday afternoon village cricket. But whereas the Havenbrook had been built as recently as 2005, my chosen destination was vastly more historic. I was going to Hambledon.

Hambledon or, more properly, Broadhalfpenny Down, situated in the south-east corner of Hampshire, is where the game began. Or at the very least, where it was gathered together and codified into the game we know today.

Just why this tiny village became known as the cradle of cricket is lost in the mists of time, but one thing is sure – its importance in the development of the sport is unparalleled. Cricket may not have been invented here – indeed, by the time Hambledon first saw action the sport had already been played in England for over a century – but this was where the game coalesced into something Michael Clarke and Craig Kieswetter would still recognise.

The greatest paradox surrounding this tiny village's pre-eminence was its sheer inaccessibility. Even my journey today threatened to put my map-reading skills to their firmest test, yet two hundred years ago it must have been like trying to get to Kathmandu. Yet despite all this, Hambledon was able to compete against 'the Rest of England' on fifty-one occasions and, what's more, trounce them in twenty-nine.

The presiding genius was the landlord of the adjoining pub, Richard Nyren. 'The General', as he was universally known, not only ran the Bat and Ball and captained the team, but also hosted the plentiful post-match dinners. This bucolic environment was further graced by opening batsman John Small and his son who played duets on the violin and cello, accompanied by vocal duets from the wicket-keeper Tom Sueter and long-stop George Leer, the latter a prodigious counter-tenor (and perhaps the first example of the ramifications of not wearing a box).

Early lithographs of matches there suggest a scene more like Gainsborough Operatic Society's production of *Naughty Marietta* than a game of cricket. Everyone is wandering around in what look like jockey caps, full-sleeved shirts, knee breeches and buckled shoes, and the main mode of fielding seems to be waving your handkerchief in the air. Even the umpires are wearing full-skirted coats and bonnets, and communicate their decisions with extravagant gestures from hands bejewelled with ornaments. John McCririck would have felt at home here.

Surviving accounts of early committee meetings, held in the pub, suggest little has surely changed in club cricket in the intervening centuries, with non-payment of subs, accusations of cheating and the dearth of practice facilities a common complaint. Indeed, one document which refers to 'a wet day, only 3 present, 9 bottles of wine consumed' would do pretty well to describe a Baldwin AGM.

Nonetheless, at its height Hambledon boasted a galaxy of world-beaters, from their demon opening bowlers, Barber and Hogsflesh, to the 'swarthy gypsy', Noah Mann, who terrorised visiting batsman for many years before falling into a fire during a post-match party. Greatest of all local legends was 'Silver Billy Beldham', described (somewhat inevitably) as the Bradman of his day, and whose ability was so great that he was paid not only five guineas if Hambledon won and three if they lost, but even a couple of quid if he deigned to turn out to practise. His energies were prodigious, as witnessed by the fact he fathered thirty children, many of them in his cottage that still stands next to the pub.

It seems incredible now, but the public bar of this unpretentious boozer in the lane across from the pitch is where this galaxy of eighteenth-century stars drank away their winnings, and also where the laws of cricket were thrashed out and the game finally meshed. For three hundred years this windswept plateau has drawn cricket lovers anxious to savour for themselves the spot where it all began. And now I was coming too.

*

It's difficult to know quite how a visit to Hambledon had escaped me. It's not as if I haven't been to similar attractions nearby. How could it be that a man whose finest years have been sacrificed on the altar of the best-loved game could have missed out on a visit to its birthplace, especially when he'd frittered equal amounts of time away at nearby attractions such as Monkey World and the Whitchurch Silk Mill.

The answer was, of course, marriage. Any marriage is based on give and take, and when you've subjected your wife to Sundays spent in a VW Golf convertible with a leaking hood while you stand about under golf umbrellas talking about how 'it looks a bit brighter over there' and 'if it stops by five we could always play in trainers', asking her to spend her one free week-end going to the cradle of cricket to watch a load of identical men doing exactly the same thing is never likely to lead anywhere but the divorce courts.

No, you show your love for your partner by driving 150 miles in a day to view rescued laboratory chimpanzees masturbating in old tyres, and items made of silk. That's what love is about.

My only impression of Hambledon had been from a documentary videotape I'd once owned, describing the history of the game. I recall little of it now, except for the establishing shot of the programme's presenter, the great John Arlott, standing next to a line of ancient beech trees and staring balefully out across the pitch.

The footage had obviously been shot in February, and far from the sun-kissed rustic idyll the programme-makers might have wished for, it comes over as somewhat inhospitable. Arlott himself looks particularly cheesed-off, with cheeks the colour of beetroot, trouser turn-ups fluttering in the wind, and the ends of his Hush Puppies stained with mud from too long spent standing about while the crew erected the dolly grip.

Yet the film-makers had still managed to transform this desolate scene into one of unutterable majesty merely by overlaying it with the second movement of Beethoven's Pastoral Symphony. The simple addition of a few bars of appropriately stirring music had instantly turned this dreary spot into one of profound beauty. Framed by swaying boughs and infused with Ludwig's incomparable melody, the scene now became poetic, timeless and full of quiet melancholy. Many years later I used the same conceit to salvage our two-hour-long wedding video with the simple addition of Frank Sinatra singing 'My Way'.

My plan today was breathtaking in its simplicity. I'd visit this mecca of the cricketing world and then relax in the snug of the Bat and Ball and watch the world Twenty20 final live on Sky Sports, thus neatly bookending three hundred years of the game in one glorious juxtaposition.

I dropped Julia at the station soon after eleven – plenty of time to drive down to Hampshire for the start of proceedings, or so I thought. But of course I'd reckoned without driving on a Sunday in Britain. Something hard-wired in me still thinks it's 1965, when your parents could take the car out for a Sunday afternoon poodle in the certain knowledge that if we broke down it would probably be Monday morning before we'd see another passing motorist. As things turned out I could have made it to Barbados in less time than it took to drive the fifty-odd miles from London to Hampshire.

To start with, there was the rain, which nowadays is always a clarion call to every single owner of a motor car to get in it and drive uselessly around looking for the nearest IKEA. You'd think people would want to stay indoors during grotty weather and snuggle down to watch the *EastEnders* omnibus. But the whole country was suddenly on the move, and their chosen rendezvous seemed to be the Marylebone flyover.

Even when I got on to the A3 my ordeal wasn't finished. The carriageway was closed near Hindhead for lane-widening, necessitating yet another detour through rain-soaked villages. The only living soul abroad by now was a bedraggled woman in her mid-fifties standing miserably by the verge behind a picnic table festooned with leaflets and fringed by deflated balloons. 'Save Undershaw', read a dank sign taped to the front of the table. She looked so unutterably forlorn that I even stopped the car and hurried over to take a leaflet in an act of entirely pointless pity.

Undershaw. The name had some special significance, but what? And then I remembered – it was the country house in which Sir Arthur Conan Doyle wrote *The Hound of the Baskervilles*. Literary cognoscenti had it that his most famous creation, Sherlock, was modelled on the Nottinghamshire bowler Frank Shacklock. Intriguingly, Shacklock's fellow fast bowler was named Mycroft.

Yet Undershaw was now derelict and apparently earmarked for demolition. It was difficult not to feel depressed that such an eminent location should be left to well-meaning housewives in Pacamacs. I gave her a feeble toot on my car horn as I drove away and she waved miserably back. Maybe some music would lift my own spirits; after all, it certainly worked for Arlott's video. I reached across and turned on the radio in the hope of finding something lively and life enhancing.

What I got was David Mellor.

My only contact with this fallen giant of Tory politics had been tangential to say the least. Many years ago I'd been due to direct his erstwhile mistress and fellow Chelsea fan, Antonia de Sancha, in a production of Chekhov's *Three Sisters* at RADA, a plan that had been cut short after the Sunday red-tops revealed she'd made love to him dressed only in a Chelsea football shirt during a break in her studies.

Naturally she'd been asked to leave my alma mater quicker than you could say Exit Stage Left, and thus our potentially historic collaboration had never come to fruition. And I'd never been able to listen to Mellor's popular Sunday morning programme 'If You Liked That, You'll Like This' without wondering whether the idea for his series came about from these exotic bouts of lovemaking and, if so, which sexual position might have been responsible.

Yet today Mellor proved an inspiring choice. Not only was his next item the very movement from the Pastoral Symphony that had done so much to turn Arlott's pilgrimage into something lasting and memorable, but, with the end of the show fast approaching, his final choice caught me utterly unprepared.

It was described as a 'newly-released CD of selected musical bon-bons' featuring the Swedish tenor Jussi Björling steaming his way through some popular musical confections of the mid-twentieth century. 'Many won't have heard of this song,' cooed Mellor, 'yet when I was growing up these sorts of plangent melodies were part of the fabric of daily life, and who better to transport us back to the quaint beauty of these forgotten tunes than the incomparable Jussi.'

Suddenly the car was filled with Björling's clarion voice barrelling through a rendering of 'Only a Rose' from *The Vagabond King*. Wyn's favourite. The sound of this sweet, simple tune, associated with the knowledge that at this moment Julia would be in the lounge of the care home, flicking through the photos and gently humming the melodies along with her mum, surrounded on all sides by the slumbering carcasses of once vibrant local citizens, had tears unexpectedly pricking my eyes. And while it might be going too far to suggest I suddenly wished she were in the car with me, I found myself quietly hoping Classic FM might be on in the lounge of the Haven-brook care home.

And then, without warning, my car headlights picked out the Old Bat and Ball, its ancient sign swinging stiffly in the after-noon breeze. I pulled into the car park, silenced the engine, closed my eyes, turned up the volume and let Björling rattle my wing mirrors with a final, glorious, everlasting top note.

I was home.

And I was in luck. A game was about to start on the ancient ground, and across the road on the pitch I could see the assorted heads of figures clad in white bobbing back and forth above the line of the hedge, while a flurry of polite applause from an unseen pavilion suggested the opposing batsmen were marching to the wicket.

This was the thing I'd come for – the holiest site in the devel-opment of the game – yet now I was here I felt strangely sheepish about lifting the veil and peering in. Instead I sat hesitantly on the pub terrace, my only companions a couple of ramblers with a muddy Labrador. But my unlikely perch proved a perfect intro-duction. The hedge prevented a direct view of play, but across from where I now sat was a gap that offered a brief view of proceedings, in line with the bowler's run-up. Even now a man swathed in pullovers and with the new ball bulging from a strain-ing trouser pocket like a life-threatening tumour stood blowing on his hands and scrutinising some unseen opposition batsmen.

My partial view followed the same identical template: the bowler setting off on a laboured run before disappearing from view, followed by anguished cries and shouts of encouragement that had presumably echoed hereabouts for the best part of 250 years. 'Lovely stuff, Ken.' 'Drop back fifteen please, Phil.' 'Another one like that, Raymondo.' I could envisage the outcome of each fresh delivery without having to move so much as a buttock cheek.

Eventually the inevitable happened. Seconds after Raymondo disappeared from view, there was a snick, a cry of 'Catch it', followed by hoarse shouts of triumph. A moment later the batsman, still encased in a helmet and arm guard, lumbered back to the pavilion.

With the drizzle abating I wandered across the road and through the gap. Even without the assistance of Beethoven the scene was instantly recognisable: the pitch, heavily scented with clover and freshly-expressed sheep dung, with the clubhouse at one end, on whose balcony a gaggle of shivering players stood swathed in jumpers.

I felt a twinge of nostalgia. The Baldwins were probably doing exactly the same thing some sixty miles along the coast even now. Their game today was against Worthing Chippendales, who, despite their title, suggestive of muscle-bound hunks batting in thongs and flinging their used cricket boxes in the direction of the tea ladies, were actually more the wooden furniture variety. It should be a good game, if only we could raise a side. The last I'd heard from Chris Buckle on Friday afternoon we'd had seven.

I hurried across to the pavilion, where a middle-aged man dressed in cricket whites and a cap sat smoking a pipe. 'Come to pay your respects?' he asked. 'Well, please don't feel you've got to be brave and stay out here. We get a lot of tourists and they always seem to feel they have to hang around outside even if they catch pneumonia. Go inside, for God's sake – there's a heater and if you're nice to my wife she may make you a cup of tea. Ask for Ros. She'll be the one keeping score.'

I thanked him and hurried in. All the clichéd images of early season cricket were on display: waiting batsmen swaddled in pads and overcoats and drumming their heels on the wooden floor; the smell of blocked drains, and the knot of loyal cricketing spouses in headscarves and sweaters huddled round a pungent Calor Gas heater. They looked perished.

Next to the doorway and peering out through a partially-open window was a woman somehow keeping score despite being wrapped from head to toe in a blanket. Having offered me a cup of tea from a flask, she invited me to pull up a chair and join her.

Ros was one of those sorts of women who'd once helped us maintain an empire. Doughty, uncomplaining and with a wry sense of humour, she kept score for all the home matches without complaint or need of an eraser. In between recording each ball she was even able to return to a pull-out Summer Special Barbecue section in the *Observer* without losing track of the total or making the slightest error.

'Look at this,' she said, turning her paper to show photographs of smiling families grilling sausages on garden lawns while children splashed happily in paddling pools. '"Twenty top tips to make your sizzling summer go with a swing". They're taking the mickey, aren't they? Are you with the opposition?'

I explained I was merely here to pay my respects, but that I'd indeed love to play here before I die.

'Well, if you ever do, remember the trick is to get forward,' she explained. 'We always have a home advantage because the opposition seem to suffer from collective amnesia. They get seduced by the short ball, go back, and next thing they know, bingo!'

As if to prove her point, there was a howl of delight, and the next moment a second opposition batsman was surveying his shattered stumps. 'See what I mean?' she continued with a malicious twinkle.

'You obviously know your stuff.'

She took out a pencil sharpener and began twizzling. 'Well, when you've crucified the best weekends of your lifetime trying to ingratiate yourself with a husband in the entirely futile hope that a bogus interest in sport might somehow result in him helping you with the housework, the only compensation is a certain knowledge of events. Otherwise you really are wasting your time, aren't you?'

The more we chatted, the more I liked her. Despite her tone suggesting she was the epitome of middle-class conservatism, one entirely in keeping with the Range Rovers parked behind the pavilion, the Mulberry bags and the designer sweaters, she admitted she was a Green Party activist, and was still celebrating the triumph of the party's leader Caroline Lucas in becoming their first ever MP.

'Of course, we knew the Labour Party candidate would never win. No hair, you see. You can't win an election nowadays without hair. The days of Clement Attlee have long gone. Mind you, I hope that odious David Milliband doesn't get the chance to have a go at the top job. I shared a car with him once and all he did was fiddle with his BlackBerry.'

Our conversation broke off while she helped an injured fielder who'd bruised his thumb to find the first-aid box. He looked blue with cold. 'Look, let me put you out of your misery,' she said as she returned to her post. 'There's really no need for you to suffer just because we've got to. Cricket can be so fascistic as a sport, don't you find? I give you special personal dispensation to go over to the pub. The weather is due to perk up later on and we'll still be here. Besides, they stop serving at three. Go on, I won't tell anyone.'

At first sight, the interior of The Bat and Ball seemed much like any other boozer, except that every available inch of wall space was covered with images of cricket. The range was breathtaking, from faded prints to snaps of TV stars and half-forgotten celebrities enjoying a charity thrashabout on the pitch across the road. Yet despite the profusion of knick-knacks and memorabilia on all sides, it was difficult to absorb the true significance of my surroundings.

Where once Nyren and his chums had sat down and decreed the permitted width of a cricket bat and the introduction of the third stump, people now guzzled suet pudding and custard and talked about the latest evictions from last night's episode of *Britain's Got Talent*. Nothing wrong with that, of course – it's what you're supposed to do in pubs – but sadly it felt no more special than if I'd popped along to my local. Was it really round these rickety old tables that the laws of cricket were codified and refined?

I shut my eyes in an effort to conjure up the scene, and a woman at the next table immediately leaned over and asked if I was feeling unwell. She had the sort of rosy cheeks and green-wellie no-nonsense attitude that you'd associate with a dog breeder or the wife of a disgraced Tory cabinet minister.

'You interested in the sport?' she asked once I explained the reason for my apparent anguish. 'Thought you were. Want me to show you around?' This was what I'd always hoped to find: a woman who ran a pub and was fascinated by cricket.

Veronica proved an excellent guide. On one wall, just above where a simpering young couple sat reading out automated horoscopes to one another from their mobile phone, she indicated an aged document, the first ever mention of cricket in these parts: '*Lost at the cricket match on Broadhalfpenny Down, a yellow and brown spaniel dog, of the setting kind, with a mottled nose which answers to the name of Rover.*'

'Impressed?'

'Wonderful.'

'Well, if you like that, you'll like this,' she continued in an unconscious echo of my journey here. We moved on to another part of the premises. More artefacts were jumbled together on the far wall: an early scorecard and a photograph showing CB Fry and a portly Gilbert Jessop standing on the pitch some time after the Great War. Finally she led me to a dimly lit alcove. 'This is what most people come to see.' She pointed up a small rectangle of paper in a tiny frame. 'It's only a photocopy but still … '

The item, dated September 1771, and signed in Nyren's own hand, was the very document that forever defined the dimensions of a cricket bat. So this was to blame for my lifetime of thick edges to slip and pitiful snicks to the keeper? '*In view of the performance of White of Ryegate on September 23rd, four and a quarter inches shall be the breadth forthwith.*'

Veronica briefly explained the story behind this piece of hurriedly-drawn legislation. The aforementioned White had apparently come out to bat on this very ground with a piece of willow considerably wider than the actual stumps. He couldn't lift the bat and the bowlers couldn't see the wicket. After one of the more futile afternoons of sporting endeavour, Nyren had decisively addressed the matter with the assistance of a quill pen and a lathe. Two hundred and fifty years on and with the Twenty20 Final now only minutes away, the bats used today by Kevin Pietersen and Cameron White would still adhere to the regulation four and a quarter inches.

Speaking of which … 'What time does the match begin?' I asked my guide, who was now clearing away the tables.

'It's any time now,' she answered. 'But you're not planning to watch it here, I hope. This is a pub, not a sports bar. You'll have to go to the Golden Hind in Horndean – it's only a few minutes away. Jake will give you directions.'

Living in London, I hadn't contemplated the possibility that a pub so profoundly associated with sport might not have satellite coverage, yet there was something comforting in the fact that the Bat and Ball still did what such places are supposed to do – provide a refuge from the world outside rather than an extension of it. Armed with a set of directions scrawled on a handy menu by Jake, I set off for Horndean. As I was about to leave a final offering caught my eye: hanging above the bar, a framed print of WG Grace at the wicket – the one everyone knows, taken from side on, with him standing at the crease with his front foot upraised at the toe in that customary fashion that makes him look as if he's just stepped on a tin tack or is about to commence a spot of line dancing.

No inscription, no explanation – just a single weary phrase in response to the presumably thousands of enquiries from bewildered foreign tourists freshly arrived to pay homage at this cricketing Mecca.

'NO, HE DID NOT PLAY HERE!'

I'd never been to Horndean, and had I not been in hot pursuit of a satellite dish I probably never would have gone. Yet this small

Hampshire town, whose name means 'valley of the dormouse', must once have been the sort of place to send Lewis Carroll drooling into his dog collar, with its duck ponds, flower-strewn meadows and tiny children bowling hoops along a dusty road heavy with the scent of trodden grass. What could possibly improve such a place? OK, throw in Gales, one of the finest small breweries in the country, and you're damn near to being in Paradise.

The town had even boasted its own light railway that ran a distance of six miles through villages with names straight out of Flanders and Swann's 'The Slow Train'. Even its less salubrious attractions had acquired a sort of bucolic notoriety, none more so than the local swimming pool, which had been created for about fifteen quid by quick-thinking local councillors, simply by lining the ground floor of the local workhouse with a polythene tank and renaming it. With its grimy water, lack of daylight and the air of misery and death that seeped through its walls, it had allegedly been the most unprepossessing civic leisure facility in the south-east – although I imagine the 'Hacienda Men's Only Sauna and Plunge Pool' I recall stumbling into in Brighton while a teenager would have run it pretty close. The memory of two gentlemen in Y-fronts playing ping-pong beside that filthy Jacuzzi will stay with me until the day I die.

No, all in all Horndean had obviously been quite a place. But now, surrounded on all sides by light industrial estates, this rural idyll seemed to be little more than a profusion of mini roundabouts and convenience stores, and had a thoroughly downtrodden look about it. Even the brewery was closed.

I drove around the one-way system several times in search of the Golden Hind, peering out of steamed-up windows and thoroughly enraging cars full of motorists on their way to Morrison's (since the closure of Gales, the town's largest employer), until I spotted a telltale Sky logo draped above a doorway at a busy intersection.

With its impressive frontage and prime location slap bang on the main road, the Golden Hind must once have been an important coaching inn on the route from London to Portsmouth. But little remained of its old Pickwickian glory now. The outside looked shabby and run down, exactly the sort of establishment that would prefer to show all-day satellite sports in order to bump up its profit margins than give the tables a good polish and steam-clean the carpets.

I parked the car and wandered in through a side door to the public bar. But even before I'd stepped over the threshold it was evident today's game had got off to the worst possible start for any red-blooded Englishman.

Not that England was doing badly. On the contrary, they'd won the toss, inserted the Aussies and already claimed the early scalps of opener Shane Watson and David Warner. No, the problem today was in the Sky commentary box, in the shape of my personal Antichrist. Even the fact we shared a Christian name (my first, his middle) had once nearly been enough to persuade me to change mine by deed poll. Now my teenage nemesis was pursuing me again.

If you'd told me back in 1972 in that park in south London that the individual who single-handedly brought us sledging, player power and the ritual of brazenly readjusting his box in between every delivery, would cause me even more misery after his career than during it, I would have called you a fool. Yet the decades that had followed Ian Michael Chappell's retirement from the Australian captaincy had, if anything, been even more awful. At least when he was playing you didn't have to listen to him.

When I'd first encountered him he was just another of that breed of fair dinkum Aussie batsmen that stretched back through Bobby Simpson to Bradman and beyond. Gutsy, combative and Australian to his core, Chappell was a thorn in our flesh all right: but that's what you expected.

Yet it was his destiny to be handed the captaincy at just the time when they'd lost the urn in 1970/71. His promotion to the helm coincided with the emergence of two of Australia's greatest fast bowlers ever to wear the baggy green cap, and under his merciless direction, Lillee and Thompson were to rip up the cricketing rule book and turn it, at least for Brits, from the best-loved game into theatre of cruelty.

As everyone knows, it's not the dog's fault, it's the owner. Cocky, garrulous, dismissive of anything to do with the old country and old manners, he trained his human attack dogs by having them hang from tree branches by their jaws for hours on end and then setting them both on anything with two legs and an England cap. Which turned out to be mostly my boyhood heroes.

The result, of course, was misery and humiliation for all England fans. And having successfully dismantled the old-fashioned courtesies of the game, he now got to work on its mechanics. No wonder, then, that when Kerry Packer came along a year or two later and decided to turn my game into his own private fiefdom, it was Chappell at the side of his throne peeling the grapes.

When Chappell finally hung up his cap at the end of 1975, I silently thanked my God that we'd seen the last of him, and yet like some cricketing version of *A Nightmare on Elm Street*, he'd proved impossible to kill, so that just as you were panting on the edge of the bed with the bloody dagger still in your hand, he was sitting bolt upright behind you, now having discarded his bat for a microphone and his baggy green for a panama hat and a piebald moustache that looked as if it had been purchased in a fire sale at Ellisdons.

The great Arlott himself had once called Chappell, with sublimely damning understatement, 'a cricketer of effect rather than the graces'. That he of all people should have inherited the great man's mantle seemed beyond endurance. Even as I entered the bar I could hear those jarring cadences, somehow disinterested and menacing all at the same time: the sort of guy who asks you how you are and then, before you can answer, tells you.

'A good part of captaincy is instinct,' he was saying to anyone who'd listen. 'You know, you have to get up into the batsman's ribcage, tuck him up, cramp him for room … ' The match was barely two overs old and already he was into cruise control. I gritted my teeth and strode in. With luck there'd be such a crowd in front of the television that most of his pronouncements would be drowned out. I could only hope there'd be a corner of the bar left for me to stand in with a decent view of the screen.

But to my surprise, the bar was virtually empty. My companions were a trio of paunchy middle-aged men camped round a circular table in front of the screen, and a gaggle of pock-marked teenagers – although strictly speaking the latter couldn't be called spectators as they'd already abandoned the action at Bridgetown for a game of darts.

The final occupant, at least, offered the prospect of greater companionship; a man in his early fifties, with thinning brown hair carefully combed à la Charlton across his forehead, and bearing a striking resemblance to Leonard Rossiter. He was sitting on a scuffed leather sofa and sipping a pint of lager with the utmost care.

A local club scorer perhaps? Or some ageing club cricketer whose own match had been rained off? Whatever his reasons, here, at least, was surely someone with whom I could savour the experience. I offered up a sheepish smile to my companion and edged round the sofa beside him. Yet even before I'd sat down, a rasp of delight from the other drinkers indicated high drama at Bridgetown.

Whatever criticisms might be levelled at Twenty20, you can't accuse it of holding back. Instant action is what it promises, and instant action is what it delivers. The match was barely fifteen deliveries old, yet umpire Aleem Dar was already raising his finger to send a third Aussie batsman back to the dugout. Brad Haddin was simultaneously staring incredulously at the umpire and vigorously rubbing the side of his chest.

'He doesn't seem to like the decision,' I suggested mildly to my new friend. 'Thin inside edge off a straight one, was it?'

'Plonker,' he murmured, turning to face me for the first time.

It was difficult to know how best to respond. Was his comment aimed at Haddin for being out, the umpire for giving the decision or me for having the temerity to open my mouth?

'He's not your favourite then?' I continued.

'Arsehole,' he continued, with contained savagery. He lifted the glass to his lips as if measuring out a quantity of nitroglycerine and took an imperceptibly small sip before replacing it on the table next to him.

It was difficult to know whether the man regarded me as an ally or an irritant, but either way it was the last word I was to get out of him for many minutes. Indeed, the general atmosphere was equally muted. Funny, I'd imagined the place stuffed to the gunwales with Portsmouth FC supporters, each dressed in Pietersen replica England shirts and singing bawdy chants while a team of sweating barmaids ferried trays of lager and complimentary roast potatoes with which to soak up the booze. Here we were, on a Sunday afternoon in May, with the cricket world's most important populist showcase under way, and with Hampshire's own star batsman one of the crucial players – and yet the bar had all the vibrancy of the Havenbrook care home.

It wasn't long before the cameras broke away from the stuttering action on the field to concentrate on more garish treats, in particular a man in the crowd dressed as Queen Elizabeth, complete with realistic facemask and white ankle-length ball gown, who was trying to start a Mexican wave. I sensed my companion stirring once more, though this time it was at least a recognisable sentence, one that included nouns, verbs and a proper overarching sentence structure.

'They're all bastards.'

'Do you mean the crowd, the Aussies or the Royal Family?' I replied.

'They just won't lie down,' he continued. 'However many times you stamp on them, they always come back. You watch now.' His manner suggested if I didn't watch now there'd be a whole heap of trouble coming my way. He sat back, an air of utter despondency enveloping him like an overcoat. Yet who could blame him if he spent his leisure hours in these dismaying surroundings?

There was an air of decay about my other drinking companions as well. One of them had a huge beer gut drooping ludicrously over a pair of combat fatigues, and none of them looked like they'd seen daylight for many weeks. And no wonder. A glance at the blackboard showed that for anyone prepared to give their lives away here, the Golden Hind and a subscription to Sky TV offered the complete alternative-lifestyle package – lower-league football play-offs on Monday, Leicester City versus Blackpool on Tuesday, the Stan Jameson darts knockout final on

Wednesday, Kilmarnock versus Ross & Cromarty on Thursday, Man Utd versus Wigan, Rugby Sevens, the FA Cup Final, each event segueing seamlessly into the next until death finally provided an intermission.

If indeed Horndean was the valley of the dormouse, the scene here was surely some alcoholic version of the Mad Hatter's tea party: these men nursing never-ending pints to an endless procession of sporting telecasts, of which none could recall beginning and which were destined never to end.

In truth, there was precious little to get excited about this afternoon. With the exception of a late assault by Cameron White, the Aussies seemed curiously muted, and the cameras were soon trawling the crowd, at one point panning to a line of gyrating Caribbean cheerleaders in skin-tight hot pants, each undulating orb watched over with a mixture of embarrassment and incredulity by a nearby security guard.

Australia eventually limped to 147, and no sooner had they set off for their dugout and the changeover than Chappell was back on air and vibrating my fillings once more. 'It's all about self-belief at this level,' he chattered. 'Every bloke out there has the technique and the experience, that's a virtual given at international level, but when it comes down to it ...'

I rose and edged my way out of the bar. Outside in the street it was cool and damp. I could feel a migraine coming on.

When I returned twenty minutes later the interval was still in session, and the Sky cameras were using the opportunity to show some panoramic shots of the island, a sky of pure duck-egg blue framed by waving palms.

Less salubrious were the cutaways to the England balcony. Graeme Swann lolled, feet up on the balustrade, his face crayoned in garish white sunblock overlaid by black-and-red shades, while next to him Pietersen sprawled in his pads, his moussed hair glinting in the sun and strange tattooed hieroglyphs shimmering on oiled forearms. The Aussies looked even more louche, disporting cut-away sleeves and muscles the size of ham hocks. The whole scene looked more like a convention of porn stars than anything Richard Nyren might recognise.

When the match restarted, batting suddenly looked much easier, and perhaps fortified by the knowledge that they were chasing a below-par total, Pietersen and Kieswetter were soon rattling the score along without incident. The only time their reply faltered was midway through England's innings when the electronic sightscreen got stuck, leaving the two batsmen having to pick the ball out from what looked to be a giant crossword puzzle.

Nobody seemed sure whether it had gone partially white when it should have stayed black, or partially black when it should have stayed white, but in either case Pietersen was having none of it and a lengthy delay ensued while the authorities sent for an electrician to reboot the thing. But unless there was a major failure of nerve or electricity supply, England was nearly home and dry.

By now the light outside was beginning to fail, and sensing the imminent end of the match the barmaid here in the pub had switched all the fruit machines on. Time to go. Even as I stood up and fumbled for my car keys, Kieswetter thumped another brutal four and Chappell was on to it in an instant. 'You've got to look for positives, you've got to hit the middle of the bat smack hard, you've got to practise hard in the nets, no use just turning up and hoping it will happen.'

I gave a final weary glance at my companion, still sipping his original pint across the table from me. Whatever else, I was determined to form one final fragile strand of heart-to-heart dialogue with him before leaving this place.

'Jesus, I'll be glad when Chappell puts a sock in it, won't you?' I remarked.

'Wanker,' he said by way of response.

For the first time this afternoon, I couldn't have put it better myself.

As I drove back to Hambledon, I found myself speculating on the events of the afternoon. If ever a day had been a game of two halves, this surely was it. Up on Broadhalfpenny Down things had changed hardly at all since Nyren had perfected his straight bat; a helmet here, an arm guard there, and perhaps the odd expletive when fifty years ago a 'drat' would have sufficed, but in all other respects Sunday afternoon cricket here would have been as instantly recognisable to someone arriving in a Ford Prefect as it would in a G-Wiz.

Indeed, were such time travel possible, a visitor from the 1930s set down outside the Bat and Ball today would have thought nothing at all had changed, with the game's rhythms and rituals as timelessly familiar as the smell of linseed oil or the stench of a newly-cut Scotch egg.

But plonk such a visitor in front of the TV at the Golden Hind and he would think he was watching an episode of *Flash Gordon*, particularly when assailed by images of people in outlandish costumes surrounded by ferocious jets of dry ice and with Ian Chappell as the Ming of Mongo.

An old edition of *The Cricketer* magazine I have in my possession, published not long after the inception of fifty-over cricket back in the 1970s, contains an article by the redoubtable Swanton. In it he'd attempted to crystallise, for younger enthusiasts, the seismic effect of condensing the natural rhythms of the game into a truncated form.

'It will be difficult for younger readers to realise how different was the face of English cricket before the introduction of the first limited-over competition,' he proclaimed with typically stately prose, going on to admit that for all its faults, its introduction 'has been a boon in some respects'. You can almost hear his teeth grinding as he commits the words to paper.

Swanton's words had been written forty-one years ago. Yet now even fifty-over cricket, the form of the game he found most threatening to tradition, seemed impossibly quaint and meandering when compared to this new kid on the block. During a dinner I'd attended a couple of years ago with one recent ex-England captain, he'd stated categorically that with the advent of T20, the fifty-over form of the game would be dead within a decade; and one can only imagine what Swanton would have made of today's nuclear-powered high jinks.

And what would be the memories I'd retain from today's encounter? Would it be Pietersen's fifty, or that desperate run-out, or those clubbed sixes high into the crowd? Once upon a time such acts of mayhem would have been sufficient to merit an entry in my Letts schoolboy diary: *Went to Hove today: Tony Greig hit a six*. Yet now T20 had made such things commonplace. No – my memories would be of those cheerleaders with the quivering posteriors, the line of men in Lycra catsuits or the bloke dressed as HRH. The memory only retains the memorable. And in T20, drama is commonplace.

I suppose my desire to get back to Hambledon to see the denouement of the game there was in some ways a desire to finish my day with some simple fare after the diet of cricketing pop and chips. But when I arrived it was obvious the match had long since finished. Through the gap I could see the solitary figure of a lone groundsman dragging the covers across the pitch, and by the time I'd locked the car and wandered across, he too had vanished.

I toyed briefly with a warming pint in the snug with Ros and the players, but it was a long drive back to London, and besides, I would be an interloper over there, nodding gamely back as they regaled me with games and participants I had neither witnessed nor cared about.

Yet still I lingered. With the match long ended and night falling, Broadhalfpenny Down now looked much like it must have for nigh on three hundred years: the line of trees, with rabbits venturing gingerly out from the undergrowth for their evening meal; the twinkling lights of houses on the horizon; rooks cawing in distant boughs, and in the centre of all things, twenty-two yards of God's most priceless earth. I almost fancied I could see the rotund Arlott standing amongst the shadows.

Except, of course, he wouldn't be here. He'd be over in the pub ordering another bottle of claret and fishing about in his briefcase for a corkscrew.

I got back to London soon after ten and picked up Julia from the station. The trip to see Wyn had gone well – they'd even had a game of Scrabble in the garden, an encounter Wyn had won on a triple-worder with onyx. They hadn't heard David Mellor's programme, but the day had ended with a sing-along to a Max Bygraves compilation CD in the lounge.

Come to think of it, today had been successful all round, what with England triumphing in Barbados and a vital edging piece inserted in the jigsaw of my own cricketing history. Though the last word on this slice of priceless cricketing heritage should be left to the great Arlott himself.

'If you walk up the road from Hambledon,' he wrote, 'past Park Gate, towards Clanfield, you will come to an old redbrick inn, bleaching in the sun: across the road from it there is a great bare Hampshire down. Don't walk by without looking at it: it's the home of the giants – the old inn is the Bat and Ball and the down is Broadhalfpenny Down, the home of Hambledon, the greatest single club in the history of cricket.'

6

Royal Muse

Imagine a schoolboy dream actually coming true.

You're eleven. You're now old enough – just – to play with a proper hard ball, and with the addition of pads, batting gloves and the true emblem of a burgeoning adolescent, a plastic box to protect your newly descended testicles, at last you're beginning to feel like a real cricketer. Where once the highlight of your week was feeding the ducks in the park or playing on the swings, now the only thing you long for is the chance of a game of cricket with your dad on a Sunday afternoon.

One such occasion arrives. Benny and Peggy announce they're taking you out for a drive to the nearby resort of Hastings, a time-honoured ritual in the Simkins household and one that has been going on for as long as you can remember. You know the routine – fish and chips on the prom, a brief constitutional, and then a long leisurely drive home through the countryside, taking care to stop off at an elegant spa town on the borders of Sussex and Kent where your mum likes to have a cup of hot chocolate in a favourite tea room of hers.

And now, having done all that, Dad has taken you across the road from the café to a gently sloping area of parkland, and has offered to bowl to you for half an hour before setting back for home.

You twist your set of child-sized stumps into the grass, strap on your pads, inch your perspiring fingers into your batting gloves and waddle to the wicket to start your innings. This process in itself has taken up nearly ten minutes, but never mind: still another twenty to go. And after several ecstatic overs of clobbering your dad's gentle donkey drops to all points of the compass, you turn to find that amongst all the dog walkers and picnickers enjoying the grass alongside you, England's most glamorous young professional player is watching from a nearby bench.

It's every schoolboy's fantasy. The perfect blend of workaday reality (the picnic), the improbable denouement (England's champion stumbling upon your efforts on his day off) and the wildly romantic – he strolls over, lays a gentle hand on your shoulders: 'I've been watching you, young man. Stay there a moment. I'm just going to have a word with your father.'

This delicious scenario actually took place – at Wellington Rock Park in the centre of Tunbridge Wells, to be precise.

Well, OK, not the last bit – being signed up on the spot – but the rest of the story happened just as I've described. It may not seem so much now to jaded middle-aged sensibilities, but to an 11-year-old it was everything. For a brief, blissful interlude one summer's afternoon I lived out my greatest fantasy – executing what I imagined was a batting masterclass in front of Sussex's most influential player and the nation's rising hero.

I can still recall both him and his girlfriend on that wooden seat now, forty years on. The girl was an attractive blonde of the sort that in only a few months' time would begin to inundate my teenage dreams, but back then I gave her no more than a passing glance. No, it was the sight of her male companion that sent an electric bolt contorting through my body.

And there could be no mistake. He was instantly recognisable: the lean yet towering frame, his trademark shock of straw-blond hair fluttering in the breeze, and those curiously strangled guttural vowels. It was Tony Greig.

At the time Greig wasn't yet the internationally known figure he was soon to become. The swift ascent to England colours and hence to the national captaincy was still a few years away. But that it would eventually prevail wasn't in much doubt, certainly to anyone who watched him playing cricket at Hove. Tony Greig had one thing you can't learn in the nets or even out in the middle – he had star quality.

The politics surrounding this brash, cocky suntanned six-footer who played for Sussex and England but who came from South Africa were well beyond me at the time, but I already knew, albeit only instinctively, that his personality and will-to-win had been forged in circumstances quite unlike Shoreham-by-Sea or Burgess Hill.

Brash, bumptious and oozing self-belief, he was somehow different to the other cricketers on the county circuit, if only because he seemed entirely at ease with glamour and celebrity in a way that normal county pros weren't back then. I'd watched him with increasing devotion ever since his arrival at Hove back in 1967.

And now he was watching me.

Goodness only knows what he was doing in a suburban park when he should have been playing for Sussex (although the fact he had his arm in a sling presumably had something to do with it). All I know is that his unexpected and highly implausible arrival at Wellington Rock gave me a thrill I never forgot.

In truth, the denouement was somewhat anticlimactic. Having missed a wide half volley outside the off stump and waddled down to deep third man to retrieve the ball, I returned to see Greig and his girlfriend already crossing the road towards the town centre. A moment more and they'd disappeared from view. They never even looked back. But never mind. I'd been able to indulge one of my great sporting scenarios: the small boy given the chance to show what he could do in front of a leading player of the game. Even my imaginary Owzthat world was never this good.

For many days afterwards my heart missed a beat whenever our phone rang at home. Maybe, maybe, just maybe, this was the call from the Sussex Secretary following up Greig's recommen-dation. 'Michael, Arthur Dumbrell here, we've had the devil's own job tracking you down, but Mr Greig was insistent ... '

A couple of years later I returned to Tunbridge Wells to watch Sussex play against Kent in a three-dayer. Greig took eight wickets for 42 in the Kent innings, his finest ever bowling stats, and his status as the hero of Tunbridge Wells was confirmed. No rediscovery of my cricketing past, present and future would be complete without a revisit. And with a T20 match scheduled this evening, Wednesday 9 June – particularly one between Kent and Sussex – I needed no second prompting.

I don't know why I'd never got round to revisiting Tunbridge Wells in the intervening four decades. What had taken me so long? I suppose having spent most of my adult life trying to avoid Nigel Farage, why risk spoiling all that good work?

The town's image as a bastion of ultra-conservative values has been immortalised in the fictional character of the morally outraged resident, 'Disgusted of ... ' Thus the popular concep-tion of this small spa town nestling in the weald of Kent is of a town full of bristling colonels and UKIP supporters, writing indignant letters to the *Daily Telegraph*, usually in green ink, frequently commencing with a curt form of address: 'Sir, am I alone in thinking ... ', and fulminating about the latest EU directive governing the curvature of bananas, the compulsory wearing of goggles during the conker season or the elevation of that ghastly screamer from Pineapple Dance Studios to the cult of media celebrity.

Residents may complain about the unfairness of this stereotypical image, yet only last year, former soldier 62-year-old Stefan Gatward embarked on a one-man campaign of what he described as 'grammatical vigilantism', and painted in the missing apostrophes on all the town's street signs. You don't find that sort of thing in Hackney.

Yet it seems I might have pre-judged this elegant resort. Recent evidence suggests 'Disgusted' was actually invented by a member of staff on the local newspaper, who, alarmed at the lack of contributions to the letters pages, began inventing bogus missives in order to generate copy.

Now, in the twenty-first century, there were signs that this pillar of archaic propriety was at last crumbling. Apparently you can purchase counter-intuitive T-shirts in the High Street with the logo 'Delighted of Tunbridge Wells' without being branded a dangerous subversive, while the town briefly even boasted its own super-hero, a strange masked individual dressed as a monkey and attired in a cape, who has been spotted helping old ladies across the precinct, returning discarded supermarket trolleys and picking up litter.

No greater testimony to the loosening of civic stays is required than the fact that the former child of Satan, Roger Daltry of The Who, has been allowed to open a trout farm in the vicinity.

The old Nevill Ground, situated in the side streets amongst the twitching curtains, has hosted its own annual cricket festival for many decades; indeed, with its spectacular profusion of rhododendrons circling the boundary, it can reasonably claim, along with about two dozen other venues, to be 'the most beautiful ground in the country'.

Kent were playing Sussex in a T20 match here tonight, and given the town's reputation for gentility, with luck the floodlights would come with a hint of apricot while the normally blaring bursts of ear-splitting music between each wicket might with luck be replaced by something more soothing – perhaps some Mantovani or Bert Kaempfert.

That's not to say the old Nevill hasn't seen plenty of drama in its time. Little 'Tich' Freeman took sixteen for 82 here against Northamptonshire in 1932 (he named his retirement cottage Dunbowling), while the luminous left-hander Frank Woolley composed some of his sweetest music on the famous old strip. Stirring names, and no doubt stirring times: yet the Nevill's only truly unique claim to cricketing fame is that it's the only ground in the world to have been subject to an act of terrorism by women's libbers.

Days before the commencement of the 1913 season, the original pavilion was burnt down by militant suffragettes, and although they left no clue as to the reason for their actions, apart from a singed photograph of their beloved leader on the outfield, it's safe to assume it was in protest against the incarceration of Mrs Pankhurst in Holloway prison. Sir Arthur Conan Doyle, who by then was living in nearby Crowhurst, lambasted them as 'female hooligans' and compared the attack on the pavilion with 'blowing up a blind man and his dog': which suggests that, whatever else, metaphors were not the great author's strongpoint.

I arrived and checked in at the Lansdale, a once elegant but now slightly run-down warren of rooms just behind the town's elegant Georgian arcade known as The Pantiles.

Mid-morning is always a bad time to check in anywhere in Britain: not only it is impossible to throw off the vague suspicion among the hotel staff that you might be an escaped murderer on the run, but it's in the crack between the staff clearing up from overnight but not yet having tarted things up for the next arrivals.

In order to get to the reception desk I had to pick my way over piles of discarded bed sheets, some with unsavoury discolorations, while from every corridor came the low, throaty hum of antique vacuum cleaners. The woman at the front desk was elbow-deep in paperwork, and from the shelf behind her a transistor radio blasted the voice of Jeremy Vine asking the nation if Prime Minister David Cameron should really visit Afghanistan.

'Business or pleasure?' she asked as she laboriously filled in my reservation form.

'It's a bit of both,' I replied, going on to explain my purpose in coming here. I mentioned that I had several hours to kill before the game, so might she, I wondered, have any suggestions for how best to spend my time, anything a bit quirky perhaps, off the beaten track?

'Quirky … ' she repeated uncertainly to herself as she processed my credit card. 'Well, there's the derelict site of the boarded-up cinema.'

'What's the story behind that then?'

She shook her head. 'There isn't one,' she said sadly. 'It's just the derelict site of a boarded-up cinema.'

My room was certainly quirky and off the beaten track. Whether or not the receptionist had responded to my cricketing motif I couldn't be sure, but she'd booked me into an attic room the size and shape of a cricket net: about thirty yards long and hardly wide enough to move about in unless you traversed sideways. The remote control for the TV at the far end of the room didn't function, not because it was faulty but simply because the beam didn't extend that far.

It was only when I glanced out of the window that I realised the serendipity of my choice. My view looked directly out on to Wellington Rock, the very patch of grass on which my fifteen minutes of sporting fame had occurred nearly half a century ago. Even the bench looked to be in the same position.

Gazing out now, I felt a slight stab of regret at the memory of my old dad trundling in off his three-pace run up in his shirt and braces, his fingers still stained with newsprint of three hundred Sunday newspapers. As a kid I had no idea of just how hard both he and Mum toiled to keep me in gym shoes and batting gloves, yet now from my elevated perspective it seemed incredible that either of my parents had sufficient energy to do anything on their half-day off other than flop on to the sofa and fall sleep, let alone drive all over the south-east with their sport–mad son.

Feeling a wave of melancholy washing over me, I roused myself and closed the window. Dad wouldn't want this. He'd stand me up straight and remind me there was a world to discover out there. I grabbed my windcheater and set off to explore.

Tunbridge Wells owes its fame to its celebrated spring waters, discovered by accident in the seventeenth century and which soon acquired a heady reputation for restorative powers. Within a couple of years of the spring's discovery, the town was full of Regency toffs who flocked here to cure the dyspeptic effects of their diet, which from the look of the recent TV series *Supersizers* seemed to consist of eating entire sheep heads in aspic.

Today it's one of only three towns in the country that are permitted to put the official 'Royal' on their street signs. (The others, if you're going to a pub quiz this evening, are Leamington Spa and newly-crowned Wootton Bassett.)

The sense of gentility even extends to the shops. Take the specialist cookery store next to the tourist office, for instance. The windows and interiors were festooned with just the sort of thing that would be indispensable to Julia if only she could cook. For someone whose only piece of essential kitchen equipment is the telephone number of the local Chinese takeaway, it was like stepping into a magical emporium. Odd contraptions with bulbous handles and sliding apertures were hanging from every available wall space.

I wandered around in this culinary Aladdin's cave, examining all sorts of bewildering artefacts whose purpose could only be guessed at. How on earth had I managed to get by without such indispensable items as aluminium lolly moulds, medium ribbon apple scrapers, crêpe flippers, ceramic sharpeners and ice-cube moulds in the shape of false teeth?

With the afternoon already well advanced I set off on my quest to sample the town's famous waters. Almost at once I got lucky. A few yards away along the street, I saw an elderly woman wearing a mob cap who stared balefully up at me from below pavement level. As I peered down she fluttered a fan hopefully in my direction. I'd found my dipper.

Lillian was one of a number of volunteers who manned the attraction throughout the summer months and dispensed samples of the town's particular brew in glass goblets to passing tourists. At one end of her pit was a stone trough with some of the murkiest water I'd ever seen lying sullenly in the bottom.

While I sampled a cupful of her brew, she explained to me all about dipping and dipperdom. The sample I was now attempting to force down was indeed from the very chalybeate spring that had first attracted polite society all those years back, and although the actual source was somewhere beneath the adjacent Boots the chemists, it was still possible to relive the piquant sensation of imbibing water suffused with the taste of rusty horseshoes.

She also offered guidance in what she called 'the language of the fan'. According to Lillian, a closed fan touching the right eye meant, 'When might I be allowed to see you?'; a half-open fan close to the lips meant 'You may kiss me'; while drawing the fan across the forehead indicated, 'You have changed.'

All well and good I suppose, and no doubt quite enough to occupy polite conversation in the eighteenth century, but hardly profound enough to answer life's big questions, such as, 'Is the hokey-cokey really what it's all about?'

Thus refreshed, I decided to explore further. Up in London the new Conservative-Liberal coalition cabinet may be rumoured to be preparing for savage expenditure cuts, but if so the news hadn't yet reached this part of Kent. The town centre had a well-heeled air to it, with bespoke butchers and sleek delicatessens selling toasted figs and fresh local asparagus tied up in designer rubber bands; while the hairdressers were full of opulent women reading gossip magazines while blonde lovelies fussed about, pasting goo into their hair and wrapping it in tinfoil.

I ended up spending the remainder of the afternoon in the Opera House with Ron and Larry. Built in 1902 and opened by the great actor-laddie himself, Sir Herbert Beerbohm Tree, the premises was still far and away the town's most impressive building, and had once even boasted a statue of Hermes on its roof. The item had only been removed because its nakedness offended certain prudish members of the community, including, perhaps, the individual who had been going around painting apostrophes.

Yet this temple to the artistic muse had followed the same inexorable decline as so many establishments in the UK, becoming a cinema, a bingo hall and now, in its current incarnation, a sports bar.

Larry and Ron were also in town for the cricket, but had arrived deliberately early so they could sit indoors and down pints. Larry worked for the National Blood Transfusion service while Ron was a bus driver. They knew little of their celebrated surroundings other than that the exterior was featured in the Morrison's supermarket Christmas advert, the one in which Richard Hammond advanced through snow-covered streets with his trolley piled high with Christmas goodies.

Ron had even worked on the project as an extra, and spent some time explaining to me in exhaustive detail exactly where I might see him if I cared to watch the commercial again. He was easy to spot, he assured me, as he was heavily featured twice – fifteenth in the queue for Santa Claus, and also briefly glimpsed later on, next but one to the person standing beside Denise Van Outen in the shot where she's walking down The Pantiles arm-in-arm with Hammond and a pantomime horse.

When I explained that it might be quite a job summoning up such a clip in mid-June, he smiled knowingly and began rummaging in his haversack. Luckily for me, he explained, he had his PC with him, and the bar was on Wi-Fi. Two minutes later we were all watching the advert on YouTube.

It turned to be rather good fun, a bit like a Christmas version of *Where's Wally*. Several times I was convinced I'd spotted him, but each new sighting was answered with a shake of the head and a recommendation to view the item again. The trouble was that there were about three thousand other extras similarly rugged up in woolly coats and hats, all looking identical. But having spent years visiting friends and acquaintances backstage at the conclusion of shows, the delicate matter of assuring him he was wonderful, darling, when I hadn't even noticed him was never likely to tax my considerable resources.

We left the bar soon after five and wandered back through the town in search of the ground. It wasn't difficult to find, as the distant *whump-whump* of pulsating hip-hop music could be heard echoing round the surrounding streets and expectant punters were approaching the entrance from all directions. I stood patiently at the end of a lengthy queue while a burly security card riffled through my consignment of rail receipts and leaflets about the language of the fan in search of evidence of al-Qaeda. Having been given security clearance, I was finally allowed in.

The Nevill was certainly lovely, but more than that, it was full. There must have been nearly 6,000 crammed inside. The sun was hot, the air was sweet, the rhododendrons were partially out, and Kent were batting. Summer was in full swing.

As I arrived the players were already making their way out on to the field. It wasn't easy to find a seat, yet eventually I located one next to a family already knee-deep in burgers and pop. Soon the ball was being clubbed to all parts of the square, which is just what we all wanted. The Sussex opening bowler Martin-Jenkins claimed the early wicket of Joe Denly, but that only provoked his opening partner and club captain Robert Key into renewed fury.

There is a feeling in the Kent cricketing community that Key's international career has suffered because he carries a bit of weight (his nickname is 'Pudding') and doesn't take life too seriously. How else can you explain the omission from the national side of a player who scored a double hundred and a ninety in the same Test match? Yet Key follows in a long tradition of portly belters stretching from Gatting and Inzamam-ul-Haq, through Milburn and Shepherd back to Warwick Armstrong and the great WG himself, and very nicely they've all done too. Key was soon impressing his point in the only way he knew by clumping the ball to all points of the compass, and long before I'd finished my first platter of chips Kent had added 47 for the second wicket.

Yet when Key was eventually dismissed having one yahoo too many, his departure went almost unnoticed. It's not as if the crowd weren't interested – it's just there was so much else to see and do. There is something almost unendurably poignant about watching the English outside on a fine summer's evening. Locked up indoors for so long each year, waiting patiently for a chance to get on the shorts and T-shirts in God's good air, by the time some decent weather finally comes along we get impossibly over-excited, like a dog who's been waiting all day to be let out for a run.

The atmosphere tonight was like some huge family barbecue. Weddings were discussed, photos of new-born babies were handed around, jokes were told and retold – there was hugging and back-slapping and laughter and discussion of problems at work and the onset of varicose veins and whether or not they were hoping to go over to Australia at Christmas to see their grandkids. The air was thick with the sound of beery laughter and chit-chat.

The players, too, seemed to catch the spirit of the crowd, with those fielding on the boundary signing autographs between balls. The spectators in return supported both sides at once, applauding Sussex's Matt Prior after he juggled an improbable catch at long on, and then cheering a bright fifty by Kent's Darren Stevens, whose late heroics hoisted Kent's total to an eminently defendable 163.

During the interval I wandered out to have a look at the pitch. Nobody's quite sure why cricket fans do this, but it remains one of the traditions of the game, and I was pleased to see this spurious ritual still being observed tonight. Spectators were gathered at both ends of the wicket, nodding knowingly to one another and pointing out scuff marks and boot imprints as if deciphering an ancient burial site.

Actually, I do know why we do this. It allows all of us bumbling, incompetent middle-aged men to fantasise about what it might be like to play there for real. We may nod sagely about types of soil and its propensity for taking spin, but there's a parallel dialogue going on in the privacy of our imagination.

If we try hard, we can almost imagine ourselves batting on this very surface, carving Luke Wright away to the deep point boundary or hooking Simon Cook for six. Pity us. Because it's all we have to cling on to.

During my brief tenure at the crease I got talking to two men, one of whom was called Mr Crampton, and the other, most wonderfully, Mr Jelly. Mr Jelly had come back specially early from work in London to see the match, and was obviously enjoying himself or, to put it another way, was pleasantly drunk.

His main topic of conversation was not Kent's progress in the Twenty20, but his daughter. She wanted to be an actress, and he wasn't sure how best to advise her, as he knew absolutely nothing about the profession, employed as he was in the diplomatic service.

She was nearly sixteen, he explained, but he'd heard somewhere that the business was massively overcrowded. I mentioned that I knew something of the business, albeit from a dinosaur's POV. Would Mr Jelly perhaps like me to suggest some possible ways forward for her?

'That would be wonderful, thank you.' He gripped my wrist gently, whether in grateful affection or to steady himself, I couldn't be sure.

'Well,' I began, 'she mustn't be discouraged by what she

reads in the press. Although it's true that 98 per cent of all actors are unemployed, what they don't tell you is that—'

'It's just I saw her in her sixth-form college's production of *Bugsy Malone* and she really was terrific. I mean, terrific. I know I'm her father and all that, but she genuinely surprised me. I think she might have something.'

'Well, in that case, has she considered doing a course in musical theatre? It might be—'

'And she's very good at impressions. She takes her mum off round the dinner table, and she's really got her off to a tee.'

'Ah well, of course, variety is a different thing—'

'And she's hoping to get some work as an extra. She was on the advert Morrison's shot here last autumn, and she's thinking it that might be a good way to start.'

'Ah well, the thing about extra work—'

The conversation lurched back and forth like this for many minutes, Mr Jelly never quite allowing me to come to my point before jumping in with some new testimonial about his daughter's theatrical ability. 'Would you like to see a photograph of her?' he eventually asked, but his fingers were already fumbling in the back pocket of his jeans. As he did so the penny dropped: Mr Jelly was not seeking practical advice at all, merely reassurance that the light of his life would be well and happy and not have her heart broken by either professional disappointment or the machinations of some disreputable luvvie.

I assured him she looked lovely, that whatever she did would turn out for the best and that she would assuredly become a household name. Which, come to think of it, with her surname, was not beyond the bounds of possibility. As long as her Christian name was Jilly, immortality was surely already within touching distance.

By now the five-minute bell was already ringing and Key was leading his Kent players out on to the pitch. As I said goodbye, the taciturn Mr Crampton mentioned something I hadn't noticed: namely, that the Nevill Ground didn't possess any floodlights. It was already past 8pm and now the sun was going down it was distinctly gloomy. 'I'm not sure they'll see much by the time this is through,' he remarked.

To judge by Sussex's response they'd obviously come to the same conclusion. Prior and his fellow opener, the pugnacious New Zealander Brendon McCullum, went about their response as if they had a train to catch. The Kent opening bowler Simon Cook came in for especially tough treatment, seeing his eighteen deliveries bludgeoned for 35. But that's the odd thing about T20. Normal rules simply don't apply. Cook's teammates seemed thrilled with his endeavours; in fact, any bowler who manages to limit the batsmen to less than twelve an over gets a pat on the rump and a series of high-fives. Mayhem is the order of the day, and merely preventing runs being hit is the signal for wild celebrations.

As darkness fell the match simmered nicely to a climax. Detractors of this curious form of the game argue that once one side is too far in front the contest becomes both meaningless and boring. But here the match see-sawed back and forth in tantalising fashion, with Sussex continually losing crucial wickets just as they threatened to overwhelm their hosts. At least I think that's what was going on: frankly it was becoming difficult to follow the path of the ball.

The match ended in high drama. With the lights of the club-house shining brightly, Sussex needed three off the final over. The crowd, who for some while had hardly looked up from their pints, now fell genuinely silent. This, after all, was what they'd paid £25 for.

The first two deliveries from opening bowler Azhar Mahmood to Sussex captain Michael Yardy yielded nothing, as each effort was punched straight to fielders in the covers. Off the next delivery, however, Yardy larruped the ball to the square leg boundary for four, and Sussex had prevailed by four wickets.

The result sparked a pitch invasion, the like of which I hadn't witnessed since the good old days of the 1970s. Young boys streamed on from every direction, many clutching autograph books, while the players fled from the pitch leaving the poor abandoned umpires feebly waving the uprooted stumps at anyone daring to approach. Afterwards the crowd gathered in front of the pavilion, while hundreds more played their own games of impromptu cricket on the outfield. I picked my way in between, dodging missiles like some geriatric break-dancer, and stood in front of the clubhouse. Someone had put 'You're Beautiful' on the turntable and its lilting beat echoed through the evening air.

By now it was nearly 10pm and the crowd were drifting off in the dark. Out on the grass, players mingled freely with friends and well-wishers, and I noticed Kent wicket-keeper Geraint Jones signing autographs at the head of a long queue. My drinking pals Ron and Larry were waiting sheepishly in its midst and waved shyly over at me.

'I am used to Tunbridge Wells: we are all hopelessly behind the times.' So said a character in EM Forster's 1908 novel *A Room With A View*. On the evidence of tonight, perhaps that was the reason for the town's quiet but beguiling charm.

Back at the hotel I sat in the open window, breathing in the warm air and staring across the arterial road at the dim shape of Wellington Rock. My brief brush with sporting glory seemed an age away. Dad had been dead nearly a quarter of a century; in fact, it dawned on me that I was older now than he had been when we'd played our game here.

And what of Tony Greig? Having been one of the architects of Kerry Packer's World Series cricketing circus, he relocated to Australia, where he carved out a new career as a pundit and entrepreneur. And very nicely he has done too. Back then his act of treachery in using his position as England captain to secretly recruit half the team to a rival enterprise seemed to my middle-class sensibilities an unforgivable act of betrayal. Greig, however, had no such qualms. 'I have sacrificed cricket's most coveted job for a cause which I believe could be in the interests of cricket the world over,' he proclaimed. Maybe, Tony, maybe. But you made one awestruck teenager feel pretty foolish for a time …

I closed the curtains and lay back on the bed. Time heals all wounds, I suppose. Whatever his faults – and he had many – Greig's presence on that bench that Sunday afternoon provided me with a few moments of sublime fantasy, and I will always thank him for spending a few moments watching a hapless kid sloshing a cricket ball round a small park when he could have spent the time snogging a gorgeous blonde.

Even now, forty years on, the memory of that interlude still has the power to comfort me when things fall apart.

7

Leggings Before Wickets

'We have another caller on the line. It's Michael from Brighton. Michael, you're through to *Call Your MP*. What is it you'd like to ask Sir Kenneth?'

I remember the incident as if it were yesterday. A summer's afternoon some time in the mid-1980s. Instead of lounging on Brighton beach amongst the holidaymakers, I was sitting in my small bedsit just off the seafront with the phone receiver pressed to my ear and a furious expression on my face. My local radio station, BBC Radio Sussex, were broadcasting their regular afternoon phone-in programme, one in which listeners with too much time on their hands could speak to their local elected representative and let off steam about their everyday civic concerns – usually the amount of graffiti or the state of the municipal flower beds.

Normally I would prefer to take my eyes out with an oyster pick than spend a glorious afternoon such as this stuck indoors listening to some old conservative grandee answering questions about parking restrictions and rubbish collection rosters. But my heritage was at stake.

'Yes. Hello. What I want to ask Sir Kenneth is this. As Member of Parliament for Hastings, how on earth can he possibly condone the plan to concrete over the cricket ground in the centre of the town simply in order to create another shopping centre? Isn't he aware just how precious the central cricket ground is? Doesn't he know the special place it holds in the history of the sport? Hasn't it occurred to him that apart from the ground being the only green space in the entire town centre—'

'Thanks, Mike, I get your drift,' interrupted the presenter. 'You're clearly referring to the proposed development on the site of the current Central Ground at Priory Meadow. Well, Sir Kenneth, Mike's obviously a cricket fan. What's your response?'

The smooth, well-honed vocabulary of the Conservative Party swung into action. Sir Kenneth Warren had been the town's MP for nearly thirteen years, and having survived the political furnace of the House of Commons, it was hardly likely that some luvvie whippersnapper on a local radio show was going to disturb his equilibrium.

'You've no need to worry, Michael: you'll still have your cricket. The developers are building a brand new facility on the edge of the town, and I can guarantee that the name of Horntye Park will soon be just as celebrated and revered in the professional game as dear old Priory Meadow is now. But if I may say so, it's also important to focus on the tremendous retail opportunities being offered, ones that will greatly enhance the overall shopping experience for local residents ... '

Long before he'd uttered that dread phrase, 'boosting the local economy', I'd fallen into a stupor, staring bleakly out at the sunshine and recalling those words of John Betjeman in his mild but deadly lament to a vanishing England, 'The Town Clerk's Views':

So let us hear this cool careerist tell
His plans to turn our country into hell ...

By the time I'd come to my senses I was already being muscled off the airwaves in favour of the next caller, a woman who wanted to know what Sir Kenneth was going to do about the amount of dog dirt on the promenade at Bexhill-on-Sea. That telephone call had been nearly three decades ago. Now I was on my way back to Hastings to find out what had happened to Sir Kenneth's grand designs and whether his vision had been worth it after all.

> The sea is near. The channel winds blow up from the west and bring the screaming gulls, and the slanting sunlight shines back off distant windows. High above, the ruined castle looks down on the intimate oasis of peace amid the busy town.

So wrote the cricket writer and local resident Gerald Brodribb at just about the time the developers were submitting their balsa wood models to the town hall for final approval. If his words read like an epitaph for a vanishing Britain, it's hardly surprising. Located slap bang in the town centre, the old Priory Meadow ground hosted matches for nearly 140 years and was the beau idéal of what a provincial ground should be: friendly, unpretentious and, most importantly, at least for the residents of this cluttered little seaside resort, a haven of calm and tranquillity amid the clog of traffic and commerce.

The venue was synonymous with spectacular innings, nail-biting finishes and improbable bowling figures: some of which I even saw. Suffused with the essence of sea air, cheap boarding houses and 'Kiss Me Quick' hats, it was almost as if anyone who played there felt compelled to entertain, their very participation in the game an extension of a Donald McGill postcard.

WG scored two of his biggest hundreds here, Ranjitsinhji played his last innings and Gilbert Jessop hit a century of such speed and power (including 26 off one over) as to make Adam Gilchrist look by comparison like Alan Carr; while Denis Compton liked the ground so much he broke records with almost as much regularity as the windows of the surrounding houses. One of the most celebrated photos of the old Brylcreem boy shows him swaggering back to the pavilion, bat held aloft, having just broken the world record for both the number of runs and the number of centuries scored in a domestic season. From the look on his face, Hastings was going to be hard pressed to hold him that evening.

But even when the cricket was dull, it was a joy to be at Priory Meadow. Pressed upon on three sides by tottering houses, you could find fun and frolics merely by relaxing in your deckchair and looking up at the tiny back-room windows of surrounding properties: figures hunched over kitchen tables, old ladies tending their house plants or talking to pet budgerigars and young girls straight out of Edward Hopper paintings, leaning out with their elbows on the sill and their faces turned to the sun.

However, the cricket was rarely boring enough to merit scanning the horizon. Given the diminutive playing area, runs were plentiful once you'd got your eye in, and third-day declarations by over-ambitious captains frequently blew up in their faces. I myself witnessed some memorable innings, including a century by Allan Lamb of Northants of a fury and intent that only a sudden and inexplicable demotion from the England national team can engender in a sportsman.

So what had happened? Where had it all gone? Well, some time in the mid-1980s, some bright spark on the town council decided the town might benefit from more acrylic underclothing. And so this ancient and venerable ground was compulsorily purchased, and before you could say 'I'll see you in Courts', it had been razed and replaced by the magnificent new Priory Meadow Shopping Centre, all 420,000 square feet of it. And where Dexter and Ranji had once wove their magic, now harried shoppers ambled up and down searching for six packs of stay-fresh socks and extra large boxer shorts.

In truth I'm doing the place a disservice. In addition to pants you could apparently also purchase bras, children's clothes, jewellery, greetings cards, chemist's sundries, mobile phones – in fact, just about everything else a local resident could possibly need, except of course a quiet, green space in which to sit with your kids and contemplate life for a brief moment.

The loss of this splendid old ground is a prime example of the homogenisation of professional cricket that has taken place in the last forty years. Just as the supermarkets have colonised our high streets, driving off small, bespoke corner shops where the owner knew your name and often had your weekly shopping waiting for you even before you'd left your house, so cricket too has been forced into the same configuration.

Thus for every Swalec and Rose Bowl that has sprung up in the attempt to attract the big matches and the big money, many more smaller venues have disappeared under the bulldozer, the names of the fallen reading like some cricketing Thiepval: Leek, Burton-on Trent, Cleethorpes, Stroud, Hinckley, Monmouth, Dudley, Frome, and the magnificently titled Vista Road recreation ground, Clacton-on–Sea. At the going down of the sun, we will remember them.

In fairness, not all have suffered quite the brutal fate of Hastings, insomuch as some have managed to hang on to their playing area even if they've lost their elevated status. But others are now housing estates, carpet warehouses, lorry parks – or shopping malls. And with each new closure, the visceral connection between the game and local communities dies another small death. The tragedy of Hastings is that despite boasting such a rich heritage, it counted for bugger all once the accountants got to work with their spreadsheets and calculators.

And what a heritage it was. Cricket matches had been played in the town since 1744, including such intriguing contests as 'a Grocer versus four friends', 'One arm versus one leg', and one I'd especially like to have seen, 'Corinthians versus masticators'.

Once the site had been purchased by a group of local philanthropists, it was soon in demand not only for cricket but also as a much-needed civic amenity. One photograph taken in 1869 shows an election rally, while others depict drill parades for recruits to the Boer War, women's archery contests and, in one especially exotic image, two teams of muscular young men in capacious shorts engaged in a game of something called Push-Ball, in which the competitors seem to be attempting to manhandle a giant balloon back and forth across the outfield. It looks like a cross between a football match and an out-take from the opening credits of *The Prisoner*.

In 1868 the visiting Aborigine team displayed their skill here in boomerang-throwing, while in 1880 even the mighty Yorkshire deigned to pay a visit, the cream of England's bowling attack being clattered to all parts of the county by a local favourite with the splendid name of Herbert Pigg.

What's more, the residents of Hastings loved it. A match here in 1893 attracted sixteen thousand spectators, while another in 1932 saw twenty thousand crammed inside. Even in the mid-1970s when I regularly made the trip over from

Brighton, a Sunday League match between Sussex and local rivals Kent would regularly result in 'Ground Full' notices posted up well before the commencement of play. I'd even played here myself a couple of times, for my school in our annual encounter against Hastings Grammar, scoring 0 in my only appearance in 1972, and operating the giant scoreboard as part of my duties as twelfth man the following summer, an occasion I'd found vastly more enjoyable.

During the last professional match in August 1989 before the bulldozers moved in, Sussex lost heavily to Middlesex and Mike Gatting made an undefeated century. I'd attended the game in person and my main memory was not of the cricket but of the otherworldly atmosphere in which it had been played, as if nobody could quite believe what was about to happen. Upon departing the ground at the end of hostilities, I'd not even looked back. A bit like Trevor Howard when he leaves Celia Johnson in the railway station buffet in the last reel of *Brief Encounter*, I knew that the affair was over. Lingering for one final hand squeeze would surely only prolong the agony of separation.

In truth the 1980s were a bit of a balls-up for Hastings generally. As well as the destruction of Priory Meadow, several leading Victorian landmarks were either pulled down or left to decay beyond repair, including the town's second biggest hotel, the Royal Victoria, and the resort's spectacular open-air swimming pool. Still, it wasn't all bad. At least they got a McDonald's.

So what of the new ground? Thirty years on, was the space-age replacement Horntye Park on the lips of Geoff Miller and David Graveney when they gathered at Lord's to synchronise talent-spotting duties? Did Radio 4's Garry Richardson wake up each morning thinking, I must remember to mention yesterday's extraordinary events at Horntye Park on my bulletin?

Well, no. There'd been hardly any mention of cricket being played there in the two decades since Sir Kenneth's honeyed assurances. So what had gone wrong? Why hadn't there been uproar from the local populace? One long-term resident provided a hint of the underlying reason. My mate Colin has lived in the old town there for many years. 'Simmo,' he'd said when I asked him about it, 'you're talking about a town which is currently trying to prevent the building of a new world-renowned art gallery on the seafront in order to preserve a coach park. They do things differently here.'

I set off to pursue my enquiries the morning after the match at Tunbridge Wells, but as the train rattled through the Kent countryside, I was filled with conflicting emotions at the prospect of reacquainting myself with my old haunt. After all, seeing it buried under three acres of marble was going to be poignant. And even without that, my relationship with Hastings over the years has been a complex, not to say controversial one, and I wasn't entirely sure of my likely reception once I stepped from the train.

The reason for my disquiet was because of a more recent association with this small seaside resort, one that still left me a little uneasy about showing my face here. In the autumn of 1998 I'd spent a week here portraying the town's most infamous alleged murderer in a reconstruction for the BBC TV series, *Trail of Guilt*. The case itself, something of a *cause célèbre* both here and up at the Old Bailey, had briefly thrust this sleepy little town into the national spotlight, when Sion Jenkins, a local schoolteacher, had been convicted of killing his foster daughter Billie-Jo. With the Beeb looking for someone to portray the miscreant on film, and with my bearing more than a passing resemblance, I'd been chosen to portray Hastings' most notorious resident.

My week here had proved unsettling. Quite apart from the constant threat of being rugby-tackled between takes by some well-meaning pedestrian attempting to effect a citizen's arrest in the mistaken belief the town's most infamous villain had escaped from custody, I was forced to drive around the town in a facsimile of Jenkins's iconic white sports car with a burly cameraman wedged into the passenger seat. Each successive take was watched with barely disguised hostility by local residents and, truth to tell, I'd been so relieved to get to the end of the shoot that I'd skedaddled on the first train back to London without stopping to pay my respects to the ground.

Still, the incident was over a decade ago, and in any case Jenkins had since been acquitted on appeal and was now living a quiet and sober life elsewhere in the country. At least, that's what I told myself when the ticket inspector at the barrier asked to see my ticket. Did his eyes narrow slightly as he handed it back, or was it just my imagination? The sooner I could lose myself in a crowd, the better. And I knew just the place.

It didn't take long to find the shopping centre. For one thing I knew the route so well from the station I could have walked there with my eyes shut, and for another, the developers had erected a tasteful monument outside the entrance to the beautiful old ground they'd so comprehensively trashed. Handily positioned in front of Thornton's chocolates and beside a stall selling organic dog treats stood a 10-foot-high bronze statue entitled 'The Spirit of Cricket', and depicting a batsman pulling a cricket ball round to leg off the back foot.

Can you remember the trademark swivel shot employed with such devastating effect by 1970s West Indian batsman Roy

Fredericks? Particularly the example in the first World Cup Final at Lord's in 1975, the one which not only rocketed to the boundary but resulted in Fredericks treading on his stumps in the process? Well, imagine that recreated in burnished bronze, but with the face of the BBC economics correspondent Hugh Pym in a sunhat stuck on the top, and you've got 'The Spirit of Cricket' as envisaged by sculptor Alan Sly.

In the pavement a few feet away, an inscription read:

THE SPIRIT OF CRICKET

Unveiled by HER MAJESTY THE QUEEN to celebrate the opening of Priory Meadow Shopping Centre. Priory Meadow Shopping Centre is built on the site of the former Central Cricket and Recreation Ground on which the game was enjoyed for over 130 years.

Commissioned by Boots Properties PLC.

In fairness the sculpture itself was a capable enough representation, yet a closer inspection soon revealed several anomalies. Just as Roy Fredericks had done back in 1975, Hugh Pym was not only swivelling, but also had his posterior parked delicately on top of the bails. His back foot, too, seemed to be surreptitiously treading on the base of the wicket. Was this just a cunning piece of design to lend strength to the edifice, or was Mr Sly, perhaps a secret cricket fan, making a coded protest against the act of civic vandalism that had spawned his artwork? I'd like to think so.

After a brief pause to pay my respects, I walked in past Clinton's Cards and a stall selling tiny novelties in aid of the

Huntington's Disease Association, until I found myself in the cool, antiseptic embrace of the main thoroughfare. It felt odd to think that where I was standing now, surrounded by young mums pushing prams, I'd once sat all day in the boiling sun eating Cheesy Wotsits and watching Imran Khan.

Did any of these shoppers have the first idea about the significance of the spot through which they now moved, grazing on pre-packed sandwiches or slurping cans of fizzy drink? I decided to ask the nearest employee to hand, a young Thai woman working in a Pick 'n' Mix stall.

Her answer surprised me. In broken English, she explained she knew all about the famous old ground, and admitted that many shoppers she served during her daily duties expressed their sadness that this arcade had ever been allowed planning permission.

Admittedly I've filled in the gaps in translation. Her actual words were, 'Thuh people here, theh remembuh the cricket, and ah sad.' But I knew only too well what those limpid green eyes were trying to convey. Yet I found her comments strangely comforting, and expressed my gratitude in the only way I knew how, by buying 400 grams of yoghurt raisins.

Apart from the spindly statue outside in the street, all other evidence of the mall's illustrious past seemed to have airbrushed out of existence. Perhaps there might be something on the first floor. I followed a sign directing me to the grandly titled Central Control Office to pursue my investigation.

My journey necessitated me using a lift, a trip that placed me alongside an elderly couple who themselves resembled characters from one of McGill's postcards – he, short and rotund, with scarlet cheeks and perpetually harassed expression, she an ample-bosomed galleon in a bright red polka dot dress with flesh spilling out of every gap. We passed the time waiting for the automatic doors to close by smiling shyly at each other, and by the time it finally jerked into life were talking like old friends.

'Get what you want, did you?' said the woman, looking at my bag of sweets. I offered her one, and confessed the purpose of my trip here today, to discover the truth about the strange case of Priory Meadow.

'Oh, I remember the ground well,' said the man huskily. 'I came here as a kid. I saw Doug Wright here several times; we used to get on our bikes after school and hare down here, caught the final couple of hours and I never once recall being asked to pay.' But he admitted the town had changed. 'It's easier to find drugs in this town now than a bloody plumber,' he said. 'Never mind, that's life.'

The main control centre turned out to be a drab office lit by sickly fluorescent tubes. At the far end a smart-suited woman was sitting behind a desk energetically clipping lots of pieces of paper to lots of other pieces of paper, and as I approached a walkie-talkie crackled into life, someone requesting a cleaner to attend to a spillage in Holland & Barrett.

I explained the purpose of my visit, including my strange, unformed passion to plant my feet once more on the site of the famous old turf, and waited for her to press the alarm. Yet instead of summoning security, she brightened immediately.

'Oh yes,' she replied. 'I remember it well. My dad was opening bat for St Leonard's first eleven, so he used to bring the whole family down here on Saturday afternoons. I used to operate the scoreboard sometimes. Shame it's gone.' She had no actual memorabilia to show me, but instead directed me towards to a gloomy corridor leading to the management toilets. Next to a sign declaring 'Dogs die in locked cars' was a single framed photograph, sole testimony to the site's illustrious past.

Taken in May 1951, it showed the then Princess Elizabeth, now our Queen, visiting the ground to accept the deeds of Hastings castle. On either side of her are two neat lines of young girls, each waving tiny Union flags and curtsying gravely as she passes. The grass beneath their feet is strewn with either daisies or confetti, while behind stands them a throng of loyal celebrants and beaming parents, each of them captured in mid-cheer.

The photograph is a particular moment caught in time: redolent of fondant fancies, *Muffin the Mule* and *Mrs Dale's Diary*. This must have been about the last time you could capture such an image as this: lines of young children executing a perfect curtsy and each utterly content to be dressed up to resemble their mothers.

Indeed, if you concentrate hard enough, as I did, I swear you could almost hear the sound of Bill Haley in the far distance: or perhaps it was just the muzak drifting up from the mall below. No matter – within a couple of years 'Rock Around The Clock' was going to unleash a cultural firestorm that would do for this sort of artless vignette for all time.

Just as I was exiting, the woman called me back. 'Sorry to ask,' she said, 'but don't I know you?'

'I don't think so.'

'I'm sure I know you from somewhere. Aren't you off the telly?'

'I think you've got somebody else. People sometimes mistake me for Jeremy Vine.'

'No no, I know him. He's younger than you are. Oh, it's on the tip of my tongue, that'll be bugging me all day.'

It didn't take long to finish my cross-examination of Priory Meadow. Now it was time to put out a search warrant for

Horntye Park, and I soon found myself strolling along the main promenade. A once thriving fishing town, Hastings seafront nowadays has a distinctly threadbare look about it, with tatty hotels nose to tail with 1960s apartment blocks and garish arcades. Even at eleven on a Thursday morning, the pubs and bars were full of men nursing pints and reading the *Racing Post*.

Still, at least it was having a go. The crazy golf was already open, while the air buzzed with the synthetic tootle of slot machines. In the distance I noticed a seafront miniature railway trundling along, the only occupant a frozen-looking driver.

Things looked up a bit in the old town. This ancient warren of alleyways and winding medieval lanes had been jazzed up, pedestrianised and, according to a blue plaque, reopened by Bernard Bresslaw. Yet even here, where you might have thought the town's cultural ambitions would be most vividly pursued, the residents' implacable objection to the proposed new art gallery on the seafront was evident. The Jerwood Project may be fully funded by a private foundation with impeccable credentials, yet virtually every shop window on the main drag was festooned with a sign proclaiming 'Save Our Stade', the old Saxon word for 'landing place' and the official name of the precious coach park currently threatened with demolition.

I wandered into a shop selling bric-a-brac, in which a woman with alarmingly hennaed hair was sitting on a chair surrounded by what David Dickinson would describe as 'ephemera' and my old mum, somewhat more succinctly, as 'old tut'.

No sooner had I entered than she was on her feet and asking if I'd like to sign the online petition. But why, I wanted to know, was there such opposition to the scheme? Wasn't it a heaven-sent opportunity for this struggling resort to regain some of its old lustre? Hadn't she heard of St Ives? A struggling fishing port, it had been revitalised into a mecca of both tourism and culture simply by the building of a branch of the Tate gallery.

But Henna woman was having none of it. Long before I'd finished, she was shaking her head in vigorous denial. 'That's rubbish,' she replied, 'we rely on that coach park. That coach park is where everybody gets off. Take that coach park away and how on earth are people going to get here? Most of the folk have trouble walking – if they remove that coach park there'll be nowhere for them to sit, they can't have a pee and the coaches will have to drop them on the outskirts of the town.'

She ranted on, peppering each sentence with the phrase 'coach park' until I wanted to scream for her to stop. Her message was unequivocal: the ability to stagger no more than thirty yards to purchase a stick of rock or find a working toilet was far more important for the town's commercial prospects than any arty-farty nonsense about exhibitions showing unmade beds or sharks in formaldehyde. By the time she'd had finished she'd almost persuaded me modern art was responsible for every modern failing from the war in Afghanistan to the demise of Woolworths.

My next witness was St Clements Caves, a series of dank-smelling subterranean chambers carved out of the crumbling sandstone of the clifftop, and an attraction I regularly visited with my long-suffering parents when I was young, as part of our ritual Sunday excursions. Priory Meadow may have long gone, but I was pleased to see this at least still survived.

Originally used by the town's smuggling community to hide their contraband from the prying eyes of the customs officers, the soft sandstone chambers had been excavated and enlarged until they were big enough to justify charging trippers a couple of bob apiece to meander through. I recalled the straggling complex of tunnels and passageways as being largely empty and deliciously silent, exuding little more than a strong and vaguely alarming smell of damp earth, one that never failed to excite half-fearful imaginings of being buried alive or having your head split clean open by some wandering axeman freshly escaped from the local mental hospital. Just the sort of thing a ten-year-old kid requires from a cave, in fact.

But in the intervening decades the clammy hand of the PR consultant had been hard at work. What had once been a crude but eerily memorable sensation had now been rebranded 'The Smuggler's Experience', complete with gift shop, glossy brochure, assorted waxwork figures, interactive exhibits and commensurately inflated entrance fee.

My guide for the tour, 'Hairy Jack', was a virtual pirate whose grinning face, framed by a dodgy-looking set of false whiskers, appeared on the walls and ceilings wherever you went. It was like being given a guided tour by a combination of Merv Hughes and Justin Lee Collins.

'Ah-ha, my hearties, I don't like customs officers and I don't like you,' he roared the moment I set foot inside the first cavern. 'But come 'ere and I'll tell 'ee a tale of contraband and treason, of strange lights and sudden gunshots … ' In a commentary punctuated every four or five seconds by bursts of maniacal yokel laughter, he explained all you could ever need to know about smugglers and smuggling, plus quite a lot you didn't.

Even when there was a brief pause, it was filled by sound effects of donkeys walking on cobbles, distant gunfire and the ticking of clocks. With nothing to still their over-excited sensibilities, crocodiles of oversexed Italian teenagers shrieked and shouted their way through the tunnels, dropping popcorn everywhere. In one chamber there was even a selection of whirring fruit machines, as if the organisers had admitted defeat and bowed to the inevitable needs of uninterested foreign exchange students. I quickly tired of the clamour and returned to the surface – needless to relate, by the only route available, through the Smuggler's Experience gift shop.

Now the proud possessor of an 'I Love London' commemorative coffee mug, I returned to the prom and fortified myself with a portion of cockles purchased from a seafood stall decorated with a pirate flag and the warning, 'He who gets shot, deserves it'. Speaking of which, it was time to bring Horntye Park in for questioning.

It took me a while to find the place. For a start nobody seemed to know where it was, and even when I eventually got some coherent directions, the walk involved a steep uphill climb for nearly half an hour. Long before I reached the top I had to stop for breath and steady myself on the shoulders of passing pensioners.

Yet the nearer I approached, the greater the feeling I'd been here before. Then I realised why – Horntye Park had been built right next to Hastings police station, the very building in which my felonious doppelgänger had been taken after his arrest, and in which I'd subsequently reproduced some of his most dramatic testimony for the delectation of TV audiences.

As I passed the entrance to the station, a police car swung in from the road, and the driver briefly scrutinised me through the windscreen. Was it my imagination, or did his brow furrow slightly? I turned my coat collar up and hurried on up the hill.

Set back from the road, partially secreted up a concealed driveway, Horntye Park was indeed quite some facility. In addition to a pristine playing surface protected by state-of-the-art pitch covers, I spotted tennis courts and what looked to be an all-weather hockey pitch.

And yet there was something dispiriting about the place. Everything looked as if it had just been freed from its protective bubblewrap. I walked round the boundary until I came a large steel-and-glass clubhouse and tried the main door. It was locked. After several minutes of vainly jiggling handles and pressing entryphone buzzers, a couple of middle-aged women hove into view and entered by another door further along I hadn't previously noticed. As I followed the women up the stairs I passed adverts offering to host your wedding reception, while in the distance I could hear the familiar *thwuck-thwuck* of a squash ball against a wall.

The top gave out on to a spacious landing off which could be glimpsed various-sized function suites, one of which already seemed laid out in preparation for a wedding reception. It was deserted. In a far corner I spotted a couple of framed photographs and tiptoed across to have a look. One showed the South of England XI versus Bradman's 1948 Australians on a sunkissed afternoon in the aftermath of the war, while next to it was another image of the very moment in 1947 when Compton broke the record for the highest number of runs in a single season. The war may barely be over, rationing may still be in place and drab austerity the order of the day, but, as Cardus famously wrote in one of his essays, 'There was no rationing in an innings by Compton.' His tally for that summer was a staggering 3816. Sixty-odd years later, Marcus Trescothick would utterly dominate the domestic averages with a measly 1817.

A voice sounded behind me. 'Can I help?' It was one of the women I'd followed up the stairs.

I unfurled a reassuring smile. 'I'm just visiting the town and was wondering if I could ask you some questions: is county cricket ever played here?'

The woman seemed wrong-footed by my query. 'No, no, you've got the wrong place,' she replied nervously, 'this is Hastings cricket club. You're thinking of the old ground down at Priory Meadow – that was knocked down some years ago. In any case, we're not really open just now.' She cast a nervous glance across at a young man in an adjoining office as she spoke. He was staring intently out and his hand was hovering towards a phone on his desk.

'But – forgive me – wasn't this new venue supposed to take over duties? I understood this was specifically intended as an alternative venue?'

'We did,' she answered, 'we did play county cricket here, but ... ' She tailed off.

'But what?'

Her response was left dangling in the silent air, for her colleague in the nearby office was talking to someone in a low tone, his hand cupped over the receiver. Perhaps it was my natural unease associated with the town, but I suspected any moment now I'd be asked to leave the premises by a couple of beefy security guards. Whatever else, my presence here was undoubtedly sticking out like a dog's balls. It was time to go. I thanked her for her time and began retracing my steps. I was barely halfway back down the staircase when she called down to me.

'I'm sorry, but don't I know you?'

'I don't think so.'

'Aren't you the chap who used to present *Crimewatch*?'

'That's Nick Ross.'

'Funny ... I could have sworn ...'

On the train back to London I reviewed the evidence. The town had got its shopping complex all right, but the other part of the equation seemed to have been conveniently forgotten. But if so, who was the culprit? There were fingerprints all over the crime scene, but whose were they? Hastings's? The developers? Sussex? Or the most likely miscreant, the crushing realities of modern economics? After all, most people nowadays would bite your hand off if you offered to concrete over that bit of grass and replace it with a Waitrose. Knowing you can find fresh kiwi fruit within a fifty-yard radius of your settee seems to be an essential component of modern living these days. In which case, who were a load of dewy-eyed old duffers like me to deprive them?

Betjeman had summed up what was now the prevailing wind as far back as 1954. Perhaps the only wonder was it had taken so long.

'I cannot say how shocked I am to see
The variations in our scenery.
Just take for instance, at a casual glance
Our muddled coastline opposite to France
Dickensian houses by the channel tides
With old-hipped roofs and weather-boarded sides
I blush to think one corner of this isle
Lacks concrete villas in the modern style.'

Some weeks after my return, I read an article in the local paper. A mural had appeared on a wall at nearby St Leonard's, showing a tiny infant in beach hat and sunglasses happily making a series of traditional sandcastles on which the Tesco logo is emblazoned.

As a pictorial comment on the town's continuing moral anguish, it could hardly be bettered. Yet even as the council were considering how best to remove the offending eyesore, rumours were now spreading the progenitor was no less a person than the infamous graffiti artist, Banksy.

So was it graffiti or art? Or even, whisper it softly, piercing social comment? I'd like to think it was a bit of each. Donald McGill he may not be, but Banksy, if so it proved to be, obviously has his finger on the pulse.

Oh well. Whether they hired a high-powered jet-wash to zap the mural to oblivion, or charge an admission fee to view it, I hope the good burghers of Hastings were happy with the outcome.

8

Dead Sert

One of the most famous photographs in sporting history – indeed, in social history – was taken outside Lord's in the summer of 1937.

In this iconic image, known to posterity simply as 'The Toffs and the Toughs', the viewer's eye is taken to the two 'toffs', subjects also of the gaze of the three 'toughs', standing alongside them. Each is wearing a top hat, a sleek waistcoat and a starched white collar beneath an immaculate morning suit. Each sports a fresh carnation in his lapel. Both carry gleaming canes and have small weekend cases positioned beside them on the pavement, each one highly polished, the gleaming studs and pristine clasps reflecting brightly in the morning sunshine.

The boy on the far left – young Peter Wagner of Russ Hill, near Charlwood, Surrey – is gazing intently off camera. What is he staring at? Perhaps it's his butler, currently labouring towards him up St John's Wood Road, waving a monocle and shouting, 'Sir, crisis averted – Cook found it in your kedgeree!'

His companion, Timothy Dyson, the taller and on the evidence of his expression the surlier of the two, has his hand placed delicately in his trouser pocket as if taking care not to spoil the nap, while the other is positioned on top of a cement bollard that rises out of the pavement nearly up to his midriff.

He has that resigned, world-weary 'You can't get the staff' expression that only true aristocrats can manage, the sort of look that suggests he's just been told the second assistant pheasant beater has overslept. He and his young companion bring to mind the playwright Alan Ayckbourn's famous phrase: 'Some people are born with a silver spoon in their mouths. Others have an entire canteen of cutlery.'

'The Battle of Waterloo was won on the playing fields of Eton.' So said the Duke of Wellington. And, indeed, anyone seeking to understand either English cricket or English life in the last two hundred years would be advised to study this photograph or, better still, pay a visit, as these boys are doing, to the annual Eton versus Harrow cricket match.

The oldest competitive cricket fixture of them all, its ancestry predates even the Battle of Trafalgar; by the time this photograph was taken, these two bastions of private education had already been locked in annual cricketing combat for 132 years. Charles Wordsworth, nephew of the poet William, played four times in the early nineteenth century, as did Lord Byron, who competed in the first match and who observed of the post-match celebrations, 'We were most of us very drunk and we went to the Haymarket where we kicked up a row, as you might suppose when Etonians and Harrovians meet in one place.'

Other celebrated participants include Gubby Allen, BJT Bosanquet (creator of both the googly and newscaster Reginald) and our own dearly beloved Henry Blofeld, who managed the dubious privilege of becoming the third victim of the only recorded hat trick in the history of the contest.

So huge were the crowds in the fixture's heyday that it resulted in the implementation of the first boundary rope to keep the throng of spectators at bay, and it says everything about the hold this sporting institution once had over British life that for many years even the *Daily Mirror* sent a special correspondent to cover the game.

Early newsreel footage of these annual encounters, just after the Great War, show the playing surface during the lunch interval buried beneath toppers and parasols, as polite society claimed their God-given right to amble back and forth across God's most exclusive piece of real estate. Even today the annual match attracts greater crowds than a Middlesex home game. Beyond the confines of this most ancient of cricketing enmities there might be world wars, civil insurrection and Lady Gaga, but for a precious day at Lord's every summer, it's always Pimms o'clock.

Perhaps it's no surprise the game has proved such a fertile breeding ground for future cricketing stardom. After all, privilege and background is woven into the fabric of the sport like the red and gold stripes on an MCC blazer.

Almost as soon as the game was codified and structured by the Victorians, it became stratified into amateur and professional, with the delineation between the two camps clear-cut and formal. The amateur, regardless of his age and status, was inevitably addressed as 'sir' by the professional, and there was never any doubt who took preference in the minds of the authorities. Before the reluctant selection of Len Hutton in the early 1950s, no England captain had been a professional – indeed, such an appointment would have been unthinkable, which is why an earlier candidate, Wally Hammond, had to turn amateur simply in order to qualify for the job (and even Hutton only managed it because the pain of having lost to the Aussies for nearly three decades outweighed all other considerations).

The progress of first-class cricket is littered, indeed shaped, by this quiet, deadly divide. As late as the 1950s, professionals with long associations with their county could expect to be summarily shouldered aside in favour of some dilettante under-graduate who'd finished his term at university and was now free for a game or two. In any case, lest anyone forget their place, the two classes frequently changed in different dressing rooms and entered the field of play by different gates.

This caste system was rigidly observed, even after careers were long finished. The story goes that when CB Fry, in many ways the examplar of the amateur ethos in all its glory and arro-gance, was doing a spot of summarising in 1940 during an early cricket commentary on BBC radio and was asked by his fellow commentator, 'And what did you think, Charles?', he replied, 'Commander Fry, if you please,' and refused to speak further.

Better still is the case of Fred Titmus when he played for MCC versus Surrey in 1950. 'Ladies and gentlemen, a correc-tion to our scorecard,' stuttered the announcer over the public address as he came out on to the field. '*FJ Titmus* should, of course, read *Titmus, FJ.*' And even now, public announcements at the home of cricket are occasionally made by the actor formerly known as Nigel Pargetter in *The Archers*. The choice seems appropriate, because if there should be a place where you can still taste the faint tang of how it all once was, Lord's on a summer's afternoon is surely it.

I'd always wanted to attend Eton v. Harrow, but until now had shrunk from doing so. I suppose I felt there was something faintly humiliating about gatecrashing a party to which I was so palpably not invited. And yet this oldest of cricketing enmities had always exerted a strange pull over me.

Having grown up on a diet of Jennings, Billy Bunter and *Tom Brown's Schooldays*, I'd always been fascinated by the life of a boys' boarding school. What might my footling abilities have amounted to if they'd been nourished in this most fertile of sporting soils? Would I have remained an inept also-ran, destined to nurdle insignificant twenties and thirties, throwing in from the deep like somebody doing a bad impression of Larry Grayson? Or would my bowling action, instead of a cricketing freak of nature, have developed into a genuinely potent weapon?

What might have been attained if only I'd had a cool twenty-eight grand a term to throw at some batting coaching from gnarled ex-pros and a limitless supply of fags to bowl at me morning, noon, and night? The answer, I knew, would forever remain lost in the fog of conjecture. But at least by seeing a game for myself I could glimpse, if only dimly, the potential benefits of nurture harnessed to nature. And 2010 was surely the year in which to do it, as it marked the centenary, not only of the greatest match in two hundred years of the contest, but arguably the greatest match in all cricket history.

I'm talking, of course, of 'Fowler's match'.

The details of the encounter, played over two days in the summer of 1910 when the Golden Age of cricket was in its fullest flood, are worth a brief retelling. In front of a capacity crowd of some twenty thousand, and despite an attack of measles that had threatened to decimate their dressing room, Harrow notched up 232 before reducing their rivals to the original Eton Mess, 67 all out.

Following on, Eton fared little better, but with Mater and Pater already stowing the Veuve Clicquot into the trunk of the Hispano-Suiza, enter the Eton captain, one Robert St Leger Fowler. The son of a Cambridge Blue and great-great-grandson of a bishop, he led a fierce counter-attack that hoisted Eton's total to 219, an effort that, according to *The Times*, could not 'be praised too highly for its courage and dash'.

But Fowler wasn't finished yet. Opening the bowling he took the first half-dozen opposition wickets, and before you could say 'six of the best', Harrow found themselves on 39–9, still fourteen runs short of victory. So sudden was their collapse that the last man, the Hon RHLG Alexander (later to become Earl Alexander of Tunis), entered from the tea tent still clutching a half-eaten cream bun.

When he too finally succumbed with Harrow still nine short, Eton had pulled off the greatest comeback since Lazarus. Such was the significance of the occasion that a subsequent congratulatory letter addressed simply to 'Fowler's mother, London' successfully reached its recipient.

It was Saturday 26 June 2010, a hundred years almost to the day since Fowler's heroics. And outside the temperature was already climbing into the mid-twenties. A full day's play at the home of cricket was guaranteed.

I'd originally resolved to be at Lord's well in time for the start of the match at noon, but at the last moment my plans were blown off-course, this time by the offer of a free seat at a dress rehearsal of Verdi's *Simon Boccanegra* at Covent Garden.

There was a time when if anyone had suggested I consider giving up a live cricket match in order to watch grand opera, I'd have called them a madman. After all, my tastes in music are decidedly middle of the road. I've always considered any art form that expected you to pay £150 a seat and still not leave you time to snatch a pint before the last Tube home to be distinctly dicey.

But this offer was something a bit special, if only for the presence in the title role of the great Placido Domingo. With tickets for performances allegedly changing hands at £500 a pop, it was not an experience to be passed over lightly. In any case, perhaps a quick dip in the rarefied world of grand opera would be ideal preparation for the day ahead, and with the dress rehearsal beginning at 10.30am and the match not scheduled till noon, I should be able to catch some of the most hummable melodies and still be at St John's Wood in time for the opening over.

But I'd forgotten it was grand opera. *Simon Boccanegra* had first to be elected Doge of Venice, then he had to make an acceptance speech, then he had to realise it would allow him to marry Maria who had been imprisoned by her father Fiesco because she bore Simon an illegitimate child; and after several more twists and turns he finally had to persuade his nemesis to make peace, only to subsequently discover Maria's dead body just as he was proclaimed Doge to the jubilation of all Venetians.

Far from a description of the entire opera, that's just a précis of the prologue. In addition, there were a further three acts, each one necessitating intervals of half an hour while more elaborate scenery was manoeuvred into position.

At one point I'd despaired not only of missing this year's Eton v. Harrow fixture but next year's as well. I'm not proud of the fact, but I was the only one in the entire auditorium who cheered when the hero finally drank from the poisoned water pitcher he'd been circling round for the previous forty minutes. Whoever said, 'The opera began at six, and three hours later I looked at my watch and it was 6.20', must have attended an occasion such as this.

The taxi dropped me outside the Grace Gates just after 3.30. I may be sixty-three years late, but he was still there, standing exactly where the photographer had captured him back in '37. His garb may have changed during the intervening decades, but he wasn't fooling anyone. He even had his hand on the same bollard.

He was a teenager, with a mop of tousled hair and holding a fox terrier on a lead. As I emerged from the cab he was speaking into a mobile phone. 'I'm going to put Milo back in the Jag, but he'll need some water so I'm just telling you because I don't want to get it in the neck if it goes all over the upholstery.'

Where his predecessor's legs had been encased in pinstripes with a crease sharp enough to open letters on, he wore the modern equivalent – crumpled Gieves & Hawkes shirt and a pair of bright pink chinos, below which a pair of suede shoes peeked out with that carefully distressed look you just know has only been obtained at great expense. The finishing touch was a pair of electric blue socks. He was fooling no one. Winston Churchill and Stanley Baldwin may once have run our lives from behind a wing collar, but Boris chic is nowadays the mark of the true toff.

My sense of being an interloper only increased when I tried to gain admittance. Despite my opera pass artlessly peeking out from my breast pocket, I was dispensed a ticket by the gate steward with what can only be described as tangible distaste, before being thoroughly frisked at the turnstile. But who can blame him? Allow some simmering anarchist in here with a bomb strapped to his waist and you'd wipe out most of the government front bench for the next two decades.

Having gained security clearance I hurried in by the nearest available entrance, which happened to be the lower tier of the Tavern Stand, the power base of the Harrow massif. There must have been upwards of two thousand, the vast majority of them boys, gathered in a huge quivering mass of teenage testosterone. A few hundred yards away their detested rivals, the Eton posse, were similarly grouped in the Mound Stand, if anything in even greater numbers and even fuller voice.

A glance at the scoreboard revealed the reason for Eton's ebullience. Having scored 205 earlier in the day, they now had Harrow tottering on 12–3. Even as I hurried to my seat, the fielders were celebrating the latest wicket with a volley of high-fives, while in the middle their young captain was already practising his hand at the sort of rabble-rousing speech that would one day stand him in good stead at PM's Question Time.

Meanwhile the next Harrow batsman, a willowy teenager with a ready likeness to a youthful Imran Khan, was plodding out to the wicket. If any youngster seemed to have the cares of the world on his shoulders, it was Yunus Sert.

Poor chap. I'd spent much of my early years imagining myself in just such a nightmare situation: stepping out on to the famous old Lord's turf in pursuit of a hopeless cause and with opposition supporters baying for my blood. A century ago the intrepid Fowler had managed to surmount his funk and pull off a famous victory, but heroics such as his were few and far between, particularly in matches such as this. A victory for Eton later this afternoon was surely only a matter of time.

I parked myself as discreetly as I could amongst the sombre Harrow contingent and studied the electronic scoreboard. The illuminated names read like something from a Rowan Atkinson sketch: Bunting, Pratt, Ballantyne-Dykes, Vandarspar, Pearson-Jones, Tidbury. Lord's looked at its most imposing this afternoon, particularly with five thousand revellers roasting in the afternoon sun. The fixture may have lost its grip on the national psyche, but this was the type of attendance the average cash-strapped county could only dream of.

But there was nothing cash-strapped about my surroundings today. The sweet scent of affluence hung in the air like incense. A woman near me in a Nicole Farhi dress was spooning crème fraiche on to some home-baked ciabatta festooned with smoked salmon, while her husband uncorked a bottle of champagne with the expertise of someone who had spent his life doing little else. I sheepishly opened my own packed lunch – a carton of Ribena and a Londis own brand Pork 'n' Pickle pie – and settled back to watch.

The next half hour proved something of an education in itself, in that there was hardly a delivery or a stroke that wasn't straight out of the MCC coaching manual. Twenty20 may have taken hold of the lower classes, but I had the distinct feeling that the only reward for a reverse sweep in these sanctified surroundings would be a public thrashing in the Harris Garden. Runs, when they came at all, were pursued by fielders who had already acquired all the skills they'd seen on TV – sliding stops, relay throws, and a readiness to shy at the stumps in the full knowledge someone would be backing up. After forty minutes of some of the tensest and most elegant cricket I'd seen all season, the score had barely crawled above 30.

The atmosphere in the stands had a similar air of effortless authority. Everywhere the talk was of endowment plans, the soaring cost of equine veterinarians and approaching skiing holidays in remote Swiss villages. One proud father in a lightweight tailored suit was telling a neighbour about his son, who had recently got a placement from the school to work on the Large Hadron Collider in Geneva. It makes a change from Saturday mornings at Greggs the bakers.

Eventually I got talking to a couple who looked straight out of Universal Casting for *Brideshead Revisited*. I'd assumed that Rollo and Elspeth were courting, but they turned out to be first cousins, and were here to cheer on a relative who was playing for Harrow.

Rollo in particular was looking forward to seeing his old school give the opponents what he called 'a good spanking'. He'd only left Harrow a few months previously, yet admitted he

was already working for the government, and indeed was anticipating an imminent meeting with the new education secretary
Michael Gove some time in the next few weeks.

'No, really, I know Gove does that *Newsnight Review* thing
and he comes over as a bit of a twat, excuse my French, you
didn't hear me say that, did you, Ellie, but when you meet him
he's absolutely pukka,' he assured me, giving his cousin an affectionate squeeze to allay her feminine sensibilities. 'Lovely fellow.'

Elspeth leaned across and introduced herself, offering me a
perfectly manicured, lily-white hand. She was here on her day off
in between working as an administrator for a London university
and being a party planner.

Fortified by frequent glugs of what he described as 'the old
vino', Rollo was soon extolling the values of 'the old alma
mater'. He'd just offered to sing a snatch of 'the old school
song' when thankfully he was distracted by Sert, who unleashed
a cover drive of sublime elegance, the ball racing up the hill to
the Warner Stand, where it clattered against the boundary
boards with a satisfying smack. 'Good shot, run them up,
Harrow!' he bellowed, rising unsteadily to his feet.

Over in the Mound Stand the Eton posse were also on their
feet and attempting to drown out Harrow's muted applause with
some new, even more bellicose offering. What Sigmund Freud
described as 'The narcissism of small differences', in which we
direct our resentment at people who are nearly like us but not
quite, was now evident in all its animalistic glory. The air was
filled with a rousing chorus of 'We're going to get a wicket in a
minute' to the tune of 'She'll be coming round the mountain
when she comes'.

'Bloody arses,' said Rollo, looking across at them with a stare
of infinite contempt. 'They won't be laughing when we've given

them a good spanking. I reckon we can do this. I tell you, Malcolm, there's a whole generation of Etonians who never saw a victory in the whole time they were at the awful place. Isn't that wonderful? Good health!'

I was anxious to discover more about daily life at Harrow, but by now Rollo was in loquacious mood, and my attempts to steer the conversation proved fruitless. 'I mean, just look at this,' he remarked, flailing his hand towards the pavilion. 'I mean, come on, why not come for a day at Lord's? Why not come here for a day?'

I agreed it was difficult to think of a reason.

He laughed. 'Good answer, good answer. No, I mean, take Ellie for instance, she may not know her googlies from her silly whatevers, but is there any better place to be in the whole wide world than sitting here, on a beautiful summer's day, watching the cricket and seeing someone get a good spanking?'

I agreed I could think of few better ways to spend my time, particularly if Ellie was involved somewhere along the line. Rollo was warming to his theme. 'The point I'm making is,' he continued with a doggedness matched by Sert out on the pitch, 'as long as there are some good strokes, that's what it's all about, isn't it?'

'Oh, Rollo, do shut up,' countered Elspeth. 'You're lapsing into hyperbole.'

She poured him a fresh refill and for the next few minutes he busied himself by texting furiously on his BlackBerry while I watched the cricket. It wasn't difficult, for there was something thrilling about this new batsman, Sert. The only other comparable batsman of his age I'd ever known display such glazed-eyed determination was the young Mike Atherton. And look what happened to him.

We were soon joined by a couple of younger boys who both arrived clutching huge bags of assorted sweets from a nearby stall. Rollo introduced them to me as Rupert and Lindsay, but with their pudding-basin haircuts, spectacles and ink-stained fingers (one in particular seemed to have an entire system of mathematical equations written on the back of his hand), they seemed to me the epitome of my fictional boarding-school heroes, Jennings and Darbishire.

They were in a state of some disgruntlement, as word had just got round that the headmaster had forbidden Harrow from chanting back at the Eton supporters. 'I mean, it's so unfair. Listen to that lot over there.' We stared across at the Mound Stand, where Eton were again standing and bellowing yet another informal anthem whose words I was unable to catch.

'What are they singing?' I asked the one resembling Darbishire.

'I'm afraid I don't know, sir.'

Sir. He called me *sir*.

Within minutes we were happily debating the merits of candy shrimps versus chocolate bananas, and having gained their confidence, I gingerly broached the subject of life at school. My image of life at boarding school veered wildly between midnight feasts and tuck shop high jinks and the casual brutality of *Flashman*, and I was anxious to gain some insight into what it was really like. Did Rupert enjoy his schooldays, or was the popular conception amongst outsiders of homesickness, freezing swims, sadistic teachers and meagre and disgusting meals really true? He thought for a moment. I could tell he was wondering if I was about to follow it up with an enquiry about whether he'd ever been to male-only sauna.

When he replied it was in a low voice. 'Well, the best you can say is that it goes on behind closed doors, sir,' he said (what 'it' was, was left hanging tantalisingly in the air). 'It's OK actually,' he continued. 'We're kept pretty busy so there's not much chance to get into trouble. As long as you keep your nose clean you're left pretty much alone. It's OK, isn't it?' The last sentence was directed hopefully at Lindsay, who popped a Flying Saucer in his mouth and nodded.

Out on the pitch young Sert was now playing a blinder, hoisting his fifty with an imperious smack for four off the back foot, and following it up by driving the next ball towards us in the Tavern. A young boy of ample proportions – indeed, the only individual on either side who might even be considered for the title role were Billy Bunter's life story to be made into a movie – began lumbering towards us in hopeless pursuit.

'Run the fat man,' shouted Rollo, struggling to his feet and flourishing his glass high in the air. 'And the ground's positively shaking!!!'

Poor fat man. I watched him labour helplessly after the ball, the sound of two thousand voices mocking his every step. He could, indeed, have been me out there at his age, thighs chafing, cheeks the colour of pickled beetroot, plodding wearily after the ball with the sound of derisory laughter ringing in his ears.

With his wobbling stomach and chubby thighs, I wondered if he found life as a boarder all so very Jennings and Darbishire, as was claimed by apologists, or whether lying low and keeping your nose clean was rather more difficult once your waistline crept up to thirty-six inches. One famously overweight ex-public schoolboy, the preternaturally spherical actor Robert Morley, had once said of his time in education, 'The only way I would return to my old school would be with a sub-machine gun and a fully armoured platoon.'

Soon enough it was the tea interval, and having bade farewell to Rollo and Elspeth I set off for a turn round the ground. Lord's is a famously convivial environment for running into old friends, and despite their enmity the two camps seemed to be mingling happily. I was especially pleased to see the sweet stand now under virtual siege by a throng of excited youngsters, pockets bulging with jelly babies, fudge and gelatinous wine gums.

Then all at once, somewhere ahead of me in the throng, I was aware of some monumental force steadily approaching, and whoever or whatever it was, its every step seemed to be gradually stilling the chaotic mass of schoolboys. Conversations stopped, jostling ceased, while those positioned on the tiers above in Tavern Stand stood gaping down in awe and disbelief.

Who could it be? A headmaster? Boris Johnson? Simon Cowell?

And then I saw them. Three exquisite young debutantes in straw hats, with skin the colour of honey and caressed by diaphanous summer dresses. Each was holding an exotic cocktail with her lips pursed pertly round the top of the straw. To this day I have no idea who they were, but I reckon Annabelle, Tabitha and Su-ling would be a pretty good guess. Sixteen, ravishingly pretty and extremely rich.

The effect in such a cauldron of bubbling male hormones was immediate. The match, the confectionery stall, the various plots and schemes to have a quick ciggie round the back of the stands or to bunk off early, all were forgotten in an instant. Shirt-tails were hastily stuffed back into jeans, hair smoothed down, ties rearranged, as eyes full of deepest longing peered back at these teenage goddesses. The girls moved on, seemingly and deliberately oblivious to the trail of emotional chaos they were leaving in their wake. The ranks closed once more and, within a minute or two, normal service had been resumed.

With the post-tea session about to commence, I was keen to sample life on the other side of the divide, particularly as I'd heard that of the two schools, Eton was the more bumptious and self-confident. It wasn't difficult to find them. Eton had virtually colonised the Mound Stand, with the first fifteen rows occupied by a seething mass of sixth-formers and with the youngsters forming an adoring outer circle. Unlike the low murmur of the Harrow camp, there was an abrasive buzz of conversation and laughter about Eton that seemed altogether more combative.

I found myself sitting immediately behind a florid-faced man in his early fifties wearing a panama hat, who, by his anxious looks across at the ringleaders every time they embarked on a fresh chorus, was obviously a member of staff. Stationed on the perimeter of the mêlée, he resembled a nervous zookeeper who knew he'd mislaid his keys to the cage. It wasn't easy to strike up a conversation as he was turned away from me towards the cricket, and in any case was demolishing a plate of haddock fillets, but nonetheless by leaning in and asking to look at his scorecard, I was able to get things moving.

'Who's your money on?' I asked.

'It's hard to tell,' he said without looking round. 'It's in the balance. I reckon you could spin a coin on this one. Excuse me just a minute.' He broke off, a forkful of cooling haddock suspended mid-air. The Eton posse was on the charge again, turning to face their younger confederates gathered further back in the stand and now attempting to ignite a Mexican wave. Randolph wiped his mouth with a napkin and struggled to his feet. 'All right, now sit down, sit down, you've had your fun,' he yelled, waving a rolled-up copy of the *Daily Telegraph* at them as if attempting to flag down a passing taxi.

When he sat down again I attempted to reignite our spluttering conversation. 'This Sert chap looks good,' I ventured.

'Oh, he is,' replied Randolph. 'He's added a hundred now with this other boy. Of course I don't know much about him, but someone was telling me at lunch that several counties have already got their eye on him. Mark my words, he'll be popping up on your TV screen in a few years if he doesn't do anything silly. He bowled well, too, don't you think?'

I admitted I'd missed that part of the game, having been previously detained at Covent Garden with Placido.

'Oh how wonderful, I'm going there next week.' He turned to engage with me for the first time, directing an aroma of boiled fish in my direction. 'We've got tickets in the Grand Circle. Tell me, what's it like? Domingo should be exemplary, I imagine, and I hear on the grapevine Poplavskaya is quite something, although personally I always seem to find she's holding back. And how is Furlanetto? Up to scratch?'

I let him know that Poplavskaya had given it the gun and that Furlanetto was well up to scratch.

'Manage "Il Lacerato Spirito" all right, does he?'

I assured him he mullered it.

'Oh, I'm so glad. The piece stands or falls by that one aria I always find, don't you think?'

I confirmed that the rendering of 'Il Lacerato Spirito' had been bang on.

Randolph seemed delighted at my report. Verdi was his great passion, and he was keen to know which of his operas was my particular favourite. But just as I was about to be drawn into an increasingly implausible discussion, our attention was distracted by the fall of a wicket. Sert's junior partner in the Harrow fightback, the doughty Castleton, had been dismissed and the Etonians were on their feet once more.

'What are they singing now?'

Randolph scratched his shaving rash. 'Um … well, the basic premise is that Eton's most famous old boy, David Cameron, is the current Prime Minister, whereas the best Harrow can manage is James Blunt,' he explained. 'Silly really.' He gave a boys-will-be-boys look and turned back to the play. 'Mind you,' I heard him add with barely concealed delight, 'absolutely true, of course.'

Perhaps so – but today there was only one star. Sert was playing a blinder. Hooks, pulls, advances down the wicket, delicate late cuts sending the fielders sprawling in desperate pursuit, he now resembled a young Owais Shah at the height of his precocious powers. Yet still the Eton contingent was undeterred. 'You're all going to a minor public school,' they yelled gleefully across at the Tavern, a forest of fingers jabbing in the air towards the enemy camp.

'Excuse me a minute,' said Randolph eventually. Some telepathic decision had obviously been arrived at among the staff, and like wranglers attempting to corral a particularly lively herd of bison, he and his colleagues were now on their feet and moving in a circular motion around the perimeter of the pack.

'OK, I want all you younger boys back in the stands. Come on, back you go.' Gradually, those on the fringes of the group began peeling off and clambering noisily back across the seats.

'Sorry about that,' said Randolph breathlessly as he rejoined me. 'They'll be all right now but it's been a long day. We only need a dose of off-colour language and the next thing we'll be having the fixture moved.'

It was now past 5pm, and the match was nicely poised.

With forty still needed, the number-seven batsman, Pearson-Jones, was given out lbw, an event that provoked the remaining rump of the Eton crew into renewed vocal histrionics. But this time their offering brought out an altogether calmer reaction in my companion. Far from jumping to his feet like a scalded cat, a dreamy look came onto Randolph's features and he began waving his plastic fork gently in the air in time to the beat.

'What's that they're singing?'

He turned to face me with a faint look of bewilderment.

'Don't you recognise it?'

I shook my head. 'Should I?'

'Have a listen,' he said.

'I'm afraid not.'

'Odd. Don't tell me you don't know this, of all pieces.'

I sat in silence for several moments.

'Got it?'

I counted to three before framing my mouth into a spurious smile.

'Ah yes.'

'Nailed it?'

'Of course,' I replied. 'Stupid of me.'

'Don't worry, I can't blame you, they're hardly the chorus of La Scala, are they?' He beat the air wistfully in time as he hummed along with them. '"The Prisoners' Chorus" from *Fidelio*: never fails to move, does it? Even when mangled by oiks like those.'

'The Prisoners' Chorus' From *Fidelio*. I dimly recalled the tune from something or other. What was it? Ah yes, that advert for kitchen roll with the special super-absorbent pockets.

'Peerless,' I murmured.

It was odd. This might be the upper classes at play, but change a few vowel sounds and you could be in the stand at Grimsby Town versus Aldershot on a Saturday afternoon in November – the tribal displays, the ritual bonding, and the singing of crude anthems crammed full of incendiary sentiments designed solely to wind up the opposition supporters. The Mariners might prefer 'We only sing when we're pissing', to the tune of 'Guantanamera', but otherwise little was different.

The end, when it occurred, came surprisingly quickly. With only four needed for victory, and with Sert himself requiring a mere single for his hundred, the Eton captain made one last desperate throw of the dice in the form of yet another bowling change. But Sert merely stepped back and flogged the ball high over the boundary rope and into the grandstand. Even before it had landed he was pumping his arms joyously in the air. With a single stroke he'd won the match, scored the game's first six and secured a century at the home of cricket.

Helmet in one hand, raised bat in the other, he approached the pavilion to a standing ovation from the members and a final jabber of statistics from the public address – 159 minutes, 131 balls, 13 fours and a six.

No man amongst the rubicund faces and straining waistlines on the pavilion's famous white benches would not have dreamed of such a moment when they were his age. All the wistfulness of corpulent middle-age was etched on their faces as their new hero disappeared past them and into the gloom of the long room.

Randolph shook his head wistfully. 'What a moment, eh? A pleasure to watch. though. Sert's match, eh?'

'Sert's match.'

Well, see you at the Garden some time?'

'I hope so. Do you all go back to school now?'

'Oh yes, we have to get this lot back to Windsor, feed them and see them safely tucked up for the night. This job's 24/7. Never mind, nearly hols.'

I left the ground by the Grace Gates, allowing myself to be carried along in the crush. Already a fleet of motor coaches were quietly revving their engines all the way along St John's Wood Road, sunburnt parents waving fond farewells to their darling ones inside. For the majority of the pupils it was presumably prep, suet sponge and lights out at 10.30.

And for Sert? A Coke; perhaps something stronger if the Housemaster was feeling benevolent, and then a chance to view the backlog of messages from various county secretaries already piling up for him on his iPhone.

As I waited for the bus, a final, full-throated chorus followed me on the breeze. Their school may have been thumped by five wickets, but Eton remained unbowed. One last anthem of defiance to the departing exhausts of their oldest rivals echoed distantly up the Edgware Rd. 'I'm Eton till I die, I'm Eton till I die, I know I am, I'm sure I am, I'm Eton till I die …'

Of that I'd never been in much doubt.

When I got back home I sought out a copy of the original 'Toffs and Toughs' photograph from my bookshelf and sat scrutinsing it for some minutes. What, I wondered, happened to young Wagner and Dyson in the years after they were snapped for posterity? Was their own progress through life as polished and unsullied as the brass studs on their suitcases?

In fact, their subsequent stories demonstrate just how big a part fate plays in the great game of life, however and wherever you go to school. Of the two, the taller one, Timothy Dyson, barely lasted a year. He was only at Harrow because both his parents were serving with His Majesty's Armed Forces in India, and in 1938, while travelling by P&O to join them in Trimulgherry, near Secunderabad, he caught diphtheria and died.

His companion, young Peter Wagner, survived the war and eventually settled into comfortable affluence with a wife, three children and a daily commute from the suburbs to a brokers' firm in London. Yet having shown worrying signs of mental instability as far back as his mid-twenties, he eventually died in a specialist nursing home in Hellingly, East Sussex, aged only sixty.

In perfect keeping with the new egalitarian era that prospered after the war, his family home, Russ Hill near Charlwood in Surrey, is now a hotel for trippers needing somewhere handy to stay the night before jetting off to the sun at Gatwick airport. Yet even this is trumped by the poignant fate of Cricket St Mary in Somerset, the house owned by Timothy Dyson's cousins and where, unable to reach his parents for so much of his short life, he spent several of his happiest schoolboy summers.

Having later been used as the setting for the BBC sitcom *To The Manor Born*, it was eventually bought by Noel Edmonds and turned into the Crinkly Bottom Theme Park, home of Mr Blobby.

As a metaphor for the last fifty years of British social history, it needs no further adornment.

9

Freddie and The Dreamers

One of the more pleasurable by-products of a life spent hanging about with other actors is that you occasionally get to rub shoulders with the rich and famous. Whether it's sharing a lift with Carol Vorderman or a Tardis with David Tennant, or merely asking the chairman of the BBC if he'd like red or white, you'll eventually find yourself interfacing with the odd showbiz celebrity.

Over time you get immune to it. An occupational hazard, I suppose. And while my own career is not so much *Who's Who* as 'Who's He?', I've still managed to cut a fair few notches on my celebrity belt, from meeting Björn and Benny to sharing a dressing room with Les Dennis.

Occasionally these showbiz encounters even extend to a game of cricket. Nothing opens up people's wallets quicker than the chance of rubbing shoulders with someone off the telly. You can hardly stroll across a village green these days without blundering into some high-profile cricketing fund-raiser involving actors and entertainers strutting their stuff in aid of a deserving cause.

Thus if you are both a luvvie and a fan of the game, chances are you'll be asked along to make up the numbers. I've played in a fair few in my time, and they've provided some piquant experiences, including batting against Henry Kelly, bowling to

Nicholas Parsons, running out Mick Jagger's younger brother, and being wrongly given out caught behind by Mick McManus.

But playing alongside professional cricketers in such encounters is something quite different. They've done something you could never do. They've walked out to bat with six needed in the final over in a Pro40 final, or caught a vital catch at Melbourne when a hundred thousand Australians are baying for them to drop it. Portraying King Lear at the National Theatre is one thing. Coming in as night watchman against Brett Lee is quite another. And while I'm sure it must be lovely to be granted an audience with Nelson Mandela or Aung San Suu Kyi, a true cricket fan would swap it in a moment for the chance to have a beer with Gary Pratt and ask him to relive his run-out of Ricky Ponting at Trent Bridge in 2005.

I'd intended to use Sunday 4 July by going to see some more T20, this time at Chelmsford. Today of all days it was essential I keep busy as the Baldwins were playing at Arundel Castle, a ground once allegedly described by the great Australian batsman and journalist Jack Fingleton as 'the most beautiful in England', and very much the jewel in the crown of Chris Buckle's fixture list. With a shirtfront batting track, a rustic pavilion and the magnificent castle itself just across the boundary rope, I knew that missing this fixture would hurt more than any other. Spend the day moping around at home and sooner or later I'd only open the fridge and hit the cheese strings.

But then came the phone call that changed everything. It was from cricket journalist and all-round *bon viveur* Peter Hayter.

'Simmo. A friend of our suggested I give you a bell. I was wondering if you might like a game of cricket this weekend?'

'I can't, Peter. I'm not fit, I'm afraid.'

'I've organised a charity fund-raising match in Shropshire and one of the teams is short.'

'I'd love to but I'm out for the season. I'm not even turning out for the Baldwins.'

'It would just be some good-natured showbiz types who know one end of a bat from the other and who don't mind making absolute twats of themselves in aid of a good cause. I don't know why but I thought of you.'

'My consultant has absolutely forbidden it.'

'It's in aid of Help For Heroes. We're raising money for injured troops over in Afghanistan.'

'Peter, I know our boys are having a tough old time out there, but I've got my own health issues just at present.'

'It's just that Freddie Flintoff has agreed to play.'

'What time are we starting?'

Freddie Flintoff is probably the most instantly recognisable cricketer on earth. A natural athlete, blessed with extraordinary stamina, he's a combination of Keith Miller (prodigious drinker), Ian Botham (prodigious drinker) and Bobby Peel (prodigious drinker and the first man ever to urinate on the pitch in a Roses match). He's also the one true world-beater our country has produced since the great Beefy. Watching Freddie roaring in from the pavilion in the summer of 2009 at Lord's with only Brad Haddin standing between him and Ashes glory is still about as visceral an experience as you will ever sample in international sport.

Indeed, no greater testimony to his superhuman prowess is needed than the observation from former Aussie opener Justin 'Nugget' Langer. They had some rare tussles in recent years, and having announced his decision to step down from international cricket, Langer concluded: 'That's the overriding positive feeling about having retired – not having that big bugger charging in at me.' Nobody ever said that about Alan Mullally.

I'd watched Freddie live many times since first encountering him in a NatWest match between Sussex and Lancashire at Hove in the early 1990s, each time with an increasing sense of wonderment. I wish I could say I spotted him during that initial encounter as the world-beater he turned out to be, but in truth my memory of him that day was merely of a rather burly teenager who could obviously give the ball some humpty. Now, two decades and any number of cricketing heroics on, he was, despite being crocked, the one true rock star in the sport.

Yet Freddie has managed to engender a sense of shock and awe on the field without it spilling into off-field hubris and arrogance. He still retains a slightly sheepish quality of the wide-eyed teenager when not in cricket whites, which perhaps is why he's so universally loved – the sort of bloke you could spend a night with at your pub. That's about as high an accolade as you can achieve in this country.

Hayter's claim that the mighty Freddie would be playing at a country house in Shropshire against a load of broken-down old duffers such as myself was so unlikely I'd had to go on Google to check it. To my certain knowledge the great man hadn't lifted a bat or bowled a ball in anger since the crucial Ashes decider last year at The Oval, when he'd ended the game virtually hobbling on one leg and been ordered to take total and absolute rest from a career-threatening injury. Cricket missed him as much as he missed cricket. A personal appearance would be an unimaginable coup for the organisers.

But Freddie was down to play all right. There it was in black and white on my laptop. Downton Hall, near Ludlow; 2pm start, Grand Charity Cricket match, all proceeds to Help For Heroes and the local church fund. 'Freddie Flintoff's XI' versus 'Boycie from *Only Fools and Horses* XI'. Admission £5.

In many ways I felt I understood Flintoff. After all, there were so many sporting parallels between us, even if my own were painted on a somewhat smaller canvas. He, like me, was a batsman struggling to shrug off a reputation as something of an under-achiever. He, like me, also bowled. And, most crucially, he too had been warned to take some time off or risk a career-threatening injury. Who knew when – or even if – Freddie might ever play again? A game alongside him would be once-in-a-lifetime opportunity. I had to be there.

That evening I broke the news to Julia.

'Well, it's your funeral,' she said. 'What will you be asked to do? I thought you couldn't indulge in any sudden exertion? That's certainly the excuse you've been giving me for the past couple of months.'

I did my best to allay her fears, describing an afternoon spent in the pavilion with my foot up on a quilted cushion, watching Freddie belting sixes, while I signed autographs surrounded by grateful squaddies.

'So how far is Ludlow?'

'About 120 miles each way. But, darling, it's in aid of Help For Heroes. Those guys are doing a lot for us out there in Hellmand. If they can put their lives at risk, surely the least I can offer is a couple of puffy toes.'

'OK. But if you end up in a wheelchair, don't blame me. And I need the car this weekend. You'll have to take the train.'

With the day approaching I retrieved my kit from the loft and stood for a while in front of the bedroom mirror, checking my technique. God, it was a relief to feel solid wood in my hands once more. I took a few moments to reacquaint myself with my trademark shots: the snick past slip, the leading edge over extra cover's outstretched fingers and the smear to midwicket. All seemed well. My summer-of-playing hiatus was itself about to take a brief hiatus. Step aside, Nugget. I was ready to face cricket's most fearsome test.

The setting was indeed as magnificent as Peter had advertised. Shropshire in any case always seems to me indescribably beautiful, like an Alfred Bestall illustration in *Rupert Bear*, and Downton Hall was right in the middle of it, an imposing country house looking down a steep slope on to a cricket pitch which nestled in a natural arena straight out of *England, Their England* and surrounded on two sides by AE Housman's blue remembered hills.

It was a sultry, blustery afternoon and rain was in the air. Yet to my astonishment, despite it being nearly two hours before the commencement of the match, there were several thousand hardy Shropshire souls already encamped round the boundary line, swathed in blankets and hats, tucking into extensive picnics and looking immensely excited. What's more, their every need was catered for – with burger vans, champagne bars, beer tents and rows of mobile toilets. I'd seen worse facilities at some county grounds. What other single cricketer could guarantee such interest? The possibility of Freddie not being here was unthinkable.

I laboured with my kit bag through a vast field serving as a car park and towards a set of large marquees. Outside VIPS in linen suits and summer dresses were already sipping drinks and swapping sophisticated chit-chat. I spied one or two actors I knew – that bloke who always gets my parts in everything I go up for, and another one who's in that prime-time series where he plays that ex-gaolbird-turned-gumshoe detective. He caught my eye and I flashed him a warm, friendly, entirely bogus smile, before promising in mime we'd catch up later on. Some chance.

Inside the main tent a special VIP fund-raising luncheon was already under way, with upwards of three or four hundred diners gathered patiently in groups of eight to ten round circular tables. The smell of vinyl and trodden grass mingled with boiled potatoes and cut flowers. I recognised Essex and England cricketer-turned-journalist Derek Pringle at a nearby table and gave him a sheepish wave in the hope he'd remember me from our only previous meeting: a chance encounter in the gents' of a curry house in central Manchester back in 1992. But if recognised me, he wasn't showing it. At another table Vic Marks could be seen struggling to open a bottle of fizzy water. But of the great Freddie there was no sign. Even now a regiment of crisply uniformed waitresses were fanning out through the tent and dispensing bread rolls with military precision.

Thankfully Peter Hayter spotted me and hurried over. 'Mike, thanks so much for turning out like this. Great you can play. You'll be on the 'Boycie from *Only Fools and Horses*' team, so check with him to see where you're batting. There are some special 'Boycie from *Only Fools and Horses*' T-shirts in the pavilion, so make sure you grab one before the game begins. In the meantime, please find a seat and have some lunch, anywhere there's space, just plonk yourself down, and go easy on the potatoes, you may be doing some running around later.'

'Yes, I wanted to ask, is Freddie actually—' But he'd hurried off.

Even in the few seconds we'd been chatting the marquee had become full to bursting, and there was now barely a space in any direction. Many of the diners had already finished their starters; if I didn't find a place soon I'd miss the free trough. In the farthest corner I spotted a couple of empty seats and inched my way between the tables towards them, dragging tablecloths from their moorings with my kit bag as I did so, and poking people in the ear with my bat handle.

Eventually I arrived and, having stacked my kit against a handy support pole, I sat down. Across the table were a couple from Tenbury Wells who introduced themselves as Ron and Irene and poured me a glass of red wine while I caught my breath. Their eldest son, a keen cricketer from local team, was helping out today to make up the numbers. Within seconds I was the proud owner of a prawn avocado. Just as I was about to begin demolishing it, I looked up to find the woman now staring across at me with a smile of what can only be described as dribbling inanity. What on earth what she looking at?

'Mind if I join you?'

I turned to find Freddie Flintoff towering above me in a white T-shirt, blue tracksuit bottoms and trainers. A beefy forearm ringed by a selection of buddy bracelets was reaching out to pull up a chair. I swallowed hard.

'Please do,' I answered hoarsely. He plonked himself down and offered a huge, bone-crunching handshake. A diamond stud glinted in his right earlobe.

'Freddie Flintoff.'

'Michael Simkins.'

'Pleased to meet you, Michael.'

It's odd, isn't it? I'd spent the long hours on the train here rehearsing what I might say to the great man should I be lucky enough to catch his eye today. Thinking back now, I seem to recall my chosen questions had included, 'What are the chances of cricket taking root in China?' 'Do you believe Zimbabwe should be reallocated official Test Match status?' And: 'When would be the right time to reintroduce foreign tours to Pakistan, given the current unstable political climate?' You know the type of thing: questions indicative of a thorough knowledge of the game, yet with an understanding of the wider political and geopolitical nuances.

But as Geoff Boycott will tell you, however much you practise in the nets, it's not the same as the real thing. Nerves, anxiety, adrenaline, all can combine to derail the most assured performer once it's for real.

Now I was facing the most naturally charismatic player on the planet, my technique, too, went to pieces. I sat, struck dumb, for several excruciating minutes while we ate in complete silence. When I did eventually speak, instead of the cricketing Melvyn Bragg I'd intended to suggest, I seemed to have turned into Melvyn Hayes. How else can I explain the fact that my attempt at conversation consisted of merely reciting the names of past Lancashire cricketers?

'Um ... I first saw you at Hove actually.'

'Oh aye?'

'Yes. Early 1990s, I think it was. NatWest Quarter Final. You made two.'

'Did I?'

'Yes. I think it was two.'

'I can't remember.'

'Good side, though. Atherton, Fairbrother, Lloyd ...'

'Aye, some good players there.'

'Watkinson. Austin, I think.'

'Yup, he was good too ... '

'Gallian.'

'He were good an' all.'

'John Crawley.'

'Yup.'

What had happened? Our conversation had become something out of a Harold Pinter play. Throughout this tortured

exchange Freddie treated me with his usual mixture of amuse-
ment and guarded courtesy, but with each new name I could see
his eyes glazing over. Already people from adjoining tables were
making their way towards us, each armed with a reason to catch
his eye and a strategy for luring him over to their table rather
than remaining at mine.

Just as I was about to commence reciting the entire Sussex
team as well, help arrived in again in the form of our presiding
genius. This time Hayter was shepherding across a crocodile of
awestruck youngsters to have their match-day programmes
signed, and their arrival provoked tens more to rise from their
tables and follow suit. Soon Freddie was happily chatting away
and signing napkins to all and sundry while I helped him to some
salmon and green beans, a role I found infinitely more satisfying.

The displacement activity seemed to break the ice, and eventually our conversation became almost intelligible. He spoke
briefly about the success of his recent operation and confidence
in the rehabilitation process, resulting in his hope he'd be
appearing for both Lancashire and the IPL next year. In return I
offered a brief summary of my ongoing metatarsal issue and my
own consultant's hopes for a return to the crease for Baldwins in
April 2012.

The conversation eventually drifted, as I knew it would, on to
the forthcoming Ashes tour. He thought Strauss's men would win
the series, but confessed it was a tough call playing Down Under
with the eyes of the world upon your every failure or indiscretion.

'Was it hard for you in 06/07?' I said with as much concern
as I could. Flintoff had led England to a miserable 0–5 drubbing
four years ago, a tour popularly considered to have been the
worst organised and worst led in recent history and for which he
had copped a huge amount of personal criticism. I felt it was

important I acknowledged the pain he'd endured during that troubled time.

'Oh aye,' he said, spearing a Charlotte potato with his fork. 'It weren't a lot of laughs. But you know what a lot of folk forget?'

He leaned forward until he was nearly nibbling my ear. I almost hoped he would.

'It's only a game … '

The meal was over soon enough, after which there was all the traditional paraphernalia of charity cricket matches the world over, and the real point of the exercise – an auction of memorabilia, pairs of tickets to forthcoming sporting events and vouchers for romantic weekends in swanky hotels, then a raffle draw, and finally a Q and A with Hayter interviewing the guest star and taking questions from the floor.

On television Freddie had always appeared to me as either pissed or wary, according to whether he'd won or lost. But now, freed from the trammels of the sound bite and the misconstrued comment, he proved an eloquent speaker. In response to various questions from the floor, he argued as to why England were likely to prevail the coming winter (we're better), gave his opinions of the domestic game (too much of it), talked about his hero (Ian Botham) and admitted he was still recovering from attending a wedding reception the previous afternoon which seemed to be populated by people out of a certain TV show (*Jeremy Kyle*).

Finally he spoke about his reasons for being here today. Freddie had recently visited Helmand Province and spent some time with British troops, a trip he described as an extraordinary privilege. During his trip he'd been in the forces dining room at Camp Bastion when an alarm had warned of incoming rocket fire. 'I thought it was a wind-up but everyone dived to the floor,' he said. 'It was scary. I've seen things over there that will live with me forever. Until you've been out there yourself and seen what they do, you've no idea of the sacrifice they're making,' he concluded. 'It redefines the word courage.'

By 2pm the fundraiser was done and dusted and Boycie was shepherding his team away from the coffee and petits fours and over to the changing rooms. I found myself sharing a secluded corner with both Marks and Pringle. At one point I even managed to get to a position where I only had the two of them in my field of vision – Marks hanging out of the window making a call on his mobile, and Pringle standing in his boxer shorts eating a chocolate éclair. God, if I squinted hard enough I could almost imagine I was with them both in the dressing room at The Oval for the 1988 Texaco trophy match against Sri Lanka.

Boycie From *Only Fools and Horses* XI won the toss and batted first. I was down to bat at number five, so while I waited my turn I sat out on the balcony watching the match. By now the crowd had swollen to over four thousand with a long crocodile of cars still waiting to get in, and despite occasional sudden squalls of freezing rain blowing in from the distant hills not a soul had moved from their spot or sought shelter. If Freddie was going to bat, they were going to be there to see it.

Not that he'd get a chance if things went on as they were. Freddie was now at the top corner of the field, sitting in what appeared to be a vinyl sentry box, patiently offering his signature to a queue of excited punters that stretched halfway round the perimeter.

Eventually it was my turn to bat, but my innings was mercifully brief. Having reverse-swept Vic Marks for a two I was caught next ball trying to hit over the top in pursuit of quick runs. Still, I told myself on the way back, it's important to entertain, and my cack-handed slap to midwicket that ended up being caught at third slip had certainly done that. Naturally it was disappointing to be out in front of the largest crowd I'll probably ever play to, but never mind. It was a charity match. Doesn't really count.

During the tea interval I sat with the actor who always gets my parts, hearing him reminisce about what it was like doing all my parts, while the bloke who's big in that prime-time detective series talked about what it was like to be big in that prime-time detective series. But whoever you sat with, there was really only one subject of conversation. Would Freddie have a bat or not?

My nemesis was categorical. 'I've checked,' he said, 'and he's definitely down in the programme as non-playing captain. Anyway, look at him, that bloke's going nowhere.' He pointed out through the tent flap to where Freddie was still signing autographs, fortified only by a cup of tea and some shortbread fingers. If anything the queue was even longer than it had been two hours earlier.

The interval was soon over and with the weather beginning to close in it was time for Freddie's team to have a go. The protocol of charity cricket matches is always a delicate one, particularly when there's the obligatory run chase. It's de rigueur to let everyone have a bat and/or bowl, and possibly both. Running out old codgers who can't make it up the other end without a sedan chair is absolutely forbidden, as is swatting hapless children to all parts of the boundary. Catches must be extravagantly dropped if the batsman has only just come in, yet once he's been around a for a bit and had a good clobber he's supposed to get out so as to let somebody else have a go. Most importantly, a contrived edge-of-the seat finish is essential, if only to keep the spectators interested in watching – and donating.

In which case, it has to be said the second half of the game at Downton Hall went entirely to plan. Boycie of *Only Fools and*

Horses had obviously captained a good many such fixtures, because his tactics were impeccable, with bowlers being switched at regular intervals and the opposition batsmen all being given a chance to have a good clatter. It was all wonderfully jolly stuff and the crowd applauded anything and everything with immense good humour. Yet by 5pm the rain had set into an irritating drizzle, and with no sign of the main – indeed, the only – attraction, a slow steady stream of cars was now beginning to pull away from the car park. In theatrical parlance, we were losing our audience. Which was probably why, at the end of his over, Boycie called me over from deep point.

'Simmo, you didn't have much of a bat. Take the next over this end, will you?' Once again, his tactics were impeccable. Word had obviously reached him that my bowling action is always good for a laugh, and with Freddie not likely to participate, he'd obviously calculated that a twirl or two from his most hapless bowler might be a way to halt the exodus. But even as I was doing my customary arm whirling exercises, a roar went up that could have been heard in the next county.

Freddie had finally defeated the queue. And he was advancing to the crease, still in his trackie bottoms but now clad in pads and gloves, with a bat in his hand the size of a Canadian redwood. It was a magnificent, awesome sight.

'OK, Simmo,' said Boycie. 'Give it your best.'

My bowling maxim has always been based on the observation by Jim Sims, the old Middlesex off-spinner: 'There is a certain deadly accuracy about a straight ball. If they miss, I hit.' I don't recall much about the over, other than that the first delivery was met with a massive studious forward defensive that was received with a loud rumble of laughter. Each of my subsequent five deliveries to England's champion was gun-barrel straight and took several seconds to arrive at the other end. By the time I'd retrieved my sweater from the umpire I'd been informed that I'd been hit for a six, two huge fours and a two. The other two deliveries Freddie been unable to punish because they were so slow he couldn't get sufficient momentum to whack them anywhere.

All this passed me by, of course. All I knew was that I was bowling to Freddie Flintoff. Yet, even with me still shambling around in a daze, the next over proved even more memorable. The honour of bowling to the great champion from the other end was rightfully given to one of the very soldiers who had given so much: a young trooper badly wounded in the conflict and now back in Britain, and mastering the complexities of a new right leg made out of carbon fibre.

The young soldier, dressed in full army fatigues, galloped in with surprising speed and skill from the pavilion end and bowled what in my book looked like a half-decent delivery. Freddie dutifully belted it back over his head into a clump of distant trees, and the two men shook hands in the middle of the pitch. The next four were similarly despatched, one sailing just over my head with the speed of a guided missile and landing in the canopy of the champagne tent, where it nearly decapitated that actor who plays the butler in *Downton Abbey*. By now the stream of departing cars had entirely ceased. Even the rain seemed to have momentarily stopped to watch.

Whoever Flintoff employs at his celestial scriptwriters, they haven't lost their touch. Off the last ball of his over, the trooper clean-bowled the star attraction all ends up, and both men returned to the pavilion to a standing ovation from players and spectators. Some moment. Some over. Some player.

With that, the game had finished. Who won I neither knew nor cared. I'd bowled to the world's greatest cricketer, and been taken for only sixteen off my six deliveries: less than three a ball. If Freddie got back to match fitness I suspected there'd be some professionals in next year's IPL who would be giving their eye teeth for such respectable figures.

After the match I sat with my new chums Freddie, Derek and Vic in the tea tent, tucking into half-price scones and jam dispensed by a team of helpers from the local church and talking cricket. If this really were to prove my only outing in 2010, I wouldn't have swapped it for the world.

Eventually Peter Hayter wandered by looking utterly knackered but deliriously happy. It was too early to know for sure, but he estimated the event had raised a figure approaching £30,000. Freddie got up to join him, but just as they were leaving a woman scurried across and asked him politely for his signature. 'Could you sign it to my young son Alfie?' she asked breathlessly. 'You're his hero.'

As Freddie inscribed his name for the umpteenth time, I was reminded of something he'd said earlier in the day. 'The guys fighting each day in Helmand province are the real heroes. I just play cricket. Great in its way – but it doesn't really matter.'

Some weeks later a friend of mine told me that Vic Marks had mentioned on *Test Match Special* about some half-fit bugger having the cheek to reverse-sweep him in recent charity match. I've no idea if I was the half-fit bugger in question, but I'd like to think so.

10

George and Mildred

If it's true that the past is a foreign country, it's also true of the north.

It was that archetypal Yorkshireman Wilfred Rhodes who best summed up the divide between them and us. 'We don't play this game for fun,' he once averred. And truth to tell, if cricket in southern England is all soft corners and sunshine, its spirit crystallised by players of gentle lyricism such as May and Cowdrey, the north is all angles and hard edges – Trueman, Paynter, Leyland and, perhaps the most psychologically angular of the lot in recent years, Peter Willey, as tough as teak and gnarled as last year's pork scratchings.

Although he played much of his professional cricket in the Midlands, Willey was originally from County Durham, a place so genuinely forbidding that I've never actually dared go there. Willey's career perhaps defines better than most why we're two races bound by mutual distrust. Noted for his physical and mental toughness and bloody-minded courage, whenever he did get selected for the national side he spent much of his time in the middle facing the brutal speed of the West Indies fast bowlers, only to be dropped as soon as we faced Sri Lanka or Zimbabwe and the southern stroke-makers could be safely recalled to unfurl their silken artistry.

It had taken me till early June to venture beyond Spaghetti Junction. But now it was time to voyage outside my comfort zone. Not that I was ready, even now, to take on the real north – Lancashire or Yorkshire – at least, not yet. No, as Max Miller said when Ken Dodd asked if he'd ever played the Glasgow Empire, 'I'm a comedian, mate, not a bloody missionary.' But thankfully there was a halfway house, a comfort stop where I could reacclimatise to life in the north without feeling I had to don a cloth cap and a whippet for camouflage. A practice net for the real thing, if you like.

I'm talking, of course, about Derbyshire.

Derbyshire has always been the acceptable face of the north. Tough, gritty, knowledgeable, unadorned, but with a softer, kinder aftertaste. Derbyshire folk might moan about cricketing privilege and all those soft southern ponces cluttering up the place, but they'll eventually give you a wry grin and say, 'Still, now you're here, you might as well pull up a chair.'

There is evidence that cricket was being enjoyed in the county as early as the mid-eighteenth century, and it was certainly being played there in 1775 when one William Waterfall was found guilty of manslaughter at Derby assizes, having killed one George Twigg in a match at Bakewell. The county club wasn't officially formed until 1870, although even then the attitude of the other, more established counties towards this newcomer could be gauged by the fact that, for the first three seasons, only Lancashire would deign to come and play them.

In fact, the opening match between the two teams ended in a remarkable victory for the minnows, who dismissed Lancs for twenty-five, and this was later followed up by a victory of similarly historic proportions against Notts, although an open house held for the visitors by a local wine merchant on the eve of the match is traditionally thought to have proved decisive in the outcome.

The county nearly folded a few years later when it was discovered that the secretary, one S Richardson, had been embezzling the funds (he nearly did for Derby County FC, too, by whom he was also employed). Rather wonderfully, he absconded and eventually surfaced as court tailor to the King of Spain. Richardson's powers of regeneration and endurance are typical of folk in this part of the world, which has produced some of the most lugubrious individuals ever to pull on a pair of whites. Indeed, the county's history is strewn with huge-hearted triers who never seemed to get much of a break from either life or the authorities, but who managed to have a laugh about their misfortune rather than allow it to gnaw away at their entrails.

The apogee of this rueful spirit is to be found in Messrs Cliff Gladwin and Les Jackson. Mention these two fast-bowling compatriots from the 1950s to any Derbyshire supporter and prepare for a long ear-bending. These two doughty stalwarts were among the greatest fast-medium bowlers in the land of any era, yet between them they notched up a measly ten Tests.

Cliff Gladwin, himself the son of a former county cricketer, claimed so many scalps – 1,653 in fact – that he's placed sixtieth in the all-time list of world wicket-takers. Yet he played only eight times for his country. His partner Les Jackson was similarly productive, achieving over a hundred wickets in ten seasons with the county, and including a harvest of 143 wickets in 1958 at the stupefying average of 10.93, a statistic that has not been bettered by anyone since. Yet he managed only two international caps.

By the time I began watching Derbyshire these two were long gone, but their traditions were being nobly upheld by Mike Hendrick. Hendrick, he of the Adge Cutler sideburns, was one of a long line of Derbyshire bowlers who carried the England bowling attack for nearly a decade and who was fatally tagged with the reputation of being unlucky – and certainly in the years during which I watched him it was primarily a case of seeing him beating the bat five deliveries out of six, only to have a catch dropped off the sixth, almost always by a slip-fielder born south of Watford Gap. Then he'd inevitably strain his groin pulling on his sweater and that would be that, until the next time.

My decision to travel the 146 miles from London to Chesterfield had been prompted by a conversation I had with George Dobell, the bristle-haired chief executive of *Spin* cricket magazine. During a chance encounter on a crowded Tube train, I mentioned my summer of cricketing rediscovery, and he'd come up with the perfect combination.

'If you want to have the sort of day you remember having as a kid,' he'd said, 'do what I do. Go to Queen's Park, Chester-field. Pick a nice day. Sample some Bakewell pudding ice cream. Stay overnight so you can enjoy a bevvy. Derbyshire are play-ing Surrey there in a few days. Try to be there when Mark Ramprakash is batting, and finish off with a nice hot curry. A real ring-burner. Life doesn't get much better than that, in my opinion. If that doesn't rekindle your love of watching the game, I don't know what will.'

If I was a trifle uneasy about taking up his suggestion, it was only because my memories of Chesterfield and its environs were decidedly mixed. I had indeed enjoyed a jolly afternoon there in my early twenties when I'd been to watch a Sunday league match while working nearby, but my other visit to this neck of the woods while still a teenager had resulted in one of the most dreadful experiences of my short life, one that proved almost too graphically how easy it is for an unwary southerner to get out of his depth.

During the last weeks of the summer holidays of 1974, me and my teenage schoolmate Trevor had set out to walk the Pennine Way, starting from the tiny village of Edale high in the Peak District and only a hop, skip and a jump from Chesterfield itself.

The most famous of national walking trails offers 180 miles of the most gruelling hiking available, and demands sturdy boots, the ability to read a compass and enough Kendal Mint Cake to satisfy Mike Gatting. Having trained for our odyssey with a couple of brief walks on the South Downs with plenty of stops at pubs along the way, we arrived woefully unprepared.

The only compass I'd ever possessed had been in the insole of my Wayfinder school shoes, while Trevor's sole navigational aid was a road map of Britain filched from the glove compartment of his dad's Rover. Consequently, and with due deference to Captain Scott, our excursion turned into the most hapless and over-ambitious expedition of the twentieth century.

If you've ever attempted the route yourself, you'll need no reminding of what's in store. Out of Edale village you ascend a series of increasingly desolate ravines until you arrive at the summit on a dank plateau called Kinder Scout, a featureless peat bog permanently covered in mist and generally agreed to present the single biggest challenge of the entire journey.

Having spent our first night at a campsite in the village, we'd struggled up to Kinder where we spent the entire day traversing back and forth across the peat bogs in increasing (and increasingly desperate) circles. By 7pm and with the sun fast dropping somewhere over Manchester, we realised we were exhausted, lost, utterly alone and without the first clue how to get back down.

It was then I discovered I'd mislaid our tent pegs.

We were utterly knackered, and yet Trevor now insisted on retracing our steps in a fruitless quest to find the lost items, and with the sun long having set and him still not having returned, I convinced myself he was either dead or had been abducted by Ian Brady. With night approaching, panic seemed the only sensible course of action, and I began running back and forth along the same few yards of muddy bog yelling his name across the resounding hilltops.

Eventually he'd appeared through the near-darkness, still without the crucial equipment but now with a bruise on his forehead and a twisted ankle, the result of falling headlong into one of the peat groughs. I suspected he might be suffering from concussion, but it was difficult to tell because by now we weren't speaking anyway.

We eventually settled on spending the night out in the open, wrapped in our tent fabric and resembling some gruesome mutant cocoon from a low-budget sci-fi movie. But thank God we did: when daylight dawned we saw that our projected route back down to Edale would have resulted in us hurtling head first down a sheer drop less than twenty yards from where we slept.

Worse was to follow. Stumbling back down into the village at 6am just as it was opening up for the day, I'd parked my exhausted companion on a stone bench outside the pub and, spotting the convenience store just unlocking its doors for business, I hurried in to buy something fortifying and nutritious to replace all those lost calories. Thus armed, I walked to the far end of the village to report the loss of the tent pegs at the local visitors' centre.

As I entered the building, an official in shirtsleeves and a National Trust lapel badge was already at the front desk, helping a couple fit a battery into the back of their flashlight. The next thirty seconds remain imprinted on my brain to this day as the most shaming during my entire fifty-three years on this earth.

'Excuse me. I've come to report the loss of some tent pegs up on Kinder Scout.'

Official looks up.

'Oh, you're the bugger, are you?'

Official explains to me that a local hiker discovered the offending items on a remote path up on Kinder the previous evening, minutes before the air was rent with the screams of a terrified teenager coming from a distant hillside. He went back down into Edale immediately and raised the alarm.

'We've had mountain rescue out all night looking for you,' he says.

Cue the main entrance doors to the visitors' centre rattling open and in trudge fifteen of the most knackered, mud-spattered men I've ever seen since I watched the 1968 Rugby League Cup Final on *Grandstand*.

'It's all right,' says the man to the team leader as they file past. 'Panic over. This is the bugger.'

The team leader looks at me through two bloodshot eyes framed by dark discolorations and bags you could use to carry your shopping home.

It was only then I realised I was still holding my strawberry Mivvi. All these years later, the recollection of that single moment still has the power to tighten my sphincter. If ever as an actor I need to summon up feelings of shame, ignominy, embarrassment and humiliation, I merely have to think of a Mivvi and I'm already halfway to an Olivier award.

The town of Chesterfield (population eighty thousand) is known internationally for both its church's wonky spire and for being the residence of George Stephenson, inventor of *The Rocket* and a glass tube designed to grow straight cucumbers. It boasts a rich cultural heritage (Bernie Clifton and Emu once lived there) as well as significant sporting antecedents, from its perennially struggling football team to darts player and international comb-over champion John Lowe. It's also the home of the most important accessory in any cricket fan's inventory: Trebor Mints.

Queen's Park, however, is the town's most famous sporting landmark. Though to call it a park is like calling Frank Sinatra an easy-listening crooner. It's the *nonpareil* of parks, with sturdy Victorian benches, a canopy of magnificent trees, ornate flowerbeds, welcoming cafés and a wonderfully provincial atmosphere.

With the exception of a brief hiatus in the early 1990s, Derbyshire has been playing here for over a century, while the earliest reference to cricket in the area describes navvies in 1770 engaged in digging a nearby canal. It is reported that they laid down their shovels and picks to watch a game and refused to resume until its conclusion; a noble tradition of working life in England that has been proudly upheld to this day.

Of the ground itself I could recall little from my only previous visit in 1979, except that it was like something out of a Deanna Durban film, with a brass band playing light orchestral favourites during the tea interval and clouds of cherry blossom that drifted like pink snow across the outfield. But afterwards I'd stayed over at a small B&B near the old market square called, if memory serves me, the Mildred Guest House, in which the only other occupant (apart from the owner) had been an elderly spaniel.

'Funny, Goldie usually comes through to greet new arrivals,' the bemused owner had observed as he'd let me in through the front door. At the far end of the passageway I'd dimly made out Goldie's head, slumped at the end of a malodorous sofa and staring bleakly back down the corridor towards me.

The reason for the beast's lack of enthusiasm had been made graphically manifest the next morning. Just as I'd been about to tuck into my full English breakfast in the dining room, Goldie had tottered in and immediately commenced violently salivating on my right foot.

Sure enough, within seconds the trickle had turned into a torrent of foul-smelling stomach juices, and with me still frantically jangling the bell on the table to summon assistance, the dog had been violently sick all over my shoe, depositing most of the bottom half of a partially digested starling in the process.

That was the sum of my memories of Chesterfield. Yet the more I pondered George's proposal, the more I liked it. What's more, when I telephoned the Mildred to book a room, it was obvious the business was still in the hands of its original owner. The only sign of technological progress in the intervening three decades was an automated rendering of Scott Joplin's 'The Entertainer' that kicked in while he consulted the booking list.

The match I was going to was a four-day championship fixture between Derbyshire and Surrey – in fact, the return match from the very one I'd witnessed at The Oval earlier in the season. But, of course, that was 2010 for you – the county championship fixtures hanging horribly askew like saddlebags on either side of a summer given entirely up to merriment and hoopla.

I reached Chesterfield shortly before noon. Or rather, I reached the outskirts then. Like many places, the centre of the town seemed to have been carved up and castrated by a ring of two-lane asphalt initiated by a nightmare confederacy of town planners and senior management from Tesco.

I could see the famous old wonky spire all right, but fifteen minutes after first spotting it I was still careering round an arterial road fringed by hypermarkets that seemed only to want to take me to Matlock. Somewhere in the middle there was a charming little Derbyshire market town, but I'm damned if I could find it.

At length I skidded to a halt next to a taxi rank. A group of desolate-looking cabbies were gathered by the window of the leading vehicle, smoking roll-ups and staring disconsolately at the *Daily Star*'s indictment of yesterday's football match. England had been beaten the previous evening in the World Cup by a German team that had been younger, fitter, more technically skilled and, according to Julia, much better looking.

As I approached, one of the cabbies was drawing a huge penis and testicles on to the image of Fabio Capello on the back page of his copy, and what's more there was a queue for the pen. I fell into conversation about the previous night's debacle in Bloemfontein. 'Bad show, wasn't it,' I said, nodding at a picture of Wayne Rooney that had been given the strategic additions of a Hitler moustache, a pair of spectacles and a jiggling vibrator.

'Bloody shite,' said one, neatly summarising nearly six pages of *Sun* leader comment.

'I wonder what can be done?'

The cabbie drew deeply on his fag. 'We can start by sending all the bloody foreigners home,' he said, with a meaningful stare across at the other side of the road. A knot of Asian minicab drivers stood on the opposite pavement outside the entrance of a seedy office and stared suspiciously back. Neither group looked as if they'd had any custom for some days.

Having secured reliable directions, I parked the car in a nearby multi-storey and set off on foot. It was another beautiful morning, and every available bench and parapet was filled with perspiring office workers glugging down low-calorie drinks and hoovering up bags of Walkers crisps.

I'd arrived on market day, and the place was bristling with activity. Everywhere you looked there were stalls selling everything from home-made chutney and rolls of curtain material to pet accessories and orthopaedic shoes, while the fresh fruit and veg stands were a positive riot of improbable apostrophes. No baseball caps and urban bling here. Value for money was what counted: this was the kingdom of bowling caps, zip-up cardigans and Aertex vests.

Each item was being picked over in minute detail. One man standing on the pavement in a butcher's apron and boater was attempting to persuade an elderly shopper to purchase his firm's world-famous meat pies. Without apologising, she lifted the top casing of pastry and sniffed the contents. 'I'll take one,' she said. That was when I finally realised that *Last of the Summer Wine*, far from being a risible parody of northern market-town life, was actually an exercise in gritty realism.

My first sight of the cricket was a glimpse of Derbyshire fast bowler Steffan Jones's posterior, clad in white and moving swiftly behind a line of trees. Cricket purists maintain you cannot be a great fast bowler unless you possess a king-sized arse, a theory that, if true, condemns poor Steffan to being a chronic underachiever. Nonetheless he was toiling away manfully again today, and I followed the sight of his buttock cheeks as I walked through some trees and across a narrow footbridge.

Queen's Park was every bit as bucolic as I remembered it. The match may have been a crunch fixture between two sides desperate to climb out of the second division and watched by a crowd numbering several thousands, but it was as if the two teams had arrived in a local park and simply set up some stumps. I wasn't even asked to fork out for a ticket.

Call me a hopeless romantic, but if any place in England

seemed purpose-built for spooning and crooning under a June moon, it was here. I passed a tiny ornamental boating lake on which couples paddled about in the sunshine between nodding moorhens and majestic swans, while on the far bank stood a café proclaiming its status as winner of the Best-Ice-Cream-in-Britain award six years running.

Butterflies fluttered across an outfield girdled by an elegant circular pathway simply perfect for strolling in the evenings with your lady love. Just then a miniature steam train named *Puffing Billy* rattled past me filled with tiny tots perched on their mothers' knees and waving to all and sundry. Much more of this sort of thing and I'd be turning round in the hope of seeing my dad returning from the war.

And I was in luck. Mark Ramprakash was batting. To cricketing cognoscenti, 'Ramps' is the greatest enigma of the modern game. A supremely gifted batsman, his elegant artistry had seemed destined for international recognition from the moment he first appeared aged only seventeen. Yet despite scoring obscene amounts of runs at domestic level, both for Middlesex and more lately with Surrey, 'Bloodaxe', as he's also known (due to his notoriously incendiary temper and will-to-win), has perpetually failed to live up to his billing at the highest level. One former England teammate summed him up perfectly when I'd spoken to him of Ramps a few years ago at a boozy lunch. 'I knew he'd never make it,' he'd told me. 'He wanted it too much.'

Now aged forty-one, an age when most cricketers have already spent several years running a pub, Ramps was in the form of his life. Winning the second series of *Strictly Come Dancing* seemed to have loosened the stays of his gut-wrenching ambition, and he was playing better than ever.

But for how much longer? Rumour was rife he might be hanging up both his boots and his tap shoes, particularly since Surrey had appointed a new captain who was aged only four when Ramps played his first innings for England. If this indeed was to be my last sight of this legendary cricketer, I couldn't wish for a more sepia-tinted setting.

As if to greet my arrival he drove the first ball I witnessed down towards the boating lake for an all-run three. But I barely noticed it: instead, my attention had been grabbed by a nearby van advertising their world-famous Bakewell pudding ices. My friend George had told me on no account to miss out on this culinary experience, and having purchased an example I found a space on one of the benches and settled down for a long lick.

The other occupants were a quartet of ruddy-cheeked sexagenarians, all of whom had lived their whole lives within five miles of the ground. Jim Broadbent could have played any one of them. 'Welcome to Moaners' Corner, Michael,' said Ernie, offering his hand. 'You'll rue the day you sat 'ere. I'm unofficial president, Harold here is treasurer, Syd there is secretary, while Vic over there at the end is shit-shoveller.' They leaned across in turn and shook my hand with grave sobriety. 'There's only one rule if you're going to sit with us,' explained the president. 'To moan when we win and to moan when we lose. It's the only fun we get at our age.'

'Ramps looks in great nick,' I observed.

'Oh yus yus yus,' replied Ernie in a startling impression of Churchill the insurance dog. 'They've got ta' get him ar't or we're suhnk. Come on, move up, you lot, and give our new recruit a bit of room. Michael,' he continued, 'just move my lunchbox out of the way and make yerself comfortable.' He gestured to an empty

Tupperware container on the seat beside him containing the remains of his sandwiches.

'Careful, Michael,' shouted Vic from the far end as I leaned across. 'Don't touch owt that's been in his mouth – you'll get scarlet fever.'

Ernie wanted to know where I'd come from, and my reply seemed to enthuse him. 'I were there once,' he said with enthusiasm. 'I had to fit some windows in a big house up by Golders Green. By heck there's a bit o' money in that area. Lovely place, mind you, I'll never forget—'

'Oi, Mr President, point of order,' interrupted Vic from the end of the row. 'Why are you suddenly talking all posh? You sound like Prince Charles.'

'I've got to,' replied Ernie. 'Otherwise he wouldn't understand a bloody word I were saying.'

The Moaners proved excellent companions. It felt not so much like a cricket match as an episode of the old ITV series *The Comedians*. Wives formed a good part of their banter, and the domestic picture they painted was of a life spent placating a fearsome banshee in hairnet and surgical stockings. Their humour may have been straight out of Les Dawson's bumper joke book ('I'd rather bring her to the cricket than kiss her goodbye'), yet it was infused with obvious, if understated, affection.

'She's not so bad as long as you don't have to look at her,' admitted Harold. 'Mind you, I daren't have any drink in the house when she's around. Not that she's a teetotaller, it's just if I put a tumbler down the next thing I know she's put her teeth in it ...'

They were equally gloomy about their county's prospects, and responded to my hopes for better in the future with derisive snorts. Harold provided a thumbnail sketch of the doleful pastime of following Derbyshire. 'They'll bugger up this one an' all, you'll see,' he said of the current team.

Never mind. Today wasn't a day for worrying about results. It was a day for basking in the sunshine as Ramprakash moved seamlessly towards the hundred and twelfth century of his career. My mate George had been right. Watching this extraordinary batsman on a dreamy June afternoon with frequent refills of Bakewell pudding ice cream was, as he'd predicted, near to cricketing nirvana.

There was a old-fashioned courtesy about my surroundings, too, right through from the greetings of the gate stewards with their jug ears and bowler hats, down to the tea ladies: bustling women with helmets of steely-grey hair, clad in easy-clean tabards and dispensing great slices of Battenberg to anyone who asked. Even the Derbyshire fielders seemed to know all the spectators individually by name.

By the end of the afternoon session, Surrey had moved serenely on to 266–3, with Ramps now in the nineties. On a low, slow wicket he'd been content to collect runs mostly in twos and threes, like some cricketing Daimler accelerating smoothly away from a pelican crossing. The hundred and twelfth hundred of his career was now within touching distance.

As the players trooped off for tea I handed back my temporary membership card and bade the committee farewell. Ernie made an official toast of thanks for my time and company, finishing his brief salutation by wishing me a happier life than he'd ever managed. In return I promised to look them up if ever I was in town again, and with a final wave goodbye I set off for the pavilion. George had texted me to say he'd arranged a pass for the press box for the rest of the season, and I was anxious to sample the atmosphere inside the one here. As I left, a last snatch of conversation drifted to me on the breeze. It was Syd.

'Oi, Mr President, where you off to now?'

'I'm going to inspect the wicket, aren't I?'

'Why do you want to do that?'

'Cos everyone else does.'

'Thank God, I thought you were goin' mushrooming ... '

There have been many times when I've wondered what it might be like to be a professional cricketer. Not an international star, you understand, but a normal county pro, spending my summer days travelling back and forth across the country, playing the game I love and getting paid for it. But one ex-school colleague of mine, who indeed pursued his – and my – dream for a few years as a county opening batsman, once put me right in brutal fashion.

When I asked him why he'd chosen to chuck the job in early and retrain to be a solicitor, he'd replied he was sick of spending his life driving up and down congested motorways late at night in clapped-out cars smelling of sweaty socks, and with the sole prospect of having his head knocked off the following morning by some young West Indian quickie. This stark description of the realities of professional sport had done much to quash any rose-tinted notions I might have harboured. Yet now, as I passed in front of the pavilion windows, my faith in a more romantic image was unexpectedly rekindled.

Through the glass I could see both the Surrey and Derbyshire teams crammed together in the tiny clubhouse, and tucking into one of the most sumptuous and unashamedly old-fashioned teas I'd ever witnessed.

The menu read like something out of *The Wind in the Willows*. I spotted ham sandwiches, boiled eggs, gala pie, sherry trifle, fruit salad (the proper tinned stuff from Libby's – none of that fresh muck), catering packs of salad cream and, unless my eyes deceived me, a tin of John West pink salmon, a culinary colossus from my childhood that even now I can never gaze upon without being reminded of watching *Dixon of Dock Green* in my parents' front parlour. And in pride of place in the middle, a huge glistening bottle of Chef tomato ketchup with the words 'Chesney Hughes's own – keep off' scrawled across the label. There was even a large tin of luncheon meat with the opening key still attached to the side and waiting to be unwound. Where on earth had the tea ladies of Chesterfield obtained such recherché delights?

I pressed my nose against the glass and allowed myself some discreet salivating. The spectator sitting next to me was smoking a briar pipe, and the soft, sweet aroma of Erinmore combined with the sight of grown men tucking into crab-paste sandwiches made me want to weep. Could you imagine top sportsmen being offered this sort of thing in any other sport? Andy Murray in a crucial quarter-final on Centre Court carefully undoing a Tunnock's tea cake, or Tiger Woods tucking into a slice of veal and ham pie while ruminating an eighteen-yarder on the eighteenth at Augusta? God, I loved this game sometimes.

Ramps's moment of triumph after the break was certainly one I'll remember. With the great man perched securely on 99 and the crowd already sweeping the cake crumbs from their laps in preparation for the anticipated standing ovation, he cover-drove the toiling Tom Lungley sumptuously to the boundary. The scoreboard clattered up the three figures, and players and spectators stood as one to applaud this cricketing masterclass. I celebrated my own lesser triumph in being here to witness it by texting George Dobell to assure him that the Ramprakash hundred he'd so confidently predicted had been accomplished without so much as a spilt chance.

Yet Ramps acknowledged the applause as if he'd just been picked out at a police identity parade. His response to the standing ovation redefined the term 'surly', and I heard the pipe-smoking Derbyshire member near me muttering, 'That young man could do with learning some manners.'

Two balls later he was clean-bowled all ends up.

Even as he was marching grim-faced back to the pavilion, an embarrassed scoreboard operator was reconfiguring his total. It turned out he'd wrongly attributed an extra three runs. Ramprakash was only on 99.

Whether his loss of concentration had been due to the fact he'd just had to play-act acknowledging a hundred he knew he hadn't yet achieved may never be known, but the look on his face as he trudged murderously back to the pavilion left little room for doubt. Glaziers and bat repairers in the Chesterfield area were about to enjoy a sudden spike in orders.

With Surrey's star now out of the way, Derbyshire's bowlers were reinvigorated and four wickets fell in quick succession. Meanwhile the sight of all that food had made me hungry and I was anxious to sample some of the famously clubbable atmosphere – and free grub – that was the lot of a county press box. Having collected my temporary pass from the secretary's office, I hurried across to the tent; although to call it a tent was something of a misnomer: it was more Argos than Ascot.

In his excellent and gently moving article on the demise of cricket journalism in the 2010 *Wisden Almanack*, Gerald Mortimer, for many years the hugely respected correspondent of the *Derby Evening Telegraph*, described how, when he began work as a cricket journo in 1970, any correspondent wishing to visit

Chesterfield during Festival week would be well advised to arrive early to claim a seat. Yet if anyone was in any doubt as to the game's decreasing relevance in the printed media now, you only had to step inside the spindly marquee with its flapping canopy and loose guy-ropes this afternoon.

Once upon a time it would have been full to bursting, not only with local reporters but also correspondents from nearly all the national papers, both broadsheets and tabloids. Now a mere handful of reporters was gathered here, sprawled among half-eaten plates of chicken and trays of coleslaw, and demonstrating the time-honoured skills of their profession since time began – namely the ability to absorb the action while simultaneously maintaining a stream of conversation about bugger all. Any hopes I might have cherished of hearing some ancient cricketing wisdom or juicy morsels of gossip from the Derbyshire dressing room were soon disabused. The only argument raging this afternoon among the various correspondents was not about the cricket at all, but the question of who was the greatest comedy team in showbiz history.

As the discussion ranged back and forth I sat quietly in the corner and steeled myself to tackle a platter of congealing roast potatoes left over from someone's lunch. One local correspondent was pushing the claim of Morecambe and Wise, another was pressing for the Two Ronnies, while a third, a young man from a local hospital radio station, was making a desperate plea for the inclusion of Horne and Corden. By the time Surrey lost their seventh wicket, the debate had been settled in favour of Eric and Ernie, yet instead of ending the furore, it merely led on to an even more frenzied argument as to who were the worst in the genre, with the candidature of the Chuckle Brothers enthusiastically pushed by Hospital Radio Man, despite protests that they were children's entertainers and thus shouldn't be included in the poll.

Eventually the debate blew itself out, and silence descended as the journalists each began filing copy for close of play. With the shadows lengthening and the crowd thinning, Surrey quietly subsided to 391, and play ended soon after 6pm. The word on the street was that Ramprakash was about to hold an informal press conference over in the pavilion, an event I was cordially invited to attend, but given Bloodaxe's mood as he'd departed the field at the end of his knock, I declined the chance to listen to a stream of thunderous obscenities – after all, once installed back at the Mildred Guest House, I suspected I'd soon be offering up enough of them myself.

Having stopped off at a nearby pub for a pint of Marston's and half an hour of Brazil versus Chile on the TV, I arrived at the Mildred just after seven. The place was much as I'd remembered it, a nondescript property on a steep hill with a display of china dogs in the front window and a selection of diseased conifers in pots arranged round the front door. I pressed the doorbell and the owner, older and greyer but still recognisably the same, hobbled out from the rear parlour. Behind him, and in place of the elderly spaniel of my previous acquaintance, now lumbered a muscular Rottweiler with a startling resemblance to Brian Close of Yorkshire and England.

'Sorry about Luther,' said the owner apologetically. 'It's just we've had one or two attempted break-ins and he's for protection. He's really very friendly once he gets to know you. But I'll always be here anyway.'

Apart from an antique fax machine propped up beneath the telephone table, nothing much had changed, even down to the flame-effect electric fire in the front lounge complete with gyrating light behind the decorative coals. I was handed a set of keys (one for the front door, one for my room and another for the communal toilet) and was shown upstairs to my room. I was now ready to tackle the final item on George's 'perfect day out' checklist, the ceremonial curry. A 'real ring-burner' had been his express command. Having supped on nothing but greasy spuds and ice cream throughout the day, I was looking forward to doing culinary battle, and I set off into town with grim relish.

It had been the proprietor of the Mildred who'd suggested I try the Red Fort, a restaurant located on a busy arterial road a few minutes' walk from the house and specialising in Bangladeshi cuisine. Huge frosted windows prevented any glimpse of the interior, and the illuminated menu display case was so fogged up it was impossible to read. Just to add to the sense of mystery, somebody had leant a full-sized cardboard cut-out of Darth Vader in one of the upstairs windows.

My tenacity was rewarded by a meeting with the owner of the premises, Ashok. Despite my being the only customer, he insisted on giving me a cramped table right next to the counter and in the glare of a bubbling fish tank. No sooner had he taken my order (something called a Chilli Naga, a speciality of the house, and not, according to Ashok, for the faint-hearted) than he asked could he join me. Within minutes we were snapping poppadoms and dribbling mango chutney down our fronts like old friends.

Ashok was a sports freak. He loved football, cricket and a curious game from his home country called kabaddi, the rules of which he attempted to explain with the aid of the relish tray and various items of cutlery. As far as I could make out, it was an ancient forerunner of the old playground game British bulldog, including a neat sporting twist in that one of the players is not allowed to breathe during the contest.

So complex were the rules that by the time Ashok had finished his induction course, our table looked as if had catered for a hen party. Thankfully a squeal of ropes and ageing pulleys alerted us that my meal was on its way up from the kitchen, and Ashok broke off briefly to collect it. I was greatly looking forward to my Chilli Naga.

'Are you ready for this?' asked Ashok anxiously as he unfurled a fresh napkin and laid it on my lap. 'You will find prevailing orange and pineapple flavours, but above all you will find this very hot. This was your request, yes? Please tell me if it is not to your taste.'

I assured him I had once existed on little else, and lifted a huge, steaming forkful to my lips. It smelt delicious: a heady blend of spices and herbs, and with the unmistakable aroma of exotic fruits infused with garlic and coriander.

'You like?'

'Christ almighty.'

'Yes it's very special. *Maze karein*. Enjoy.'

As I ate, Ashok's conversation moved on to cricket, and in particular his national team. He agreed the current Test series between England and Bangladesh was a hopeless mismatch, one that did little credit to his nation's sporting reputation. The only exception was his side's star player, opening batsman Tamim Iqbal, who'd recently scored a withering century at Lord's before following it up with another 70-odd at Edgbaston. A lager-flecked photograph of his hero hung above the bar, the frame surrounded by a strand of yellowing tinsel.

'You know of Tamim?' he asked.

I nodded. In truth it wasn't because I'd lost interest, or because I wasn't anxious to communicate my opinion, it's just that it's difficult to talk coherently about professional sport through a mouthful of seared flesh. Instead I scooped up a couple of tablespoonfuls of boiled rice and gestured for him to continue.

As I ate Ashok told me his life story. Originally from Dhaka, he had lived in the UK for the last ten years and owned this restaurant for the last five of them. 'The people here in Chesterfield are very kind,' he said. 'I have had the odd problem with abuse, but look at this way – if millions of Englishmen suddenly arrived in Bangladesh, we too would feel threatened. It is only human nature. I tell you, I have been treated with great courtesy. This is God's own country. Ah, I see you too have tears in your eyes.' He reached across to the counter and handed me a fresh napkin on which to blow my nose.

'But it is changing,' he continued. 'Now there are Kurds, Poles, Romanians: when I first came here they were unheard of, but now – you see them everywhere. Some of them are dangerous people. I tell you, Michael, I don't feel safe any longer with them walking around. Does this seem odd to you?'

My reply was a grotesque hiccough.

'Yes it is indeed odd, my friend. Twenty years ago my words could have probably been put in the mouths of most of the residents here about me, yet this is how things evolve. People come, they settle, they integrate, they ride out the ethnic prejudice from the indigenous population until they, too, feel accepted, whereupon they in turn find themselves threatened by the next wave following in their wake.'

Eventually he fixed me with a look of utmost sincerity. 'But I tell you,' he said quietly, 'if Bangladesh were ever to play here at Chesterfield, I would ensure Tamim would enjoy a meal in my establishment he would remember for the rest of his life. Speaking of which, how is yours?'

'Truly memorable,' I answered huskily. 'I wonder, could I have another boiled rice and a fresh pitcher of water?'

I left the Red Fort just before ten, having eaten about five forkfuls of Chilli Naga, four servings of vanilla sorbet and about half a hundredweight of orange Matchmakers. I even briefly contemplated purchasing a Mivvi on the way back to the hotel, but decided not – no point in tempting fate. Nonetheless, I'd enjoyed meeting Ashok. In fact, I'd enjoyed the whole experience since setting off this morning. George's recipe for the perfect day had indeed been spot on.

Back at the Mildred, the front door was ajar and the theme tune from *News At Ten* was blaring from the parlour. As I stepped into the hallway, Luther the Rottweiler barrelled out, claws clattering on the lino. His owner was nowhere to be seen. Luther now had a look in his eye that I just knew was one day going to lead to the beast being headline news and spoken of in sorrowful terms by Julie Etchingham.

What would Peter Willey do in such circumstances? He wouldn't cower in a corner like I was doing, vainly scanning the hallway for assistance. He'd take the animal's front paws, bend them at right angles and sever the aorta in a single, unhurried movement.

Maybe so. But I was from Brighton.

'Good dog, nice dog,' I croaked, and hurried up the stairs. Five minutes later I was standing under the shower with my mouth open.

11

I Was There

Ever since I'd first started watching cricket, I'd always considered Glamorgan to be somewhat different. Well, not exactly different – what's the phrase I'm looking for?

A bit crap, I think that's it.

A bit crap can be very endearing when you're ten years old and you're a bit crap as well. 'Michael is not particularly adept at games but tries hard and is popular with his teammates', my form teacher once wrote on my school report. The same could be said of Glamorgan. Whenever they played Sussex I always left school for the dash down to Hove and the post-tea session with an extra spring in my step, as they were often the only team we could beat – or so it seemed. I suppose that's why I'd retained such affection for them.

The last of the original seventeen counties to turn professional, they'd come to the game as recently as 1921, which is perhaps why they still appeared to be thoroughly enjoying themselves, whatever the results. Not just their players, but their supporters as well: large, ruddy-faced men in shirt-sleeves and braces with rich rumbling baritone voices, who accepted perennial disappointment with a smile and a chorus of 'Cwm Rhondda'.

Because of their relative obscurity, the players were a nightmare for autograph hunters, as they contained virtually nobody you could put a name to. Or rather, you could put a name to them, but it was always Jones.

There were one or two notable exceptions: their captain Tony Lewis, for instance, who briefly skippered the national side, or Jeff Jones, a lanky fast-medium bowler who followed a long and distinguished line of international prospects by continually breaking down, and, even more venerable, their crinkly-haired off-spinner, Don Shepherd, who seemed to have been part of their set-up almost since their inception.

An old-fashioned type of player you could never imagine wearing anything other than blazer and slacks, Shepherd always seemed to be bowling from one end, a fact confirmed by his 2,200 wickets for his county, the greatest number of dismissals by any bowler never to be awarded an England cap. His absence from the national team sheet led to dark rumours that an anti-Wales bias existed in the corridors of the MCC. But Shepherd had shrugged off his continuing disappointment by simply doing what he did best: bowling his way season by season into the record books. His reward was a place in the hearts of all red-blooded Welshmen and now, in 2010, rightfully the presidency of the county.

Even above the name of Shepherd, however, Glamorgan cricket is synonymous with the name of one man: Wilf Wooller, or to give him the title by which he was universally known, 'that bloody Wilf Wooller'. The sort of chap for whom the word 'combative' might have been coined (though not within earshot, not unless you wanted a stream of invective in your lughole), Wooller's involvement with Glamorgan cricket, for good or for ill, lasted for over three decades, and runs through the history of the county like lettering through a stick of Mumbles rock.

A dashing if combustible sportsman, he'd first played both cricket for Glamorgan and rugby for Wales before the Second

World War, but like so many from that disrupted generation, his best years were much taken up by active service overseas. Having survived two years in the notorious Changi jail in Singapore (decades later he still refused to use pocket calculators made in Japan), he returned to the county in 1946, and having soon assumed both the captaincy and the secretaryship, immediately set about re-minting the team in his own bristling image, mainly by employing an iron fist in an iron glove.

A year later it paid off in dramatic style, when under his leadership Glamorgan won their first championship title. It was a remarkable achievement for such an unfashionable county, but there was little doubt who was the presiding genius of the campaign – Wooller, who planned meticulously for every match in minute detail, even travelling round with his team in a lorry laden with army blankets and a mangle with which to dry any pitches threatened with rain. Legend has it that when playing at Swansea he even claimed to consult the local tide tables before the toss.

Both in the press box and the field of play, he was fearless and unapologetic. Supplementing his meagre pay as a writer, he'd often roundly criticise in print the very players whom he was supposed to be captaining on the field, while when batting he'd think nothing of taking on the fastest of bowlers by any means available ('Call yourself fast, Tyson?'). When the great Peter May of Surrey found himself run out by Wooller after backing up too far at the non-strikers' end and enquired politely, 'Isn't it customary to give the batsman a warning?', Wooller replied, 'Not in Swansea.'

On another occasion, during a match against Somerset under the equally forthright captaincy of Yorkshireman Brian Close, that bloody Wooller, by now having hung up his boots but still serving as county secretary, became so incensed by Close's delaying tactics that he announced over the loudspeaker, 'In view of Somerset's negative approach to the game we are willing to refund the admission money of any spectator who wishes to call at the club office.' Try doing that today and see how long you last in your post.

Test selector, businessman, rugby international and latterly commentator, he was one of those men who long after retirement still couldn't keep away from the game he loved, which is why he found himself witnessing, albeit from behind a microphone, one of the most famous episodes in the history of the game, and one whose dewy-eyed memory drew me to Swansea for the next leg of my journey. While trying to describe those extraordinary events even Wooller, a man not known for readily complimenting any visitor from beyond the Severn Bridge, was forced to exclaim 'Good gracious' twice within a couple of minutes. As a commentating classic it may not rank alongside 'They think it's all over ...', but coming from him, it was praise indeed.

For anyone like me who cut their cricket-watching teeth in the late 1960s, the tiny tumbledown ground of St Helen's will forever be associated with five minutes of cricket mayhem. 'The old lady', as she's affectionately known in these parts, is famous for one cricketing milestone, and I'm not referring to the fact she possesses the longest flight of steps from pavilion to boundary of any ground in England (sixty-seven, to be exact). No, it was here, at this dilapidated little arena just off Swansea seafront that once doubled as Wales's national rugby stadium, that in 1968 the immortal Garry Sobers hit six successive sixes.

It's difficult now in this era of thrash and run to appreciate just how extraordinary his feat was back then. Nowadays, with bats the thickness of telephone directories and the necessities of the one-day game turning even the stodgiest blocker into a cricketing thug, such a feat would be scarcely enough persuade the average spectator to glance up from their BlackBerry.

Forty-odd years ago you didn't loft the ball off the grass before August, and only then if the committee gave you written permission in triplicate. To give you some idea, Don Bradman only hit six sixes throughout his entire international career, during which he scored nearly 7,000 runs. But Sobers didn't follow fashion so much as dance on its grave. And so on the third day of the championship match between Nottinghamshire and Glamorgan, he grasped his cricketing destiny with both hands.

The recipient of his unlikely assault wasn't canny old Don Shepherd (much too wise for that, he made sure he bowled twenty-five niggardly overs at the other end), but his more prosaic Glamorgan teammate, Malcolm Nash. Nash was a decent seam bowler but in presumably a moment of madness had decided to have a go with some spin, and his subsequent *High Noon* with Sobers ended with a world record and an unexpected glut of work for roofers throughout the Gower peninsula.

'My one aim was to persuade Sobers to hit the ball in the air,' Nash said afterwards with breathtaking sanguinity. As to whether it affected his confidence, suffice it to say he now lives in San Francisco and works for a firm that recycles plastic.

The incident has naturally become something of an urban sporting myth. I've spent time with Glamorgan supporters in all sorts of unlikely locations – in hotel foyers in Vienna, harbour-side bars in Bombay, even three hours trapped in a lift in Stockholm's highest skyscraper – and each averred they'd been there to witness the great event.

'Ah, yes, that over. Sobers the bat. I was there, see? I recollect it as if it were yesterday.' And they'll give a deep, south Wales rumbling chuckle of rueful reflection.

The explanation for this example of collective wishful thinking is explained by the fact it was captured on camera by BBC Wales, and consequently the event was reshown endlessly, even making it on to the national news. And as you'll know yourself, the memory can play funny tricks. As a result of such scheduling serendipity, 'that over' can be viewed on YouTube more than forty years on. What's more, it's glorious stuff – wondrous hitting by possibly the greatest natural athlete ever to play the sport.

Although Sobers' assault consists of six separate shots, the footage more resembles the same stroke endlessly replayed, with the director shouting 'Cut!' at a slightly later point in each take. Each instance commences with Nash lolloping in from the concrete rugby terrace end, continues with Sobers rocking on to the balls of his toes like some cricketing Nureyev, followed by a blur of the bat as it describes a murderous arc through the air, and the next thing Nash is peering in the direction of Jones the butcher to see if he can have his ball back.

Even by itself the event would be sufficient reason to justify the rail fare to Swansea, and yet history was once more in the making. For on Thursday 22 July, the off-spinner Robert Croft, one of Glamorgan's most loyal and durable stalwarts, was on the very point of completing a unique double – the first (and almost certainly the last) Welsh cricketer ever to record one thousand wickets and ten thousasnd runs.

I'd always liked Crofty. A small, combative off-spinner with all the physical elegance of a garden gnome, he was principally famous for being England's answer to Shane Warne, and for deliberately barging into Essex bowler Marc Ilott during a tele-vised match at Chelmsford (itself an action that would stir the blood of any right-thinking Englishman).

His mere presence, with those hunched shoulders and that splayed walk, was a reminder of the old days, when you could tell players apart other than by checking the number on the backs of their shirts. And having grown up a stone throw's away from the ground, he was understandably keen to celebrate the milestone here, at Swansea. Perched tantalisingly on 997 dismissals at the start of the championship match against Leicestershire the previous morning, he'd snaffled a brace before the arrival of a cloudburst that had brought proceedings to an early end. Sometime this afternoon he should finish the job, watched over by family and friends. And, as long as there wasn't a points failure at Didcot Parkway, by me too.

I spent the long train journey from Paddington catching up on national events in the newspapers: and there was plenty to enjoy, for middle England was in uproar. Footage had just been released to a shocked nation of a publicity stunt at a seaside resort on the Black Sea at which a group of Russian entrepreneurs had tied a donkey to a parachute before sending the animal on a bizarre flight high into the air.

Needless to say it had nearly caused a third world war. We may not care a toss for our civil liberties here in the UK, but by God, put a cat in a wheelie bin or tie a donkey to a parachute and you're certain to reignite the debate on capital punishment.

It had rained most of the way down, and was still spitting when I arrived at eleven, so donning a particularly hideous polythene hat bought specially for the purpose, I set off on what the ticket collector assured me was 'a brisk half-hour's walk' to the ground.

Swansea seemed a bustling enough place all right, but the economic underinvestment that habitually blights this area of south Wales was evident wherever you looked. The buildings all seemed to have been turned hurriedly into something else: the churches were now pubs, the once-elegant Victorian villas were nursing homes, while a shop that had until recently evidently sold grand pianos was now an oriental supermarket.

That's not to say there wasn't life in the old dog. My route took me past the Guildhall where graduates from Swansea University were celebrating their degree ceremony. The lawns in the front of the building were thronged with excited students in mortarboards and gowns, surrounded by friends and family and all clutching glasses of bubbly.

Girls in cocktail dresses and red stilettos tottered about in the rain amongst proud fathers and cheery mums, while a party of grinning male scholars stood laughing and joking in the dank air, sublimely happy to be through their exams and off on the next part of their big adventure. A photographer shod in the obligatory Hush Puppies and festooned with a hundredweight of different cameras fussed around, arranging them into groups for an official photo ('Now come on, ladies: if you can't see the lens, it can't see you'). It was nice to see so much optimism, although how many of them would find work was hard to predict.

A few yards further I turned a corner and suddenly found myself on a gusty seafront and staring at a huge bay of spectacular proportions. Wet sand stretched out for thousands of yards towards a slate-grey sea, and on the far side of the shoreline and framed by scudding clouds I could just make out the shape of Mumbles pier jutting out from the promenade. As for the ground itself, there was no mistaking it: the place looked exactly as it did forty odd years ago on BBC Wales's grainy footage. It reminded me of the gag, 'They dropped a nuclear bomb and it caused fifteen quids' worth of damage.' I could only hope that what St Helen's lacked in style, it made up for in atmosphere.

'First time here?' said the man at the turnstiles as I peered in through the gates. I assured him it was, before adding I was pleased to finally make acquaintance with a place forever associated with Garry Sobers' extraordinary blitz.

'I was here.'

'You were?'

'I saw every ball,' he continued wistfully. 'Bloody marvellous it was, even if we were on the receiving end. Never forget it. Though you'll be lucky to see much like it today.'

Indeed, after its overnight drenching, 'the old lady' presented a desolate spectacle. Although the rain had now ceased and the covers were off, the prospect of any play seemed a distant one. Spectators with furled umbrellas picked their way gingerly between the puddles, while in the car park a group of dispirited workmen in overalls were shovelling bags of gravel into huge potholes filled with stagnant water. Nearby a set of portable cricket nets on broken wheels sat drunkenly by the perimeter wall, the netting shredded and flapping limply in the breeze.

I picked my way round the perimeter of the outfield, traversing sodden concrete stands like an impromptu mountaineer. Now clutching my temporary media pass, I set off for the press box in the hope that it might offer some comfort from the general squalor, but it was if anything more dispiriting – a grubby room whose sole occupant was a spotty teenager surfing the internet on a laptop.

'Have I missed anything?' I asked.

'Only this.' He turned the screen and I found myself watching footage of a terrified donkey suspended by a parachute sailing high over the Black Sea.

'I mean, in the cricket.'

'Naw,' he said in a light Welsh lilt. 'It's been pissing it down. I'm only here to take Crofty's photo when he does the biz. And I'm supposed to be covering a disabled swimming gala this afternoon.'

The clip of the donkey came to an abrupt end. He switched to another excerpt, this time of an elderly man falling down an escalator at Tokyo airport. I noticed with incredulity it had had a staggering 2 million hits. No wonder county cricket was struggling to survive in the twenty-first century if this was the sort of entertainment people craved. Though come to think of it, if any one cricketer could rival the man on the escalator, surely AJ Harris of Leicestershire, the player who had been timed out in mysterious circumstances back in 2005, would be the man to do it. After all, he was playing in today's fixture for the visitors, and what with St Helen's having all those stairs ... My heart skipped a beat.

'There's another inspection in a minute so we might be lucky,' continued the youth without looking up. 'Everyone's in the bar. They're doing a carvery. The food's not great but you can eat as much as you want.'

I left him watching a clip of a man laden with a tray of drinks walking into a set of patio windows, and picked my way across to the clubhouse. My route took me past the players' balcony. Several Glamorgan players were lolling in chairs reading the papers, and in the centre I spotted Robert Croft himself, perched on the front balustrade, idly spinning a cricket ball in one hand and glancing moodily out towards the Irish Sea.

In front of him a narrow flight of cement steps led down to the pitch. There are few more desolate experiences in all sport than having to walk back to the pavilion having scored a first ball duck, and whoever had designed this particular route can only have been a bowler with a warped sense of humour. Just then a young colt in Leicestershire colours hurried past me. I asked him if he knew where I could find his teammate.

'Who? Andy?'

'Is that his name? AJ Harris.'

'Andy's not playing,' he answered.

'Not playing?'

'Nope.' He was already hurrying into the darkness of the dressing room.

'But I saw his name on the scorecard.'

He stopped and considered for a moment. 'Wrong Harris,' he suddenly exclaimed. 'You're thinking of the guy playing for Glamorgan. James Harris. He's the one down there.' He nodded to a distant figure doing gentle limbering exercises down on the outfield.

A quick look at the current averages on a sheet of paper pinned to the notice board in the clubhouse seemed to provide a clue as to my Harris's omission from today's Leicestershire team. Cricket, that most fickle of games, was again proving a hard taskmaster. So far this season he'd played only four matches, taking nine wickets for 385 (one of which he'd secured against Sussex back in April) at an unenviable average of just over 42 a piece. It wasn't difficult to conjure a likely, if fanciful, scenario from the statistics, particularly as Leicestershire was 35-year-old AJ's fifth county in nearly as many years.

I'd seen hundreds of Harrises in my time. One season they're opening the bowling, a year or two later they're being mentioned as potential England prospects, then a little while more they're third or fourth change or bringing on the drinks. Then an injury or two, or the arrival of some new player from another county, and before you know it they're working in the club's marketing department or even pushing trolleys in your local Waitrose. My Harris had been Leicestershire's leading wicket-taker last season and had even toured Australia with England 'A' back in 1996/97. So where might he be today? Languishing at some second eleven fixture? Guesting for a local club side in an effort recapture some form? Or resting at home with his knee in plaster and clinging to the hope of being able to manage some light training before the end of August? Whatever he was doing, I hoped he was OK.

As I stood in contemplation, the clouds parted and bright sunshine dazzled off the wet concrete. A feeble cheer went up from the bedraggled spectators. Even Crofty managed a watery smile.

Almost on cue a fluting voice crackled out over the loud-speakers. 'I have some better news to impart,' it began in a voice resembling a junior curate making parish announcements. 'The umpires have decided that play shall commence at 1.40 providing no further rain obviates. In essence,' he continued, 'that ensures that seventy-two overs are still calculated to remain from the day's allotted play, which will be added to the accrued remainder of the additional half-hour from yesterday's early abandonment. So to sum up … '

Fantastic. This was what I had missed from my cricket. Where else would you get a public address system at a sporting event in which words like 'essence', 'obviates' and 'accrued' were thrown around like confetti? I just had time to throw some lunch down my neck before settling down for Crofty's big moment.

There are few things we Brits like more than an all-you-can-eat carvery, and the one in St Helen's Clubhouse turned out to be a striking example of the genre, in that it was stewed, tepid and plentiful. A long table stood at one end of the room, manned by a couple of teenagers in chef's hats standing behind steaming tureens. The food inside had once been an attractive prospect, but now anaemic cauliflower and watery swede stared back up at me, and there was something about the overpowering school-dinner aroma that immediately quelled my appetite. In the end I plumped for a tuna baguette from the bar and settled down at a table next to the window. Far down below, the covers were already being removed and Leicestershire's Paul Nixon was leading some tentative catching practice on the boundary edge.

I found myself next to a man eating the largest meal I'd had ever seen. My mum always told me it was rude to stare, but this really was something. In addition to what seemed a full roast with three kinds of meat, his plate was piled high with faggots, pease pudding and sufficient mashed potato in which to mislay your cutlery.

What's more, he'd cleverly managed to buttress the perimeters of the plate with some naan bread from the vegetarian curry option. Weighted down with mashed potato, they were now doing splendid service as a means of doubling the overall surface area of the plate. I could only assume he must have once been a distinguished architect. He was sweating horribly, though whether from the muggy climate of the dining room or the effort to trying to force such a quantity down his gullet, it was difficult to tell.

On a wall above his head was a collage – six separate snaps of Sobers in full spate, somewhat incongruously framed between the stuffed head of an antelope and a signed photograph of Diana, Princess of Wales.

'That was some achievement,' I suggested, nodding towards the montage.

He turned his head with some difficulty. 'I was there,' he replied, spearing a faggot with his fork and waggling it in the direction of the photo.

'Were you?'

'Never forget it,' he said.

'Which end was he batting at?' I asked.

He looked slightly pained, and stared out of the fogged-up windows as if seeking inspiration to a difficult quiz teaser. 'Let me see now,' he murmured. 'It was at the far end, I think. He hit the last ball right over into the rugby stands. Marvellous it was.'

My new dining companion was no Russell Brand, but by my waiting patiently while he forced down another shovelful of food, we eventually struck up what could almost pass for a lively conversation. Among ten interesting facts he imparted, I learnt that dolphins are often spotted in Swansea Bay, that on a good day you could see right across the Bristol Channel to Ilfracombe: and that Rossi's parlour on Mumbles seafront does the best ice cream in the whole of south Wales.

More worryingly, he also informed me that the view from the pavilion, or anywhere else for that matter, might not be around much longer. 'See this morning's article?' he said, nodding to a damp newspaper on the table in front of him that looked as if it done service as a mop.

I stared at the headline – 'Croft closes in on historic double' – but lower down the news was more disquieting. According to sources leaked from the local council, clandestine plans were afoot to bulldoze this famous old ground and turn it into an aquarium.

With the brand new Swalec Stadium in nearby Cardiff hoovering up all the available money (or so stated the pro-aquarium lobby), it would only be sensible to rationalise Glamorgan's overstretched resources and concentrate efforts on the main venue, thus freeing up this valuable piece of real estate for the advancement of Swansea's struggling tourist industry.

'Bloody terrible, isn't it?' said my companion through a mouthful of potato. 'We knew this might happen. They've let the place go to rack and ruin and are now claiming it's not fit for purpose.' I thought back to Priory Meadow at Hastings: a unique piece of cricketing history now turned into a cornucopia for ladies' underwear. It was the same old argument that'd been used there; now it seemed St Helen's might be next on the conveyor belt.

'Oh well. I shan't be here to see it,' he said wistfully, followed by a discreet belch. 'Enjoy your day. And don't forget, Rossi's ice cream. Try the Raspberry Explosion. It's worth the journey. Any bus along the prom will take you there.' He rose stiffly and hurried off to the sweet trolley.

By now both the players and umpires were on the outfield. With the wicket damp and two new batsmen at the crease, the Glamorgan captain, Jamie Dalrymple, elected to start with seam-up, and thus the county's favourite son was sent deep to deep mid-off to contemplate his fate. I hurried down the steps and joined a knot of well-wishers sitting within touching distance of Croft on the other side of the boundary board. They were evidently a fan club, or members of his immediate family – possibly both.

Another man soon joined us and gave Crofty a wave as he took his seat. His greeting jolted the great man out of his reverie. 'You feelin' all right now?' asked Croft.

'Not bad,' replied the man. 'I'm trying to walk off all that beer you forced down my throat last night.'

'Keep walking, boyo,' replied Croft. He looked unutterably frustrated, and vented his feelings by pulling his cap down over his ears and kicking at a clod of turf.

Luckily it didn't take long for the call to arms and Croft started marking out his run-up. Spectators began emerging from the clubhouse, some still with napkins tucked into their shirt collars, while from a stand at the sea end I noticed the glint of tele-photo lenses being lined up. This was we'd all been waiting for.

It didn't take long. A quicker delivery aimed at the leg stump and a fraction short, a crude flick to leg from Leicester-shire batsman Wayne White, a blur of wicket-keeping gloves, a throaty appeal from the surrounding fielders, an upraised finger, and suddenly Crofty was doing some ancient Celtic dance in the middle of the square, legs akimbo, arms pumping as if performing a Welsh equivalent of the haka, before finally sinking to his knees. Moments later he vanished from view, smothered by his teammates. When he emerged it was to a standing ovation. Already clattering down the steps, all sixty-seven of them, I noticed the great Don Shepherd himself, blazer and slacks flapping in the breeze, clutching in one hand a bottle of celebratory champagne.

Meanwhile, a local cameraman ambled on to capture the happy scene, and for the next few minutes the square trans-formed into an impromptu party. Thirteen years after his first scalp, Glamorgan's favourite son had his thousandth wicket. Though it was just as well he managed it when he did, because even as Croft was trotting back to his position at fine leg, the umpires were gathering up the bails and running off. Huge black clouds were mustering just behind the Guildhall. No need to wait for the inevitable. Within seconds it was chucking it down.

While we waited for the storm to move on out over the Irish Sea, I joined a gaggle of local reporters in the press box as Glam-organ's hero relived his great moment for local press. His answers to the questions – did you sleep last night – are you feel-ing tired out – can you recall your first wicket – will you have a drink to celebrate – were modest and wry, but it was obvious he was hugely relieved to make the milestone, and in front of a home crowd as well. Apparently he'd already had a text from his first victim, Surrey's Graham Thorpe, to congratulate him.

By the time he'd answered all the questions in English and then again in Welsh, nearly half an hour had passed, and the rain was heavier than ever. Don Shepherd himself briefly looked in at the door to the press box. 'Bloody typical,' he said mournfully to nobody in particular. 'Nearly four weeks of Mickey Mouse cricket and as soon as we get the real thing, this happens.' He mooched off. With play out of the question for heaven knows how long, there was only one thing for it.

One of the lessons I should have learnt in my fifty-three years on the nineteenth largest island on the planet is never to make a special journey anywhere merely in order to sample ice cream. Just as with our other staple foodstuff, fish and chips, it's one of the oddities of life in Britain that everybody has an opinion on where the best example in the country may be sampled, and it's always within a five-mile radius of where they live. And it's almost always a disappointment.

My journey, perhaps predictably, turned out to be a fool's errand. Instead of whisking me along the bay to Mumbles seafront, a distance of what appeared no more than a couple of miles, the bus I joined kept turning right to make a series of lumbering detours round various housing estates. We crawled along over speed humps and through winding streets barely large enough for a transit van, flipping wing mirrors and scraping hubcaps of parked cars. Just when I thought we were about to rejoin the highway for good, the bus turned into the vast complex of Swansea Metropolitan University for yet another agonising detour. By the time I'd arrived at the Mumbles nearly an hour had passed. This Raspberry Explosion had better be good.

The resort, also known as the 'Gateway to the Gower peninsula', has something of a reputation for being a jewel in the
Welsh tourist board crown, its attractions numbering, among
others, snazzy boutiques, elegant fish restaurants and a wide
selection of arts and crafts, from Welsh love spoons to handmade
chocolate. Yet today it looked even more desolate than the St
Helen's press box. Crocodiles of bedraggled tourists laden down
with children laboured along the main thoroughfare looking for
somewhere to shelter, and judging by the length of the queue
outside Rossi's parlour it was the only option.

My experience proved every bit as frustrating as the journey
here. Preparing my order necessitated the girl who took it
making three separate journeys the entire length of the counter,
on each occasion scooping a dollop of raspberry goo from a plastic tub at the far end before returning once more to the front to
add another layer of ice cream.

Once served, I settled down at a nearby table to read the late
edition of the local paper. But it was bedlam in here: screaming
toddlers, bickering families and the screech of chairs being scraped
back and forth across the tiled floor. The dessert was impossibly
sweet and glutinous and my wafer was damp. Less than ten
minutes after arriving I'd cut my losses and was trundling back
through the university halls of residence at a steady 8mph.

But as luck would have it, I got back dead on 5pm, exactly in
time to watch Leicestershire resume their innings and promptly
lose their last three wickets inside eighteen deliveries. With the
ground once more unaccountably bathed in glorious sunshine, the
final hour of play proved the most pleasurable of the day, during
which Croft's remarkable coup de théâtre was nearly stolen from
under his nose by his Glamorgan teammate, Australian batsman
Mark Cosgrove.

Voted the 'Don Bradman Player of the Year' in 2005, Cosgrove was another in the diminishing category of players who could safely be described as big-boned. He was one of three players temporarily suspended from the Australian centre of excellence in 2007 for what was described, with unusual Antipodean diplomacy, as 'repeated inappropriate treatment of accommodation facilities'. He'd then been sacked by South Australia over fitness issues, whereupon he'd gone straight to join Tasmania and walloped 160 in his first innings for them, mostly in boundaries.

Now he was scoring runs for Glamorgan with equal rapidity. No wonder they loved the guy in these parts. In the opening ten overs this evening he splattered the Leicestershire bowling to all corners of the ground in a manner that suggested he wasn't interested in running any more than was absolutely necessary.

As I watched, I found myself earwigging a conversation between a couple of burly ex-coal miners in the row behind me. Much of their chat centred on an aspect of daily working practice I'd certainly never come across during my three years of drama training at RADA: namely, the advantages of using stone dust as a means to keep the coal dust from infiltrating your lungs while you're working underground. If my understanding was correct, strewing the substance liberally on the floor of the shaft ensured that, due to the stone dust's greater weight, the coal dust was kept anchored to the floor.

'Oh yes, I knew all about that,' his companion struck up. 'I was a ventilation engineer. I spent my life trying to calculate how much methane was in the atmosphere so as to prevent explosions.'

'Did you ever suffer one?'

'No,' replied his friend, 'plenty of dust explosions, but never a methane explosion, thank God. Funny thing is,' he continued,

'I would smoke five or six fags before putting on my lamp and getting into the cage. But when I was down there I never fancied one.' Even eavesdropping on these reminiscences was sufficient to make me want to cough.

Their conversation eventually broke off while Cosgrove essayed a ferocious hit off Leicestershire's Matthew Hoggard that walloped into the boundary board with such force it nearly tipped it backwards.

'That's it, Cozzy boy,' shouted the first of the coal-miners, rising to his feet.

I turned to them. 'Cosgrove looks good,' I suggested.

'Oh, he's a good lad, is Cozzy,' the man replied with an affectionate chuckle. 'Easy on the eye. Tell you what, much more of him and Leicester can forget about winning this match. Lovely boy.'

'So why isn't he playing for Australia?'

'Too fat. Apparently Ponting won't have him because he doesn't look the part. Suits us perfectly.'

'Well, he certainly graces the old ground,' I ventured. 'The great Garry himself would have been proud of him.'

'Garry Sobers?'

I nodded.

'I was here,' he said. 'I was sitting near just about here, a few rows down from where we are now. You know that fourth ball of Nash's over, the one the fielder caught on the boundary but cockled over the rope as he did it – you look on that footage and you'll see me about three rows back. You can see me just as he gets up and looks behind him. I look a bit different now, mind. Forty years of Edna's home cooking has done that.'

During the next half hour we watched in admiration as Cosgrove continued to pepper the boundary boards, at one point blasting six fours in ten balls including three consecutive boundaries. Yet by 6.15 more thunderclouds had enveloped the ground and Cosgrove was running, for the first and only time, back to the sanctity of the dressing room.

Even as he laboured up the steps, the spectators were already streaming out of the main gates. The locals in these parts obviously knew their weather and, sure enough, within seconds it was chucking it down yet again for the third, or was it the fourth, time in as many hours. Never mind: my day at Swansea may have produced barely forty overs, but they'd been stuffed full of natural goodness.

Before setting off back to the station, I decided to call in at the Cricketers, a tiny pub on a street corner opposite the ground. The premises had featured heavily in the original footage of Sobers as the majority of the balls had been hit over its roof, but even without this claim to fame, a cricketing guidebook in my possession, left over from the late 1990s, had recommended it as a place to drop in.

'The saloon bar has an interesting selection of memorabilia dedicated to Glamorgan cricket,' it ran. 'And bar meals are even served on old scorecards.'

Even before I stepped over the threshold it was obvious why the publication was long out of print. If ever Wilf Wooller or Don Shepherd had held pride of place on the walls of this grubby boozer, they were long gone. The place had a disinterested air about it, and of its cricketing associations little or nothing remained.

Instead, a huge TV screen draped above the bar was currently playing a garish pop music video, showing gyrating lovelies prancing round some bling-encrusted dude on a golden throne. If he'd been Garry Sobers I might have stayed, but it was obvious that many years had passed since his name had been heard in here. Or so I thought.

I bought a desultory half pint and settled down by the window, near an impossibly elderly man in a greasy raincoat who looked as if he hadn't strayed from this spot for many moons. Eventually he lifted his half pint of Guinness to his lips and supped it thoughtfully. After a long, luxurious smack of his lips, he finally spoke.

'Been to the cricket, have you?'

'Yes, I have.'

'Enjoy yourself?'

'Very much,' I answered. 'I've always wanted to visit the ground and it's been a great day.'

'Oh, it's seen some stuff all right,' he answered enigmatically. 'Garry Sobers hit six sixes off an over once.' His comment seemed to dangle in the air.

'I know,' I replied. I could see what was coming, and for once I was determined to forestall the inevitable. 'Were you there?'

'No,' said the man, once more lifting the glass to his lips. 'As a matter of fact, I was here … '

12

Boiled Beef and Carrick

It's difficult to imagine nowadays how unutterably dull Sundays once were in Britain until that wondrous day in April 1969 when John Player decided to use live limited-overs cricket to advertise its smoking accessories. Previously, the only options were to go on a picnic with Mum and Dad – Lewes or Hastings, of course, or, if memory serves me, a lay-by on the A27 between Sompting and Worthing that always seemed to hold a bewildering fascination for them – or stay in and watch reruns of *Ice-Cold In Alex* on the telly.

Not any more. Sundays were suddenly fun. Even more wonderfully, BBC2, anxious to find something to fill their schedules throughout those long desolate afternoons, began to broadcast entire matches from 2pm until nearly 7. And the new format was a perfect piece of precision social engineering. Forty overs a side, eight only per bowler, run-ups restricted to fifteen yards, a mere couple of quid to get in and the whole confection perfectly pitched to fill that twilight zone between the twin pillars of family life, the Sunday roast and *Songs of Praise*.

No surprise, then, that it was an instant success. No more sandwiches covered in exhaust fumes. No more Anthony Quayle wrestling with that bloody crank handle. There was a whole new world out there, and with the grounds knee-deep in fag-dispensing dolly birds clad in white kinky boots and with garish sashes bisecting their bosoms, it was the perfect place for dads to take the family. Even my own dad attended a few matches in those early years, and we lived in a tobacconist's shop; such was the new contest's allure.

I was at Hove for the first game there on 27 April, Sussex against Lancashire. It was the first Sunday I can ever recall doing anything other than watching juggernauts thundering past our lay-by or army trucks rolling down sand dunes. It felt good.

In fact, it felt more than that – it felt deliciously insubordinate, as if we knew that what we were doing went against the express wishes of the Archbishop of Canterbury and that we'd all return home to find our pipes burst or houses burgled as divine retribution.

The new svelte format also revolutionised the way the game was played. Such was the tactical rigidity of the professional game back then that in the first season of the contest, the Somerset off-spinner Brian Langford was allowed to bowl his entire eight-over spell, mostly to Brian Ward of Essex, without conceding a single run. 'I thought I'd play him out,' said Ward afterwards. All that was swept aside within a season or two – nudging, nurdling, keeping the scoreboard ticking over, stealing the strike, hitting over the top: these were the new skills, and everyone had better learn them PDQ. With improvisation and agility now as important as classic textbook cover drives or line and length, specialist fielders such David Hughes or Derek Randall suddenly became worth their weight in gold. By the same token, old duffers content to stop the ball with their foot, or sleek classicists who never worked the ball to leg in case it creased their shirt, were now viewed as a positive liability.

So what had happened to the forty-over formula in the decades between then and now? It seemed to have retreated into a cricketing demimonde, followed only by lonely widowers or by people who were neither traditionalist enough to enjoy the three-day game nor funky enough to get down and dirty in T20. How had this shapely young beauty aged so disastrously within a few brief decades?

'Nothing dates more than the recently fashionable': these words do not explain the premature ageing of the 40-over format, but do ring a warning bell for T20 if the authorities don't watch out.

The rot seems to have initially set in when John Player ditched its sponsorship at the end of 1986, to be replaced by Refuge Assurance. Almost imperceptibly the contest's profile started to unravel. With a special knockout finale bolted on to the end of the season, this once-simple structure became increasingly unwieldy, and with the BBC dropping their coverage in the late 1980s, attendances soon started failing. In 1993 the competition was disastrously extended to fifty overs, which pleased nobody, then forty-five, then back to its original length, and finally split into two divisions, by which time it had almost as much surgery on its features as David Guest – and with about as much benefit to its overall appearance.

The final nail in its coffin was surely the decision to free the contest from its traditional Sunday-only moorings. Shorn of its structure or symmetry, the contest had become a sprawling and amorphous hybrid, without either purpose or passion. In its current format it is known as the Clydesdale Bank 40, and who knows what will happen to it in the future?

Nonetheless, today I was on my way to pay my respects one last time to the old-fashioned Sunday League and, by chance, at a game that was both on a Sunday, and at a venue and in a town central to both my professional and cricketing education. For if there is any one place in the country in which my two twin obsessions, acting and cricket, are forever captured in perfect rose-tinted harmony, it is the small North Yorkshire coastal resort of Scarborough.

My spell in the town, spanning two entire summers in the early 1980s, owes its place to cricketing serendipity, as the local theatre company was run by world-famous dramatist and cricket nut Alan Ayckbourn. I'd auditioned for him in the spring of 1980, and later heard I owed my selection as much to my reputation as a dogged opening batsman as to any ability with comic timing or skills in delivering iambic pentameter.

It was a blissful couple of years. It was in Scarborough I'd had my first serious love affair, learnt to drive and had my first catastrophic encounter with malt whisky. A theatre-based team of actors, stage hands and hangers-on played matches nearly every Sunday, and on the rare weekends when there was a gap in the itinerary and I didn't have my Owzthat set to hand, I could always obtain a quick fix at the nearby cricket ground, where Scarborough played in the Yorkshire county premier league. Best of all, every August the ground hosted Yorkshire for a week or so of first-class competition as part of one of the oldest festivals in the cricketing calendar.

One of the advantages of having a boss who loves cricket is that the natural working patterns inexorably follow the contours of the fixture list. Thus the following summer, 1981, seeing that the third Ashes Test was scheduled to take place at Headingley, Ayckbourn did what all right-minded theatre directors should do and cancelled rehearsals for two days in order to take the entire acting company across to Leeds for the Thursday and Saturday of the game.

Alas, his timing in cricket was not quite so deft as his feel for comedy. If most cricket fans are wont to rattle off their most famous 'I was there' story at the drop of a catch, Headingley 1981, or 'Botham's Test' as it was to be forever known, was destined to become my best and only 'I was nearly there' yarn. Or rather, I was there, but not at the right moment.

The first day of the game gave no inkling of the pyrotechnics to follow. In dramatic terms it was the equivalent of watching a four-act play about suicide in rural Sweden, as Australia's limpet-like opening batsman John Dyson ground his way to one of the slowest Test centuries on record.

But if Thursday was Strindberg, the next day of our scheduled visit, the Saturday, was black comedy. With Australia having now racked up 401, England were bowled out in just under three sessions and followed on 227 runs behind. It was some time around 5pm, just as Graham Gooch was plodding his way back to the dressing room for the second time in under five hours, that Ladbrokes flashed up the latest odds on the scoreboard.

England 500–1 to win, it read.

I'm not a betting man, but I'm not a complete twat either. The official Ladbrokes odds predictor, ex-England wicketkeeper Godfrey Evans, must surely have had a brainstorm. Of course there was no way England were going to get back from this debacle, of course not. But 500–1? What was the worst that could happen? I'd lose a fiver. And the best?

I promise you my buttock cheeks actually left the seat. But the theatre press officer and cricketing sage, a man known to all and sundry simply as Woody, had other ideas. As I made to leave I felt a discreet tug on my trousers.

'Simmo, sit down for Christ's sake,' he said simply. 'Don't be a prat. Buy a round of drinks with it and save your money.'

'But it's 500–1,' I pleaded. 'It's a no-brainer.'

'You're wasting your wages. We're stuffed. This match is only going in one direction.' Always one for obeying the voice of authority, I sat down again, not knowing that even as I did so half the Australian team were at that very moment signalling for their mates in the crowd to go and put down a fiver on their behalf.

The rest, as they say, is history. It turned into 'Botham's Test', not high drama so much as the cricketing equivalent of Freddie Mercury duetting with Montserrat Caballe: ludicrous, unfathomable, preposterous and utterly memorable. Less than forty-eight hours after nearly placing a bet that would have netted me almost the equivalent of thirty weeks' repertory wages, I burst into Ayckbourn's office in unthinking delirium, sending cast and scripts flying, and dancing a highland reel with one of the greatest names in British theatre history, all the while proclaiming the joyous news that we'd won.

To his eternal credit, the exuberance of his jig even outdid mine. It was a wonderful, improbable, glorious, epoch-defining moment in my love affair with the game. What's more, it was the only time I ever witnessed Ayckbourn dance in nearly two years of theatrical first-night parties.

My return visit to Scarborough this weekend may not include a highland reel, but at least I could enjoy a trip down memory lane with a weekend by the sea and a Sunday League encounter between Yorkshire and Middlesex.

I arrived on the Saturday lunchtime after a train ride via York. The fifty-minute journey on to Scarborough on the tiny Trumptonesque branch line was always one of the joys of going there, and little had changed in the intervening years. The trees, the neatly manicured fields, tiny signal boxes with glinting windows, and dinky road bridges of the sort favoured by Postman Pat, pitchforking above the track – everywhere the sort of neatness and order you saw only in a tabletop layout at a model railway exhibition. Or my Hornby and Tri-ang long ago.

It was a beautiful late August weekend, the sort of final hurrah before we're all invited to get out the winceyette and the Wincarnis, and the resort was doing what it does best – providing somewhere for solid Yorkshire folk to enjoy some no-nonsense fun. The town has always had a loyal clientele through good times and bad, and today it was packed to the gunwales. If nothing else, it also explained the answer to one of sport's most elusive questions: who ate all the pies? It wasn't, as custom supposes, Mike Gatting, but day trippers from Leeds and Rotherham. Despite the sweltering temperatures, they sat on every available vantage point scoffing improbable amounts of meat and pastry and thoroughly enjoying themselves in the process.

If you can't beat them, join them, has always been my motto. I purchased a lamb and mint pasty from a handy retailer and sat down on a wall across from the station. The café opposite had been an eatery where I'd spent many happy afternoons refuelling between the matinee and evening performances at the nearby theatre, while briefly enjoying a mild flirtation with the girl who pushed the sweet trolley.

Where once Annette had plied me with glistening rum babas there was now a respectable travel agent's offering coach tours for local tastes and local sensibilities. No foreign excursions, with insanitary plumbing and dodgy spics making off with your hat and coat the minute you'd checked in, from this establishment. Instead the fare was as homely as roast beef and Yorkshire pudding: 'British Isles In Bloom' – 'The beautiful

Yorkshire Dales' – 'Autumn in the Channel Islands ("Bergerac country")'. What's more, business was brisk.

My route to the hotel took me straight down the main drag. Now, just as thirty years ago, it was again offering good old-fashioned value for money, such as tumbling clockwork puppies and pairs of inflatable breasts. I stopped briefly at a confectioner's and bought myself a slice of 'Malibu, truffle, Bounty bar and cherry crème fudge'. Having grown up in a sweetshop, I regard myself as something of an authority on the subject, and until this moment I'd always maintained that nothing ever devised by man could beat Mackintosh's Caramac for sheer tooth-rotting sweetness – but this was something else. The sugar rush took barely ten seconds to overwhelm me and was sufficient to give me momentary symptoms of Parkinson's disease.

The match at Scarborough's old ground in North Marine Road was not until tomorrow afternoon, but I had a lot of memory lane to stroll down first. Later on today, the Saturday, I had a rendezvous at my old theatre for a theatrical entertainment on the theme of cricket, cleverly designed to synchronise with the festival trade, but with the afternoon to enjoy before then I wanted to catch one of the town's principal tourist attractions, and an event I'd inexplicably never seen despite two years' sojourn in the town.

If there is one thing we like even more than beating the Aussies, it's stuffing the Germans, and the miniature naval battles on the lake at Peasholme Park in the town's North Bay tap into just about everything the Brits love: ice cream, boating, sunshine and Nazis. Advertised as the longest-running show of all time (it fired its first shot in anger in 1927), the concept is unashamedly old-fashioned, which is why people come here.

I'd forgotten just how different the North and South Bays were in Scarborough. No more than a steep headland separates the two, yet crossing from one to the other is still like stepping between two worlds. Where the south bay is frenzied, knock-about and full of candy floss and trips round the harbour by speedboat, its neighbour on the other side of the headland is as prim and respectable as a short story by Alan Bennett. With its neatly-tended flower beds, manicured pathways and canine-faeces receptacles you could eat your dinner off, Peasholme Park is a shining example of old-fashioned Yorkshire municipal pride. By the time I arrived it was nearly 3pm, and with the aquatic carnage due to commence at any minute, a crowd of several hundred spectators was already sitting patiently.

In front of us was a large ornamental lake, in the middle of which stood a pontoon decorated as a Chinese teahouse. The sole occupant was an electric organist, already pumping out the theme from *Thunderbirds* in between maintaining a raucous commentary.

Meanwhile, a procession of diminutive warships was already chugging ominously towards us, each craft apparently steered by a council employee secreted somewhere in the hull. Against all odds, the event has forestalled the blandishments of the PC brigade, but only just, as there's been some deft remarketing in recent years to assuage liberal sensibilities. This daily display of Lilliputian warfare was once advertised as a recreation in miniature of the battle of the River Plate, in which a victorious English convoy of destroyers tracked down and sunk the mighty German warship *Graf Spee*. But in recent times the word 'German' has been airbrushed out of the advertising material, to be replaced by the all-purpose term 'enemy', and the vessel, which was now steaming towards me at a steady 3mph, had been tastefully repainted in anonymous hues and renamed the *SS Robert Eaves*.

Nevertheless, the musical motif thundering out from the organist on the pontoon provided healthy clues to the conflict's real provenance to anyone with an IQ greater than their age: 'The Dambusters March', '633 Squadron' and Ron Grainer's theme from 'The Battle of Britain'. We may all be friends within the corridors of Brussels, but up here memories are somewhat longer.

'Good afternoon, ladies and gentlemen, boys and girls, and recycled teenagers – that's grans and grannies,' blared the organist over the music. 'Now what we want today is lots of cheering the Royal Navy, and booing the enemy any time you see them approaching so we can warn our brave lads they're about to be attacked. Come on, everyone: let's hear you boo. Imagine you've just seen the England football team playing ...'

The crowd needed no second prompting. 'BOOOO!!' we shouted in unison. 'That's wonderful, folks,' yelled the organist. 'And let's all hope we have lots of fun and a JOLLY GOOD BATTLE!!' With that he struck up a rousing chorus of 'We Are Sailing', a melody that provoked many in the audience to begin waving their ice-lollies back and forth in the air. I never knew total war could be so much fun.

In truth the conflict nearly didn't get going. As a preliminary to the main event there was supposed to be a naval beauty pageant in which all eight or so craft involved in the battle poodled round the perimeter of the lake in front of the audience. Yet it soon became clear the *SS Robert Eaves* was in some difficulty. After ten minutes of laboured progress it had slowed to a virtual stop, the worried features of its onboard controller just visible in the tiny windows on its deck through a plume of acrid smoke.

'Ooh, I think he's got some weed round his propeller,' said the organist. 'We've had a lot o' trouble with that this summer. Never mind, has anyone here got a birthday they're celebratin'?' A flurry of hands went up.

Thankfully by the time we'd sung a couple of choruses of 'Happy Birthday' and applauded a couple from Rotherham celebrating their silver wedding anniversary, the pride of the German navy had managed to limp back to base where a mechanic wearing huge black waders and a wetsuit successfully cleared the obstruction.

At last we were up and running. What's more, the massacre proved well worth the wait. For the next fifteen minutes or so the various craft pottered back and forth across the water, firing tiny fizzing missiles at one another and scaring a flock of ducks that foolishly tried to land in the middle of the war zone. But the outcome was only a matter of time, not least because there were seven British boats against one of the enemy, plus a coordinated aerial bombardment by jiggling wooden aeroplanes in RAF livery strung from undulating wires above the water. Well within the allotted thirty minutes, the *Robert Eaves* was belching symbolic smoke and hoisting the white flag, and the free world was safe once more – at least until the 5pm performance.

The spectacle finished with a final parade by the victorious British convoy, now with their upper decks removed to show the heads of the drivers, their bodies still wedged horizontally inside the hulls, who waved enthusiastically at the punters as they trundled past. A final round of applause and an admonition to pick up our litter on the way out, and it was over. Where moments before the battle of the Atlantic had been in full spate, happy families now trundled happily back and forth across the lake in rowing boats and giant pedaloes.

By 6pm I was in my seat in the studio space at the Stephen Joseph Theatre for the first of the evening's theatrical confections. The original building in which I once trod the boards is no longer in use, but in its shiny new guise in a converted Odeon cinema opposite the railway station, the repertory company still serves up popular and populist theatregoing throughout the year. And while Ayckbourn himself may no longer be in charge (although he still lives in the town), both his obsessions and those of his successor, the equally cricket-besotted Chris Monks, were reflected in the offering.

It was a short play called *Twenty:20* by James Quinn, and proved an engaging two-hander set in the England cricket dressing room during a one-day international. A young dude, loosely based I imagine on someone such as Liam Plunkett, arrives to play his first match in national colours. He thinks Don Bradman was a bowler, and can hardly concentrate on the game in hand due to calls to his agent, glugs from his canister of special isotonic drink and conversations on his BlackBerry with his *Emmerdale* star fiancée who is currently appearing on *Strictly Come Skateboarding*.

Thus he hardly notices his sole companion, the ghost of a long-forgotten star of the 1950s, who is sitting in a baggy woollen sweater and yellowing flannels in the corner of the room, nursing a cup of old-fashioned Yorkshire tea.

The themes may have been predictable, yet were strangely affecting. The old codger gently warns the kid that although the bright lights of international stardom may seem alluring, if he spends all his time sampling fashionable nightclubs and opening supermarkets rather than developing line and length, he's destined ultimately to fail. A nice touch, in amongst the gentle homilies, was an audio commentary of the match supposedly unfolding out on the pitch, conducted by the actual voice of David 'Bumble' Lloyd, and while I might not pay much to see his *Hamlet*, in the guise of himself he added a touch of verisimilitude to proceedings. The audience, mostly middle-aged couples, warmed to both the show and its comfortably old-fashioned sentiments. As I followed them out of the auditorium at the end, it was obvious from their conversation that most were intending to be at the game tomorrow.

Over breakfast the next morning in my hotel I got chatting to several other couples who were all sitting meekly at their numbered tables waiting for someone to break the suffocating silence that seems to prevail in English seaside guest houses during mealtimes. When I finally piped up, the sense of relief was as great as if I'd offered to donate a kidney. They were soon prattling away nineteen to the dozen, and all admitted they were diehard Yorkshire cricket fans who'd come specifically for the festival.

Throughout the conversation, one name above all kept being mentioned: that of Len Hutton. This favourite son of Yorkshire made some of his biggest scores at Scarborough, including thirteen centuries, and he even got married in the area, having met and fallen in love with local supporter Dorothy Dennis ('a rare case of a fan gets her man', trumpeted Pathé News in its coverage of the wedding).

Hutton is idolised in these parts, not just for his mixture of supreme determination and effortless artistry at the crease, but also for the way he conducted himself off it. Yorkshiremen like their heroes to be modest and unadorned, and Hutton was certainly that. Careful with his money, too, so the stories go. Only one of my fellow-diners had actually seen him play, yet to hear them all talking now you'd think they'd each conducted the wedding service.

Although I'd never seen Hutton bat, I was at least able to share my memory of having once fallen into casual conversation with him on the staircase at Lord's in 1986, when he was seventy. Our brief exchange had been little more than idle chit-chat between any two men who find themselves having to descend a deserted staircase together, yet I remembered him as being polite, gracious and apparently genuinely interested in my footling, tongue-tied pleasantries. Having shaken his hand at the end of our brief exchange, I hadn't washed it for a week. I may not have known much, but I knew that along with Hobbs, Hammond and Bradman, Hutton was considered to be the very best. Certainly amongst my own acquaintances, the actor Tom Courtenay and the playwright Harold Pinter both rated him above all others. And having offered up my own brief titbit, I sat back and let Harold Pinter's famous poem to his hero roll around in my head:

> *I saw Len Hutton in his prime*
> *Another time*
> > *another time*

Legend has it that having written the poem, Pinter sent it to his friend and fellow dramatist Simon Gray for his reaction. A week later he called to hear his friend's pronouncement. Gray replied, 'I haven't finished reading it.'

Since arriving here yesterday, I'd hardly met anyone who didn't claim to be attending this afternoon's game, and consequently I arrived at the ground in North Marine Road in plenty of time in which to gain a seat. Or so I thought. But such was the crush to get in that it took me nearly a quarter of an hour to inveigle my way through the turnstiles. The official capacity may be six thousand, but if so I could only hope nobody from Health & Safety was watching. The ground was rammed, with thousands in rows on the seats and more sprawled on the grass behind the boundary rope. Change the Bermuda shorts and the cans of Coke for beanie hats and pipe tobacco and it could have been the early 1970s with Roxy Music on the radio and Harold Wilson talking about the pound in your pocket.

It took me several more minutes to shoulder my way through to a vacant berth, and even then my seat was only available because a nearby sightscreen obscured at least a third of the playing area from view. I found myself sitting at what is known as the Trafalgar Square end, next to one of my breakfast companions from the hotel.

Arthur had that disarming habit of many middle-aged Englishmen of ending every pronouncement with nervous laugh, as if to say, 'I know it's silly, but there's no accounting for it.' He'd been coming to every festival for over forty years, and my gentle query as to whether he'd considered anywhere else to spend his holiday seemed to leave him nonplussed.

'Oh no, we love it here,' he said with a soft chuckle. 'My wife and I come every year. We make sure we do a bit o' sightseeing, of course, before I disappear off here for the cricket and leave her to it. We went to Whitby on Monday, Bridlington on Tuesday, Filey on Friday and York yesterday, so I've done my duty.'

'And is your wife here?'

'Oh no, she'll be a cricket widow for the next few days,' he continued, laughing nervously once more. 'In fact, she's gone on a magical mystery bus tour this afternoon. Though it's not really much of a mystery since the driver let slip they were going to Pickering. Never mind, she likes it there.'

We both agreed today's encounter promised a keen contest. Both Yorkshire and Middlesex are counties that traditionally regard an elevated status and a brimming trophy cabinet as their birthright. Yet in truth the two teams found themselves in somewhat different fettle in 2010. Yorkshire has trodden the harder but more productive road of nurturing a team of largely home-grown players, and the policy was at last bearing fruit. Favourites to win this season's forty-over competition, they were also in contention for the championship. Yorkshire folk have been conditioned to winning over many years; no wonder they were out in force today.

Middlesex, by contrast, have been lured by the honey trap of expedience, buying up disgruntled hacks from other teams and relying on a few international names to shore things up, often for only two or three weeks at a time. Their current plight, and indeed you could say the plight of the English county set-up, was reflected in the presence today of 41-year-old Sean Udal.

Having given yeoman service for Hampshire and occasionally England, he'd already retired once, back in 2008, but had not only been lured out of retirement by Middlesex but handed the captaincy, a position he'd only relinquished a few weeks before today's game. In Australia a player of his vintage, however handy, would long ago have been forced to cede his place in the team to younger, fitter guys in their early twenties. Yet here he was today, ambling around in the sunshine, bowling his little offies as he's done for the past twenty-one years, and still thoroughly enjoying himself.

Jolly good, too, you might say – indeed, I do myself. But somewhere, presumably pouring out tumblers of orange squash in the players' dressing room, was some young rookie who would have killed for a chance to pit his burgeoning talents against Yorkshire in front of six thousand people.

Arthur and I were soon reminiscing about our memories of the festival. While his memory was encyclopaedic, my own recollections were more a general remembrance of days basking in the sunshine, not being able to believe my luck that after only two years out of drama school I was being paid to spend my days watching cricket, my evenings acting in plays and, during the summer of 1980, my nights with the buxom female proprietor of a local vegetarian restaurant.

We both recalled spending an entire day (presumably the same one) watching Boycott grind his way to another of his remorseless centuries against Derbyshire, followed by a thrilling John Player League encounter against Northants on the Sunday. Arthur reminded me that Yorkshire selected a local boy for the game, Simon Dennis, a gesture that must have added a good few thousand or so to the gate receipts. 'They're no fools,' he concluded with a twinkle.

Forty overs wasn't really the type of game he enjoyed, being what he called 'an old fuddy-duddy', but he still preferred watching it to shopping. 'I reckon they'll be changing it again soon enough,' he said. 'No doubt some bright spark in the ECCB will be drawing up a proposal to increase revenue, probably by substituting stumps with goals, making the ball a bit bigger and having a new rule whereby you kick it rather than hit it. Nothing surprises me any more … '

By now the game was nearly forty minutes old, and Yorkshire captain Andrew Gale and South African import Jacques Rudolph had already clubbed a fifty partnership without breaking sweat. Rudolph is one of those curious overseas signings who are invaluable to county sides, in that they get dropped from the national side and then vent their spleen by belting thousands of runs as a domestic mercenary. And Rudolph was having a pearler of a season for his adopted club. Today he seemed hell bent on confirming his status as the leading run-getter in the competition (average 85), as well as attempting to join the select band of only three players who've ever hit a ball clean out of the ground and on to the adjoining rooftops (CI Thornton, WG Grace and Cec Pepper being the other three).

Of the thousands watching, the only contingent who weren't taking a paternal interest in Rudolph's imperious progress was a group of lads on the popular terraces who had decided to spend the afternoon stacking empty plastic pint glasses into one another in order to form a tower. By the time the captain Gale was out for 38, the edifice was already a couple of metres high and gaining tumescence at a rate that would put most of its overseers to shame.

'Feed the stick and it will grow,' they chanted, to the tune of, 'Be thou still my strength and shield'. Soon enough a rival plastic Tower of Pisa began to emerge a few rows along. Meanwhile, on a true wicket and with mercilessly short boundaries, Rudolph was happy to fill his boots. His 124 came off only 108 balls, and Yorkshire closed on a mighty 250–6. Middlesex would have to go some to make a game of it.

I assure you I hadn't intended to take a walk out to the middle between innings, but in fact such was the crush that it was the only way of getting from one side of the ground to the other. My journey was rewarded by being able to join a throng of spectators who'd gathered to watch England fast-bowling prospect Ajmal Shahzad practising on the edge of the square. Shahzad, an outside chance for selection in the Ashes party, was currently undergoing rehabilitation for an injury, and this gentle outing today was presumably part of his training schedule.

There is always something viscerally thrilling about being able to stand right next to a genuine fast bowler as he limbers up, and Shahzad didn't disappoint. So many wanted to watch him in action that his run up necessitated threading a path in between two tightly-packed columns of awestruck spectators. Each time he approached they parted like the Red Sea before closing again once he was past and craning their necks to see what happened next. Viewed this close up, even these gentle looseners seemed impossibly frightening. How on earth did batsmen ever hit a thing going at such speed?

Having stopped briefly at the second-hand book stall to purchase a dog-eared benefit brochure dedicated to Yorkshire legend Phil Carrick, I set out to find a vantage point on which to watch the Middlesex reply, and inched my way to where a distant concrete staircase offered an elevated view. Across from me, on the other side of the boundary, the VIPs of the borough congregated in white marquees, feasting in style on muffins and scones and salvers of fresh fancies. Old-fashioned hospitality is prodigious in these parts, and when full the ground still retains the feel of a JB Priestley play about it, with groaning tea tables, paper doilies and plump aldermen in straining waistcoats.

I found myself sharing my perch with a line of svelte, middle-aged Yorkshiremen in tracksuits and polo shirts. Assuming me to be some southern ponce from St John's Wood, the contingent eyed me suspiciously at first, yet by maintaining the essential tribal rituals practised the world over by Englishmen meeting for the first time – namely, avoiding eye contact, saying nothing and acting for all the world as if I hadn't even noticed their existence – I gradually began to gain their trust. My initiation was eventually confirmed when their leader glanced briefly in my direction and uttered the traditional male welcome of Englishmen everywhere.

'Fulham have just equalised against Man U.'

Of course: it was August, and elsewhere the Premier League was in full swing. I'd lived up here long enough once to know the correct response: nodding my head knowingly and pulling the corners of my mouth down. It did the trick. Within minutes we were swapping Polo mints like old friends.

These guys all looked young enough to have full-time jobs, yet their sun-beaten complexions and exhaustive knowledge suggested a life spent doing little else than watching their team. Their loyalty was entire, immovable, unapologetic and trenchantly expressed: none of the self-deprecating wryness of Moaners' Corner at Chesterfield – here, every field placing or bowling change was dissected at length. What was it Wilfred Rhodes had said about Yorkshire cricket? 'We don't play for fun.' These guys were living testimony to that.

Middlesex set about their task with gusto, and their own star batsman Owais Shah was soon scoring as freely as Rudolph had managed earlier on. With the hundred soon hoisted, the match was swinging nicely backwards and forwards. So was something else.

By now the giant plastic construction over on the popular terraces had grown into a huge and menacing phallus, teetering three or four metres into the air and waving high back and forth above the heads of the crowd. Eventually a couple of stewards moved in, but before they could take control of the situation the tower collapsed, showering those nearby with the dregs of hundreds of pints of lager. Nobody seemed to mind, and minutes later another edifice was already beginning to spring up.

Meanwhile, Yorkshire were turning the screw. Veteran Yorkshire player Anthony McGrath, bowling his medium-pace dobbers, had met with immediate success, knocking back Shah's stump with his first delivery and sending my acquaintances into fresh paroxysms of fist-clenched joy. 'Good boy, Tony,' muttered my companion as Shah trailed disconsolately back to the pavilion. 'Well done, my son.' I responded by turning down the corners of my mouth and nodded sagely, a gesture that utterly satisfied him.

With Shah's dismissal the fight temporarily went out of the visitors, and for the next hour or so they lost wickets at regular intervals, three of them going to the young leg spinner Adil Rashid. Rashid is only the third Asian player to play for the county, and by the comments of the proud quasi-parents next to me, big things are expected of him in these parts.

As afternoon turned to evening the result looked to be a formality: yet there is something about the forty-over format that can still surprise. Even as spectators were drifting away to beat the rush, a ninth-wicket stand between Neil Dexter and Toby Roland-Jones somehow added fifty in one of those curious one-day partnerships that creeps up on both the fielding side and the paying public without anyone much noticing. Suddenly, from a position of near defeat, victory for the visitors looked a distinct possibility.

The final over was a classic. With Middlesex requiring thirteen more to win and Dexter now seeing it like a football, McGrath was summoned back to arms. As he lolloped in to bowl his first delivery, you could have heard a pin drop. As it was, Dexter was unable to get the ball to the boundary in sufficient quantities, and with seven still required from two balls, victory could finally be celebrated. After five hours of terrific cricket, Yorkshire had won and God was in his heaven.

It had been just the sort of day I remembered enjoying as a young man. Sweaty, sunburnt, action-packed and entirely good-natured. Even the groups of stick-feeders had proved entirely benign. What's more, there were no referrals, no crashing music at every touch and turn, no football chanting and above all no action replays or endless hiatuses while we waited to hear the third umpire's decision. What you saw was what you got, and the game was all the better for it. Those two men in white coats out there were the men in charge, not pampered pundits cocooned in trailers with earpieces and video replays.

Best of all had been the sense of being in a community in which county cricket still mattered. My weekend in my old stamping ground had included live theatre, a cooked breakfast, Malibu-flavoured fudge, a naval battle and, to top things off, a fabulous game under cloudless summer skies. What on earth could possibly top this as a trip down memory lane?

I soon got my answer. As I left the ground I got a call on my mobile. It was Alan Ayckbourn. He'd been in one of the VIP marquees for the day as guest of the mayor, and having heard that I'd been spotted in the theatre the previous evening had taken a chance on my presence at the ground.

'Simmo, fancy coming for supper? We're having beef … '

13

Hammond's Source

It was September, and the summer was finally drawing to an end. But not quite yet. In the meantime, with bonfire night approaching, the TUC conference in full swing and a special festive mince pie section already doing a brisk trade at Selfridges, it was time for some more cricket.

You can always tell when the county championship is coming to a close, as it's the only time it gets a mention on the *Today* programme. After five months of football, boxing, tennis, golf, weightlifting and women's competitive rugby, I woke to hear Garry Richardson waxing lyrical about who might lift the pennant in four days' time.

For some counties, the season was already done and dusted. But for others this final push would be the difference between death and glory. A big hundred here, an inspired burst of bowling there, even a crucial run-out or a dropped catch: five months of blood, sweat, and toil could still hang on a single moment. No fewer than three separate counties – Notts, Somerset and Yorkshire – could still lift the title in four days' time. It promised to be one of the closest finishes in the competition's history.

Ironically, the best place to watch the pulsating climax was from my living room. Upon hearing that Sky were planning to broadcast the final round of the championship in full, I'd finally succumbed to Murdoch's blandishments and signed up to a month's trial.

The nice man at Sky who took my credit card details over the phone had assured me that the process would necessitate drilling a small hole in the masonry for the cable, a procedure that would take no more than fifteen minutes. To Julia, drilling a small hole anywhere was tantamount to removing an entire outside wall with a demolition ball, as bricks and mortar was her one guarantee of a comfortable old age once forty years of G&Ts and wasabi peanuts had stripped my stomach lining and confined me to a hospice in Finchley. Yet with the strategic repositioning of a large yucca plant, you'd never have noticed anyone had even been here.

Persuading Julia to let me sprawl in front of the televised cricket for four days would have put our marriage to its sternest test to date, except that something extraordinary had occurred. She'd spent the last couple of weeks filming a children's TV series in Liverpool, and by chance her selected hotel had also been the preferred home of the visiting Hampshire cricket team during their recent four-day match against Lancashire at nearby Aigburth. Thus she and the rest of the cast had shared the bar of the John Lennon Crowne Plaza with the Hampshire squad as they relaxed in trackies and jogging bottoms after a hard day's play. She'd even shared a brief conversation with Dominic Cork in the local M&S after their paths crossed in the frozen foods section.

Odd. A woman who hadn't shown the slightest inclination towards the game or its protagonists for all these years could suddenly describe the nature of Dimitri Mascarenhas's niggling thigh strain and the distinct scent of Sean Ervine's aftershave. In particular, she seemed keen to know all there was to know about young James Vince, their handsome strokemaker: his nickname, what sort of music he liked, and whether he preferred Radio 1 or Heart 106.2.

Once upon a time such information would have been impossible to provide even if I'd wanted to (can you imagine anyone enquiring of Derbyshire's Fred Rumsey whether he shopped in Burton or Millets?), but this sort of social titbit was common currency in cricket magazines these days, and I was able to furnish her with sufficient gossip to ensure she could hold her own in the event of a chance encounter. A couple of nights spent in the company of a troupe of muscular young athletes had brought her closer to the game I loved than nearly three decades of Sunday afternoons watching the Baldwins.

As it turned out, my carefully-planned investment looked as if it might prove, quite literally, a washout. When I tuned in on the first morning it was lashing it down at Headingley, where third-placed Yorkshire were playing Kent, while up at Chester-le-Street, Marcus Trescothick's second-placed Somerset were being thwarted in identical circumstances. And as for Old Trafford, where Lancashire were taking on Notts …

'Manchester weather is a popular joke. And I don't care what the meteorological statistics are, that joke has a solid basis.' So said the most curmudgeonly of Yorkshiremen, JB Priestley, who not only knew a thing or two about the sport but who, on the evidence of at least one actor I talked to who met him, never went anywhere without his own private supply of Izal toilet paper in his coat pocket. 'Jolly Jack' may have been notorious for his parsimony, but even this most famous son of Bradford would have let slip a cackle or two at the situation prevailing across the Pennines.

There was something strangely disarming about the ECCB's faith in the English weather. Perhaps I'm just an old-fashioned climate-change sceptic, but I recall the championship used to be done and dusted by about 6 September. A big knees-up in the Gillette Cup Final at Lord's to a full house, and the game would be put away in its green baize cloth for another winter. Now it seemed the season had to be stretched so that it reached almost up to the first Test at Brisbane.

The first day's weather turned out to be so wretched that Sky was forced to show endless replays of past glories. We had the T20 World Cup Final I'd watched all those weeks ago in Horndean, then a rerun of August's sodden one-day finale from the Rose Bowl, and with rain still falling they had to resort to the 2005 Ashes highlights. Long before the end of play I'd switched over to repeats of *Wacky Races* on CBeebies.

The following day was even worse. When I switched on at 10.30 I was greeted yet again by Charles Colvile and Nasser Hussain trying to make the sight of sodden tarpaulin seem interesting. But there was no disguising the scene outside their commentary position – it looked like Manchester on a wet Tuesday morning.

When play did eventually get under way at 4pm it was watched by a crowd you could have counted on two hands. A camera-shot over the fence to their neighbours, Manchester United, illustrated better than any journalism the gulf between the two sports. With the mighty Reds due to play Glasgow Rangers in four hours' time, there were already more people gathered in the football stadium than currently watching the cricket.

Still, all agreed it had been a miracle to get the pitch fit for play at all after such a dousing. 'Though how long they'll last out there is a moot point,' suggested Hussain. 'We have to worry about the light here come mid-September. Come 5.30 it'll be getting distinctly murky out there.'

That's what I love about cricket. It can make even the savviest pundit look a complete prat. In one respect he was absolutely correct – the players did indeed come off at 5.24, a mere six minutes before his prediction. But their departure was due not to insufficient light, but too much of it.

Just before 5.15 the clouds dispersed to reveal a huge bloated autumn sun hanging just above the sightscreen and directly behind the bowler's arm. It was now shining directly into the batsmen's eyes.

Within seconds the Notts batsmen were peering at the far end as if trying to inspect the inside of a blast furnace. Batting was impossible. The umpires wandered over for a look, picked up the bails and marched off. After nearly two days of Manchester resembling out-takes from *The Perfect Storm*, play was abandoned for the day due to too much sun.

What followed was perhaps the most memorable image of the whole summer. A lone spectator, with a pint in one hand and a pie in the other, looking round in utter bewilderment. Having sat patiently under an umbrella for the entire day, possibly two, hoping against hope for a few sodden overs come teatime, he now wore a look of total incomprehension. He would have leaned across to ask a fellow spectator what the f**k was going off out there, only there was nobody within fifty yards to talk to. No wonder cricket hasn't caught on in the United States.

With only two days left, it was time to make my final pilgrimage of the summer. And I was in luck. With isobars virtually obliterating the entire British Isles apart from a small gap over the Bristol Channel, my destination offered the only chance of some live cricket.

Gloucestershire, 'the shire of the Graces', is regarded by many as the most romantic county of all. Its history is synonymous with legendary names. The immortal WG played much of his best cricket here, as did his brothers, the mercurial EM and the stolid

GF – at least until GF slept in a damp bed and caught pneumonia. Gilbert Jessop was another giant whose presence lit up the county in its early years. And with subsequent eras throwing up such luminaries as Charlie Parker, Tom Goddard and the irrepressible David Shepherd, this was just the sort of place for sitting in a deckchair with a pint and boring the arses off those around you about the old days – which is just as well, as in recent years the club hasn't been too much to write home about.

It's one of the great conundrums of the sport that a county with such history and talent should have managed so little silverware. They've never won the championship since it was properly organised, and despite being able to supply a fair selection of the nation's greatest players, have acquired a reputation as something of a collective underachiever.

Their home ground is at Nevil Road in Bristol, a city in which I'd spent a lot of time both as part of the famous Old Vic repertory company in the mid-1980s, and later on while filming an impotent husband in *Casualty* and then a suave statesman in six episodes of *The House of Eliot*. Yet for reasons never fully fathomed, I'd rarely visited the ground. One reason was its relative inaccessibility, tucked away in a warren of side streets some distance from the centre. I always seemed to be in the centre waiting for buses that never arrived or couldn't guarantee to get me back in time for rehearsals or curtain up.

One summer I bought an old Renault 6 with the intention of using it to get to the ground on match days, but I soon realised that being the only young actor in the company with a car offered somewhat more interesting carnal opportunities than the chance to watch Jim Foat or RDV Knight.

Not that it lasted long anyway, as the car proved one of the most profoundly duff purchases I ever made. I eventually flogged the vehicle to a scrap-metal dealer. Three months later, the same car was being used for hold-ups on petrol stations in the M5 corridor, a fact I was only alerted to when the police turned up at my digs in Clifton to arrest me. No wonder I rarely strayed from the city centre.

But even when I did make it to Nevil Road, there was always something slightly dispiriting about the venue. I'd anticipated that a ground with such a rich and nourishing heritage would be a mass of ivy-clad towers and rustic crenellations, and yet, just as with the county that resides there, there's an air of something left half-finished about it all, as if underachievement and frustrated promise have seeped into the brickwork.

In fairness, the club has done its best to inject a little romance where it can. Anything and everything that could be named has been given a title, from the Jessop Stand in the far corner through to the Grace Pavilion and the Hammond Roof Terrace. There are plans afoot to expand the venue from its current basic capacity of four thousand up to sixteen thousand in order to bring it up to Test status, although nearby residents are threatening to campaign against the development. This is England, after all.

Meanwhile, both the county team and the ground itself have had a slightly run-down, dog-eared feel. Indeed, for anyone looking for spooky karmic resonances, one man's reputation still seems to me to cast a baleful shadow over the place. For if the sunny spirit of Tate pervades Hove, and Frank Woolley still imbues Canterbury with a timeless elegance, Nevil Road on a blustery day still summons up the sombre, brooding memory of perhaps the most gifted batsman ever to come from English loins, Wally Hammond.

Sport is littered with players who've been unable to fully enjoy their God-given talent, due to their time in the spotlight colliding with another whose genius has eclipsed their own. Think of Joe Frazier and Muhammad Ali, Jimmy White and Steve Davies, or Jocky Wilson and Eric Bristow. But no man was more cursed by a personal nemesis than Gloucestershire's favourite son.

In any other era than the one he played in (mainly between the wars), Hammond would surely have been described as the best batsman of all time. A player of exceptional ability in every facet of the game, he was earmarked for future greatness by no less than Neville Cardus when he was still only starting out. Having witnessed the young batsman destroy the great Australian fast bowler Ted McDonald up at Old Trafford, Cardus wrote with a passion bordering on the homoerotic: 'I tremble with delight at the grandeur he will spread over our cricket fields', and to be fair to the old boy, his premonition was pretty much spot on.

For over two decades, Hammond was unquestionably the finest batsman in the country, with over fifty thousansd runs and 167 centuries, every one of them by popular consent a miniature work of art. Indeed, his appetite for run-scoring at both domestic and international level was nearly as prodigious as his alleged appetite for sexual congress. Yet from the moment Australia's Don Bradman arrived, Hammond's career was to be fatally and corrosively eclipsed by the one individual on the planet whose skill and ambition exceeded even his own. Whatever Hammond did, Bradman did more. Consequently Hammond's name is seldom heard nowadays, despite his astonishing ability and peerless match stats.

A man of sullen and uncertain temper, slow to praise and quick to condemn, his personality was said by some to have changed for the worse after he took a mercury cure for a bout of syphilis contracted while on tour to the Caribbean in 1925. His name is rightly commemorated in the Hammond Roof Terrace at the eastern end of ground, and his face also peers out at you wherever you go here, either from framed prints in the pavilion or from the pages of any number of county histories on sale in the club shop.

Yet you only have to study the snaps of the man from 1928 onwards, forever seemingly condemned to share the lens along-side his Antipodean counterpart, to see from where his unhappiness may truly have stemmed – the Don always wearing the same sweet look of quiet, supreme confidence and Hammond looking like a cross between WH Auden's younger brother and a dyspeptic turtle, a rictus grin concealing a deeper, suppressed fury at his karmic misfortune.

Hammond's final years were troubled in the way that thwarted ambition can induce in a great sportsman. Having retired in 1947 after a glorious yet somehow joyless career, he foolishly agreed to come back for an ill-judged single appearance against Somerset at Nevil Road in 1951. But by now old and infirm, he could hardly get the ball off the square. The opposing bowler Horace Hazell recalled afterwards praying that Hammond would middle something with the bat, if only to spare everyone's blushes. He was soon out for 7 and never played again. He died in virtual solitude in South Africa in 1965. Yet such was his skill and artistry that his memory remains a burning flame in those lucky enough to have seen him.

In his excellent biography of the player, David Foot cites the time he visited a public sale of Hammond's personal possessions soon after the sportsman's death, many of which went for trifling sums. Seeing strangers guiltily picking their way through his effects, writes Foot, was 'a truly poignant tableau of acrid reflections on a gifted life that drifted into virtual anonymity'. Leaving the sale, Foot walked to his car and cried for only the second time in his adult life.

Perhaps it was the romantic middle-aged musings of an actor with too much time on his hands, too much Cardus on his bookshelves and too few auditions in his diary, but for me, Nevil Road, when cold and overcast as it always seemed to be whenever I came here, still seems to mirror the spirit of the troubled, fractious soul who bestrode it for nearly thirty years.

Or at least it had been. Then during a chance visit here back in 2007, I'd run into Bryan 'Bomber' Wells and the skies immediately lifted. The antithesis of Hammond, Bomber was one of the greatest characters of Gloucestershire cricket, one of the most loved and dearly cherished, and inevitably a man to whom unlikely stories hung like tin numbers on a scoreboard.

Our chance meeting had only occurred at all when I'd offered a casual comment to an old codger sitting in a wheelchair beside me on the boundary. But the moment I'd realised it was the legendary Bomber I knew I'd been truly blessed. For here was a man who, in start contrast to Hammond, had wrung every moment of joy and laughter he could out of his time in the game.

He'd been nicknamed 'Bomber' after the legendary British heavyweight boxer Bombardier Billy Wells, the one who'd ended up being the brawny gong-striker for J Arthur Rank movies once his fighting days were through. But there the comparison ended.

Our Bomber had both a hearty appetite and a healthy distaste for unnecessary exertion (he once made a one-handed catch on the boundary rope while drinking a cup of tea provided by a spectator); indeed, so short was his run-up that he claimed the majority of his 998 career wickets, mostly for his beloved Gloucestershire, were taken because the batsman wasn't looking up as he bowled.

Legend has it that in one match the batsman was recalled for just that reason, whereupon Bomber bowled him next ball as well. Upon being recalled a second time the batsman refused, allegedly replying, 'If you think I'm going to give him his bloody hat trick you've got another think coming.' Years later the batsman Len Hemming was asked about the incident. 'I've no recollection of,' he replied, 'but I'm all in favour of it.'

As if to prove the fact, Bomber claimed to have bowled the fastest over in cricket history, all six balls of which were completed in the time it took the clock at Worcestershire Cathedral to strike twelve (the chimes were subsequently timed at 34 seconds).

But it was his running between the wickets that marked him out as a true giant of the game. After one spectacular mix-up in a crucial county match, Bomber's terrified batting partner finally lost his temper and bellowed down the pitch, 'Bomber, for God's sake call!' to which Bomber shouted back, 'Heads!' But he was no fool: a spin bowler of spite and guile, he would have played many Tests for England had competition not been so intense. 'Cricket is the funniest and loveliest game in the world if you just let people get on with it,' he once said. I suspected that Bomber would have fitted in very well with the Baldwins.

When I'd met him, Bomber's playing days were long over. By now in his eighties and in failing health, he spent his declining days watching his beloved county and gorging himself on ice creams. But his misty memories of playing here back in the 1940s and fifties had kept me enthralled throughout our brief meeting, and it was Bomber himself who recounted the story of his only match alongside the great Hammond (the one of the champion's ill-fated return to county colours in 1951). Foolhardy it might have been, yet when I asked Bomber for his appraisal of his hero, he needed no time for reflection. 'Simply the best,' he replied.

Michael Parkinson had once come up with the perfect description of Bomber: 'there was summer in his face, and laughter in his soul.' He had died not long after our chance meeting and, without him, I sensed my visit to Nevil Road today might not be the same.

But if there was no Bomber today, at least there was Kevin Pietersen; though I imagine he may have struggled with old Bomber. Pietersen's presence today was one of the more delicious ironies of the season. Having been released the previous month by Hampshire after admitting he preferred living in swanky London to the prosaic suburbs, he'd found himself subsequently dropped by England after a series of uncharacteristically low scores, and was now bobbing about without either a county or a country. Not that he seemed especially bothered – a recall to national colours would come soon enough, and in the meantime he could hang out in the cafés and bars of the King's Road, dandling his newborn baby on one knee and a double-skinny macchiato on the other.

But the ECCB was adamant; anybody wanting to be considered for inclusion in the forthcoming Ashes tour had first to be affiliated, and thus Surrey had taken this brash colossus under their wing for the final couple of matches to spare the administrators' blushes and to give him a chance to play himself into form before boarding the plane. Hence his presence for the visitors at Bristol, playing for one load of cricketers whose names he hardly knew against another load of cricketers whose names he hardly knew.

If Grace and Hammond succinctly define two eras of the game, Pietersen surely flies the flag for cricket in the twenty-first century. It was Mike Atherton who once said, 'Pietersen is the most fascinating of the present crop of batsmen, and I suspect he would say the same', and the notion of watching this garish superstar in such prosaic circumstances was strangely enticing, not to say tinged with gentle schadenfreude. For Pietersen defined the image of the modern cricketing celebrity, born to strut upon the grand stage rather the prosaic hinterlands of Bristol.

Pietersen on form is always worth a long drive, and I'd been hoping to see him in action, particularly since he'd ended the previous day's play undefeated on forty. But as usual both fate and the UK's congested motorway system had other ideas. Cricket, always the most capricious of sports, ensured that he was out second ball of the morning with me still wrestling with the contraflow near Hungerford, and instead of watching one of the game's most gifted exponents, I ended up enduring one of the most buttock-clenchingly dull mornings of cricket it had ever been my misfortune to watch. I'm not sure of the overall session statistics – Surrey either scored forty in twenty overs, or twenty in forty – either way, it felt much the same.

A small crowd, many of whom had come in the hope of pyrotechnics, bore their early disappointment in that stoical sort of way that only county championship crowds are capable of, drowning their disappointment in cups of powdery hot chocolate from the catering trailer and yarning away about old matches and old heroes.

As Surrey trooped off at lunchtime, all out for 188, one spectator expressed it more trenchantly than most. 'What a bloody morning,' he said cheerfully in a broad Justin Lee Collins dialect. 'Bloody Surrey, pissing about like that. There's a game to be won here, and some buggers need entertaining an' all.'

'So why do you come?' I asked.

The question seemed to wrongfoot him. After a few moments his brow cleared. 'Because I love cricket!!!' he declared with evident relief, as if recalling the answer to a quiz question.

By now it was lunchtime and for the umpteenth time this season it was time to face the dismal prospect of trying to find something digestible to eat. My season had started back at The Oval with a burger-and-chips combo that included sufficient calories to keep the entire British Heart foundation on red alert; now it seemed destined to finish in identical circumstances.

I don't know what it is about catering at cricket grounds, but it's almost impossible to purchase anything that isn't designed to shorten your life expectancy. The 'bill of fayre' in the club café today offered a choice of burger and fries, pie and fries or pasty and fries. The food on view reminded me of a story comedian Chic Murray used to tell of a visit he once made to a catering truck whilst watching a football match in the 1950s. 'I'd like a cup of tea, a meat pie and a few kind words,' he said to the proprietor, who duly handed over the tea and the pie.

'What about the few kind words?' asked Chic.

The owner leaned across the counter. 'Don't eat the pie,' he answered.

I ate my meal at a greasy table, surrounded by cartons of flaccid chips, half-eaten muffins and sachets of damp salt. By the time Gloucestershire commenced their own first innings, I'd been joined by one of those curious individuals who seem to wash up at county cricket. Unkempt, clad in old jumpers and rotting shoes, he smelt of stale sweat mixed with damp dog.

Despite the shortcomings of his personal grooming regime, he talked endlessly and without pausing to anyone who'd listen of cricket and cricketers. Within minutes of being sucked into his orbit I'd been treated to a whistle-stop description of each and every Gloucestershire match throughout the summer, both home and away. Inevitably, his attention soon turned to a particularly toothsome fiasco that had occurred here a couple of weeks ago, one in which Gloucestershire had managed to lose a vital game despite dismissing the visitors for forty-four. Needless to say, Memory Man was able to describe each wicket in immaculate detail.

The remarkable thing about him was his clarity of thought. He not only seemed able to recall each dismissal, but in addition each fresh reminiscence was perfectly composed, including parenthesis, sub-clauses and tangential references. This bloke would have cleaned up on *Just A Minute.*

When opening bat/wicketkeeper Jonathan Batty was out, it sent my companion into fresh paroxysms.

'Well, of course, he's had a terrible season,' he explained. 'In fact, with his only scoring a sole half-century the entire season in fifteen matches, this latest failure will bring his overall average down to 16.3'.

A man sitting at an adjoining table piped up. 'I don't know why they ever got rid of Adshead,' he mumbled. 'He was a perfectly respectable 'keeper.'

'Ah well,' continued Memory Man, 'that may prove to be a wise choice in the long run, because if you investigate Adshead's personal website you'll see that he's planning to take time off next summer to go trekking in Kenya for charity, which surely suggests he no longer sees his future in the professional game. A pity, as he scored 3,077 runs during his time with us, as well as taking 192 catches, but at the age of thirty-one you can hardly blame him for wishing to cast his net a little wider. In fact, I understand he needs to raise a small matter of £750 in order to secure his passage, and if you study the progress of his appeal to date, you'll see that the vast majority of contributions have come from Gloucestershire members.'

His fund of knowledge really was extraordinary. I pictured him back at his tiny flat in the winter evenings, surrounded by old Wisdens and washing-up bowls full of human body parts, trawling the web for nuggets of information with which to dazzle the denizens of the Hammond Terrace the following summer.

County cricket still seemed to attract these sort of lost souls. Indeed, there is a theory among some sporting psychologists that the unchanging rhythm of the traditional four-day game provides a safe haven for a entire class known derisively as 'anoraks', troubled drifters who derive comfort and security from the endless repetition of some inane activity. Maybe, but in that case it would surely condemn fans of *Deal Or No Deal* in similar fashion.

By the time I'd extricated myself from my cricketing Ancient Mariner, the home side had lost another wicket and, with a heavily revised batting order, were struggling to make any headway. My companion had let slip that the reason for the inexplicable shuffle from the printed scorecard was because several of the team were suffering from a stomach upset and unable to stray more than five feet from the gents' (on this topic at least his details were mercifully scant). While the survivors prodded and nurdled their way towards the Surrey total, the great Pietersen stood muffled up at first slip, contemplating the scene around him as if returning to some nightmarish lifestyle he'd long thought banished forever.

I watched the afternoon session from the edge of the sightscreen alongside another lone spectator, one who seemed to be shrouded in mute dread at the prospect of the summer's end. A once good-looking man in his late forties with a rugged five o'clock shadow and a shock of swept-back hair (a bit like a young Ian McShane), his features were now racked by too little success, too much booze and nowhere near enough moisturiser. He wore a grubby spotted cravat and an old black leather car coat that smelt rather like old Holborn, a fact soon confirmed by his aromatic breath and stained fingers.

He looked freezing, yet seemed to content to stand in the strafing wind with nothing to warm him but another roll-up. Nonetheless, he admitted he enjoyed coming here. 'Not for the T20,' he continued in a husky voice, 'I hate that muck. But I like this form. It reminds me of when I was kid. Seventeen first-class counties and a tour match every year. That's what I'm used to. I spent half my childhood here.' His final phrase seemed pertinent. Like so many I'd come across, his attendance seemed not so much an affirmation of the game as it is, so much as a chance to recollect how it once was.

My mention of Gloucestershire's glory days unleashed a torrent of reminiscences, with names of famous old players tumbling out of his mouth faster than flecks of tobacco. His boyhood heroes were of a far later vintage than Grace and Hammond, but nonetheless his cheeks were soon flushing with the memory: Procter, Zaheer Abbas and Sadiq Mohammad. As he talked, a distant light inundated his bloodshot eyes, and I could envisage Gavin as he once must have been, not a broken-down drifter approaching fifty, but a handsome bushy-tailed teenager running on to the pitch at every opportunity and pestering players for their autographs before popping off to the world-famous Coronation Tap in Clifton for some industrial-strength scrumpy and a crack at the barmaid.

Inevitably his conversation turned to the legendary Lancashire–Gloucestershire Gillette Cup semi-final of 1971, a cricketing milestone and a reference point for anyone who watched sport in the 1970s, much as the Steve Davis/Dennis

Taylor snooker final achieved a decade and a half later. Gavin asked me if I remembered the encounter.

Who didn't? The match, watched at the ground by a packed house and broadcast live on the BBC from Old Trafford, had gone on long into the evening, and the longer it overran, the more it captured the national imagination. Originally scheduled to finish by 6pm, it was still being televised nearly three hours later, with half the kingdom now glued to the box and the main evening news bulletin having been shunted unceremoniously to BBC2.

This titanic struggle between the shire of the Graces and the county of the Red Rose, perhaps the greatest in the entire history of the old sixty-over competition, ended in farcical circumstances and near darkness when Lancashire's David Hughes managed somehow to larrup an over from Gloucestershire's veteran spinner John Mortimore for twenty-four, despite what Jim Laker continually referred to as 'the gatherin' gloom'.

I remembered all this of course – who wouldn't? It was undeniably one of those few sporting events that momentarily unite an entire nation and help to define a sporting decade – but despite my protestations that I recalled every ball clearly, Gavin seemed to think I didn't.

'It went on till nearly ten to nine at night,' he rasped, shaking his head at the wonder of such an occurrence. 'It was nearly dark by the time it finished; I watched it with my dad on the box, just him and me all alone in our house. He even offered me a glass of shandy.'

'I know. I saw the match on the telly.'

'And then David Hughes hit twenty-four off a single over.'

'Yes, I was watching it too. I recall it well.'

'He took John Mortimore to the cleaners. One ball, he flayed it down to deep extra cover and all the kids outside the rope came streaming on, and Mike Bissex ploughed straight into them trying to stop the ball.'

'I remember every ball,' I reiterated. But even as I did so, the penny dropped. Gavin wasn't seeking to share the drama of that evening four decades ago, but rather to relive it: not for me, but for himself. The memory of sitting with his old dad sharing his first beer was obviously a cherished one, a precious possession that still warmed him through the foggy uncertainties of middle age. And nothing, least of all me, was going to stop him now.

His rhetorical narrative finished (as I knew it would) with Hughes's desperate swat down to deep point off fast bowler Mike Procter, a stroke that triggered a mass invasion of the pitch from all sides by a delirious Lancashire crowd. Having completed his tale, my companion broke into a grin, revealing a line of yellowing teeth.

'What a match. Pandemonium. We may have lost the bastard game but I'll never forget it. And I watched it with my dad.' He fumbled in his pocket and commenced rolling another ciggie, a procedure he undertook with infinite care and in complete silence. Only when he was satisfied with it did he look up at me again. 'Six weeks later he was dead.'

By the time he'd run out of both Rizlas and recollections, it was nearly tea and Gloucestershire took the decision to declare in the hope of presumably setting up a run chase some time tomorrow afternoon.

'Are you staying on?' asked Gavin hopefully.

'I'm afraid not,' I replied. 'I've got an important meeting.'

'Pity,' he said, shaking my hand with surprising tenderness. 'You got me reminiscing there. I feel a whole lot better.'

It was time to go. After all, I had one last port of call, perhaps the most piquant of them all, and I didn't want to be late. As I passed the far end of the ground in my car I glimpsed Pietersen's muscle-bound frame high up on the pavilion balcony. With his Gucci wrap-arounds and a mobile phone clamped to his right ear, he looked less like a professional sportsman and more like a refugee from a Hollywood movie. It's cricket, Jim, but not as we know it.

Just then my mobile pinged. It was a text from my cricketing journo friend, George Dobell. 'Just heard' – it read – 'Jimmy Anderson posing nude for next month's edition of *Attitude*. Gawd help us all.'

The mere idea of it was sufficient to make me brake sharply. What on earth would the ghosts of Nevil Road have made of such shenanigans? One of their number, and England's leading fast bowler to boot, stripping bare for a gay magazine centrefold? Of one thing I was sure: Wally Hammond would have disapproved of any player exposing his genitals with such abandon – unless it was him, of course.

And Bomber? What, I wondered, would he have made of it all?

His reaction, I felt sure, would be somewhat different. In fact, I could almost imagine his voice, full of good humour and West Country wisdom, ringing out during the photoshoot …

'I don't know what that young man's got on, but it needs ironing … '

I was still laughing when I pulled into the car park at Clifton College.

14

Bristol Cream

CB Fry's *Gallery of Famous Players* first appeared in the book-shops in the summer of 1899. At the time of publication, nearly every one of the hundred and fifty or so individuals selected for this ultimate coffee-table tome were in their pomp. Fry himself, a man of brisk opinions and brittle prose (colleagues are inevitably described as possessing 'extreme merit' and 'consider-able vim', while Harry Baldwin, the rotund Hampshire bowler whose walrus moustache and prodigious waistline inspired the name of my own team of Sunday afternoon occasionals, is described with damning condescension as 'the ideal practice bowler'), clearly set out to celebrate the very best in thrusting manhood. Indeed, his was one of the very first books to attempt to capture cricketers in motion, and their confidence and joie de vivre is evident in every page, captured either in mid-leap or in the act of essaying some extravagant shot.

It was a good time for those lucky few in Fry's curtish delight. Cricket was the national sport, both Queen Victoria and WG Grace were still on their respective thrones, and the British Empire covered half the earth. Many of the chosen ones were themselves national celebrities: their deeds recorded, their opin-ions listened to and their company sought.

Yet with hindsight, one only has to begin turning over the heavy, brittle pages to be reminded of how difficult life became for many players once the cricket stopped, the crowds dispersed and they could no longer get either their leg, or arm, over.

No pension plans or media punditry to fall back on back then. Unless you had a private income (thankfully, many did), the only things certain were a spreading waist and diminishing income. Take the opening page of Fry's book, for instance: little Johnny Briggs, standing at the crease with raised fists as if about to attempt ten rounds in a fairground ring. This phenomenal left arm bowler, by repute 'as resilient as a rubber ball', who once answered a charge of insobriety from a colleague with a demonstration of trick bicycle racing, was in the very summer of the book's publication basking in the glory of being dubbed 'Wisden Cricketer of the Year'. Yet within three short years he'd died in a mental asylum aged only thirty-nine.

A few pages further on – page 9 to be precise – we get to moustachioed Albert Trott. An early prototype of Ian Botham in both his all-round abilities and capacity for booze, he was one of only a handful of players to represent both England and Australia. In the same summer as publication he made the most famous hit in all cricket, clobbering Monty Noble over the roof of the pavilion at Lord's, a feat that has never been repeated despite frequent attempts by generations of batsmen. Yet it was for his bowling that he most feared: described by Fry as relying 'on never-ceasing variations of speed', he could produce virtually any delivery known to man.

With age and ale taking an increasing toll, he lost his magic touch. Five days before the outbreak of war he shot himself with a Browning revolver in his Willesden lodging house, aged only forty-one. In a scribbled will he left his entire estate to his land-lady. It amounted to £4.

There are many others who failed to cope once the music stopped. Andrew Stoddart, after Grace the most celebrated sportsman of the time, killed himself in circumstances similar to Trott; while Nottinghamshire's infamous blocker William Scotton cut his throat in bed, trying vainly to catch the flow in a basin so as not spoil his landlady's sheets. Most piquant of all was little Arthur Shrewsbury, the man forever linked with one of the most famous quotes in cricketing history ('Give me Arthur,' proclaimed Grace when asked with whom he'd most like to open the batting); he looks happy enough in Fry's gallery, standing with weapon raised *à la* Graham Gooch, yet he shot himself through the head four years later, having previously purchased the wrong calibre bullets, and only seconds after wounding himself in the flank during a previous botched attempt. No wonder he considered he'd lost his touch.

Each had once strutted upon the very grandest of sporting stages, yet all were ultimately overtaken by depression, ennui and a gnawing fear of a penurious and anonymous future.

Yet compared to those who followed on their heels, they had it easy. The next generation really did cop it, as their best years collided full tilt with the war to end all wars. Between 1914 and 1918, at least 210 professional cricketers answered the call to arms in the Great War. Thirty-four didn't come back, while those that did found the world unrecognisable from the one they'd left.

Their names, too, form a doleful catalogue. Albert 'Tibby' Cotter, the Australian paceman, who at Gallipoli compacted a ball of mud into his hand and, tossing it up in the air, pronounced, 'That's my last ball, Blue, something's going to happen.' Having been commended several times for his bravery, he was shot at close range during the battle of Beersheba.

Kenneth Hutchings of Kent, who had scored a hundred for England at Melbourne in 1907/08, had his life ended by a German shell, while Percy Hardy of Essex slit his own throat in the gents' lavatory at King's Cross Station, having been unable to face the prospect of returning to France. And then there was the demise of perhaps the greatest of them all, Kent's Colin Blythe.

Having headed the national bowling averages for the past three years, Blythe enlisted for service despite suffering from epilepsy, and died in the mud of Passchendaele in 1917. Ninety-two years on and with Ricky Ponting's 2009 Australians about to invade our country, England captain Andrew Strauss and his England squad laid a stone cricket ball at Blythe's grave in Flanders during a team-building exercise (all, that is, except for Freddie Flintoff, who overslept and missed the bus).

Great names all: and individuals who'd continued to flicker back and forth across my own imaginings in the forty years since I'd first read of their exploits. Now, in the gloom of a West Country evening, I was about to pay my personal respects to one of the greatest of the fallen.

Arthur Collins's candidature in any gallery of cricketing greats is beyond doubt, particularly when you consider he achieved his unique and wondrous record in 1899, the very year of Fry's glossy tribute. Yet you'll find no mention of him there: how could you, when he was barely thirteen years old at the time of his feat. Nowadays his name is only recognised by historians and librarians. Yet the inspiration he offered to all a fat, freckly, cricket-mad teenager was incalculably profound.

If ever you find yourself trapped at a party by someone droning on about cricket and need to discover if they're a genuine gripper (the term given to the sort of obsessive who takes your wrist as he speaks and is still holding it the next morning) or merely masquerading as one, just ask them this simple question: 'Who has made the highest ever score?'

If they answer, 'Brian Lara, 501 not out', then relax. Have another drink. You're OK. Really. No need to claim you've left the gas on or spotted an old school mate on the other side of the room. You're talking to a lightweight. They'll soon run out of steam and move on to some more pleasurable and inclusive topic, such as the correct method of growing cacti or their recent caravan holiday in the Lake District.

If on the other hand they offer up, 'AEJ Collins, 628 not out for Clarke's House versus North ... '

Well, you weren't planning on leaving any time soon, were you?

If I seem to know the answer myself, please don't feel the need to panic. It's only because, like young Arthur, I was thirteen once, and when you're thirteen and can only regard the prospect of batting long enough to reach double figures as some impossibly distant fantasy, having a real-life role model such as Collins makes all the difference between persevering or throwing in the towel.

Until I stumbled upon this unlikely sporting superstar, courtesy of a slim, coffee-stained volume in my local second-hand bookshop, I'd had to be content with facsimile male role models for my inspiration. The *Valiant*'s square-jawed Captain Hurricane, looking like Fred Trueman on steroids; Roy Race, speeding down the touchline for Melchester Rovers: or the inimitable Alf Tupper, the Tough of the Track, who ran in bare feet and lived only on fags and fish and chips, and who surely found physical expression decades later in the guise of Phil Tufnell.

But from the moment I read about Collins, I had no need of heroes fashioned out of pen and ink. Give me Arthur.

The reason for his elevation to folk hero was a single mind-boggling innings of 628. That he achieved it when aged only thirteen is truly remarkable. That it took him nearly a week to do so is more sensational still. But most miraculous, at least viewed through the prism of twenty-first century mores, is that despite the instant and national fame it heaped on his willowy young shoulders (one publication proclaiming 'he has a reputation as great as the most advertised soap'), he still retained a quiet modesty, a sense of proportion and an unwillingness to hog the limelight. Try suggesting that to Justin Bieber.

I first came upon Arthur and his magic bat while thumbing though the shelves of my local second-hand bookshop, Holley-man and Treacher, a splendid old establishment in Brighton town centre, watched over by a couple of middle-aged men with thinning hair and fondness for Pringle sweaters. I spent most of my time and almost all of my precious pocket money in this establishment when I was young, poring over old biographies and tour diaries of long-forgotten series. Indeed, I seemed to be the only person who was remotely interested in buying them, which I suppose is why they were always on the shelves.

Many of the volumes I'd thumbed through so many times I could almost recite the contents from memory, and even though I knew my schoolfriends, who preferred to spend their precious funds on Pink Floyd LPs or the latest Monty Python compendium, viewed my obsession with bewilderment border-ing on unease, it never struck me that my lifestyle choices were in any way odd. Each book offered identical reminiscences and stale controversy, but I devoured them as if they were *The Lord of the Rings* or Peter Benchley's *Jaws*. And yet the slim volume hidden between them that described Collins's improbable heroics revealed a life far more thought-provoking than anything penned by gnarled old ex-professionals: and all for 75 pence, some damage to front cover.

On a warm Thursday afternoon in 1899, young Arthur opened the batting in an inter-house match on the smaller of the two pitches that form the hub of Clifton College, a celebrated private school for boys perched high on Bristol Downs between the suspension bridge and the forbidding walls of the nearby zoo.

Clifton College already had something of a distinguished reputation in cricketing circles. WG Grace scored thirteen of his centuries on the main pitch, and even sent his sons there to be educated, while another old boy was Sir Henry Newbolt, who commemorated the main square with the immortal lines, 'There's a breathless hush in the Close tonight', and went on to crystallise the moral code of a doomed generation: 'Play Up, Play Up, And Play the game', perhaps the most unwitting paean to the futility of the war that was going to do for so many: including, sadly, young Arthur.

The fixture in which Collins was playing was an inconsequential one, just one of hundreds of inter-house games designed to encourage the collegiate motto: *Spiritus intus alit* ('The soul nourishes within'). Nobody, least of all Arthur himself, expected the school's strict routine to be unduly troubled by proceedings. After all, they were only kids.

Going in first, he scored his first run at 3.30pm. By the time play ended for the weekend he'd made 508 more, and on his arrival back at the crease on Monday it was to find the ground now resembling a cricketing Mecca, with a substantial crowd having gathered from far and wide to see just how high he could go. They were in for quite a wait. By the time he'd unstrapped his pads for the last time, he'd been in for nearly a week and walloped 146 boundaries; and even then his innings only ended because he ran out of partners. As a consequence he briefly became the most famous sportsman in the land: feted and photographed wherever he went.

It's not difficult to imagine what such overnight fame and celebrity would have spawned had he managed it a hundred years later, though it's safe to assume an appearance on *The Alan Titchmarsh Show* would have been just the beginning. Yet perhaps it's just as well he missed out, for Collins was no Kevin Pietersen. Notoriously reticent and agonisingly shy, he considered his sporting heroics to be the worst thing he ever did and couldn't wait to sink back into grateful obscurity.

The most famous picture, taken in the heady afterglow of his extraordinary marathon, suggests just how heavy the legacy of celebrity is already bearing down on his young shoulders. He stands queasily in a typical artist's studio of the period, in front of a faded backcloth of flowers and ferns that make it look like he's been snapped in John Emburey's daughter's florists.

His garb is a creased cotton shirt, shapeless white flannels held up by a snake belt, a pair of pads that look as if he's crawled his way to six figures rather than run them, and finally a pair of co-respondent shoes of the sort made popular by Brian Johnston. It's his face that betrays his unease with new-found fame. Fair-haired, with an unhealthy pallor borne of too many hours hunched over Latin primers, his face is etched with suspicion blended with simmering unease. 'What' – his expression seems to be saying – 'on earth have I done?'

I could tell him what he'd done. He'd given hope and comfort to generations of hapless schoolboys. Whenever I found myself in a school cricket match shambling back to the pavilion for yet another duck, I would sit in a dark corner of the changing room, draw out the slim volume depicting Collins's unlikely triumph and run my fingers gently down the cover illustration. 'Never mind,' it said to me. 'There's always next time.' Sporting glory *was* still possible, with a little application and a lot of luck.

Clifton College and the pitch on which Collins achieved immortality is a mere ten-minute drive from Gloucestershire's ground at Nevil Road, and I arrived to find not only my own parking permit but also a cup of tea waiting for me at the entrance. My guide was a bright, friendly woman named Lucy who worked as part of the administration staff. When I'd telephoned her earlier in the week to ask if I could look around, I'd envisaged having to explain the purpose of my request in exhaustive detail, but the moment I'd mentioned the name of Collins it was as if I'd uttered some cricketing *Open Sesame*. 'Oh yes, young Arthur,' she responded. 'I know exactly who you mean. We get a lot of calls about him. When would you like to drop by?'

Her only misgiving was that the actual scorebook in which his feat was recorded, and the item I most desired to see, was currently on loan to an American university and thus would be unavailable for inspection. 'It's something of an icon, you see,' she explained. 'You'd be amazed the requests we get to borrow it.'

The college itself was much as I'd always imagined Nevil Road would be until I actually went there – a picture-postcard jumble of ancient buildings and ivy-clad turrets round which crows flapped and cawed. Lucy welcomed me in through the main doors and showed me to her office, where she produced a large bunch of jangling keys from her desk drawer. As I followed her across to the playing fields, she attempted to give a full description of the school and its workings, one I noted was full of pleasingly old-fashioned terms such as refectory, crammer, big school and sanatorium.

If ever proof was needed of the change of seasons, our brief promenade provided it. The cricket pavilion was locked and bolted, while the outfield of the main pitch, Newbolt's famous Close, was covered in a luxuriant covering of thick grass. Rugby posts dotted the horizon, and in the far distance a gaggle of schoolchildren rugged up in pullovers and caps were streaming across a quad. Powdery leaves blew about at our feet, and there was rain was in the air.

On the far side we came to a flight of steps cut into a grassy slope, beneath which was a diminutive playing field, a toddler version of its more famous counterpart, a cricket field in minia-ture. 'This is it,' she said almost apologetically. 'Not much to see, I'm afraid, but there we are. Welcome to Collins's piece.'

As an arena of special sporting significance, it was, to say the least, underwhelming; it would have struggled to accommodate a game between the Krankies and the Diddymen. Barely sixty yards long, the boundary on one side of the wicket was barely seventeen yards. Yet what had I been expecting? And more to the point, what should I do now I was here? Take some photos? Leave some flow-ers? Read aloud a section of the MCC coaching manual?

Instead I stood and let my imagination have a quick turn around the square. From somewhere in the vaults of my memory, probably A level English, I found myself recalling lines from Siegfried Sassoon,

I see them in foul dug-outs, gnawed by rats,
And in the ruined trenches, lashed with rain,
Dreaming of things they did with balls and bats,

And mocked by hopeless longing to regain
Bank-holidays, and picture-shows, and spats,
And going to the office in the train.

Lucy now shepherded me over to a small, discoloured commemorative plaque set into the far wall behind the bowler's arm. It read: '628. This innings is the highest recorded in the history of cricket.' An incongruous touch was provided by the nearby zoo in the loud, lazy and utterly bloodcurdling roar of a lion. I felt a shiver of something indefinable skitter up and down my back.

'Cold, isn't it?' said Lucy. 'Let's go indoors. Would you like to see the memorial display case? It's over in the library. There's not much to see, I'm afraid, without the scorebook, but I think there are some commemorative plates and a couple of photos and suchlike. You might as well. I've told the librarian to expect you.'

We hurried across to a modern purpose-built block, where we were welcomed by a prim young woman whose name I instantly forgot. In fact, I forgot just about everything else as well, because I found myself being handed the very scorebook I'd been informed was currently in Wisconsin being pored over by baffled American teenagers.

By stupendous fortune, the librarian explained, the item had been returned by special courier the previous day. Take my time. No hurry. Having handed over to me, she even stepped back several paces as if completing an ancient ceremony. I turned the fragile volume to the light and inspected it between gently splayed fingers. All I needed now was a pair of white cotton gloves and Hugh Scully.

In truth, the item itself couldn't have been more prosaic. Titled simply, 'Limp Pocket Scorebook', it was tatty and faded and had obviously been simply fished out of the college stationary cupboard in April 1899 and put to work. Now, 111 years on, it was bound together by little more than yellowing Sellotape and flecks of brittle glue. Yet flicking through the ten or so games contained within its tissue-like pages, it was obvious that Collins's magnificent feat was no sporting aberration.

I'd imagined his innings to be something of a one-off, yet his name appears in almost every column in every contest, either knocking up some considerable score (the week before his big one he'd scored a century) or taking a hatful of wickets. Collins 31; Collins 4–34; and in one improbable entry, Collins 9 wickets in an innings – all of them bowled. Finally I turned to his 628 not out. The precious double-page entry, the one that has been reproduced in countless anthologies of the game and which had been my constant companion as a teenager, I now held between my big fat fingers.

As a kid I may once have thrilled to the touch of a cricket ball still warm from being rubbed on Tony Buss's groin – but this was something else. Yet the overwhelming feeling that Collins's innings aroused in me was not so much a sense of wonder at the sheer extent of his endeavour, or even suppressed glee at the gruesome bowling figures, but a profound sense of sympathy for the poor sod deputed to keep score: one EW Pegler.

You can imagine the scene. The headmaster is striding purposefully across Upper Close, his master's robes flowing behind him like an academic Dracula, when suddenly he spies some poor hapless juvenile on his way for a quick fag behind the bike sheds. 'Pegler,' he bellows, 'whatever you're doing, stop it at once and come over here. They need someone to keep score for the house match. Even you should be able to manage that, and for goodness' sake try and keep awake. If I hear of any mistakes or crossings-out, it'll be six of the best for you, you miserable boy … '

On the evidence of these faded figures, Pegler would have happily settled for a sound thrashing had he known what lay in store as an alternative. It was evident from his increasingly anarchic handwriting that some sort of nervous collapse overwhelmed the poor lad. The opening entries are neat enough, regimented numbers criss-crossing the page in crisply sharpened pencil, but as Collins grinds inexorably on from ton to ton, poor Pegler's endless rows of numerals begin straggling back and forth across the page and up the margins, while the names of the bowlers are crossed out, replaced, then crossed out again.

Poor old Pegler. Years later, and by now a distinguished commander, he admitted the overall total may have been twenty or so runs adrift, but defended his mathematical incompetence by claiming he'd been 'much badgered by masters and reporters' throughout his sojourn on the scorer's table. 'An inky boy is defenceless against grown-ups,' he concluded with typically martial understatement.

I gazed upon the booklet for some minutes, turning its flimsy pages back and forth in reverent silence while Lucy and the librarian watched me discreetly from afar. Somewhere in the distance the chapel bell sounded six o'clock, and outside the windows the lamps of the main quadrangle were now twinkling in the dusk. Eventually I nodded for the librarian to step forward, and in an act of the gravest solemnity handed it back into her custody. A moment more and this jewel in Clifton's crown was once more restored to its rightful place under lock and key.

Afterwards Lucy offered me a glass of sherry in her office while I chatted to her colleague, an elderly ex-master called Raymond who confessed he spent his declining years beavering away at an unofficial history of the school.

Raymond turned out to be something of an aficionado on all things Collinsian, and filled in the gaps of the boy's short and tragic life. Like so many young men at the turn of the twentieth century, he ran headfirst into the Great War, which erupted only months after he'd left military college at Woolwich. Along with half the young men of fighting age, he soon found himself in France for his awfully big adventure, the one that would be over by Christmas.

Yet even had such a wretchedly misplaced estimate proved accurate, it would have been cold comfort to Collins's young bride Ethel. Having already been mentioned in despatches in the opening weeks of the war, her husband was killed during the first battle of Ypres on 11 November. His body was dragged back to the trenches across No-Man's-Land and hurriedly buried, but in the continual chaos that flowed back and forth across this God-forsaken spot in the following four years, his grave was lost. His details now are only commemorated on the Menin Gate.

'Par for the course, I'm afraid,' Raymong assured me. 'Of the twenty-two boys who took part in Collins's match, sixteen never made it through to Armistice Day.'

After a final vote of thank to my hosts, I returned to the car. Before leaving the house earlier today, and in anticipation of this possible final detour, I'd popped my old copy of Fry's famous book on to the passenger seat, and having now completed my quest, I sat in the car, lit by the sickly orange glow of a street lamp, turning over the pages for the first time in years and staring at these strange, surreal figures from a bygone age.

My final journey of the summer had book-ended the game in perfect parentheses, at one end a schoolboy prodigy who barely survived a month or two into the Great War, while at the other an individual whose every posture and pose defined the way ahead for the game, a lifestyle strewn with unimaginable wealth, opportunity and conspicuous show. Only a hundred years separated Pietersen and Collins. It seemed a lot more.

It was many moons since I'd last glanced at these sepia-tinted heroes. It's easy nowadays to regard such figures with their straw hats, spreading waistlines and slatted pads as something both laughable and foolish. Indeed, it's equally easy enough to laugh at Newbolt's poetic legacy that guided their conduct. Even as a teenager I remember thinking they and their surroundings looked distinctly quaint. And the game, and its sporting codes, had changed immeasurably more still in the intervening half-century. I could almost hear Nasser Hussain snorting with derision. 'Look, the game's changed, it's no longer tea on the lawn and jolly good show and one to get off the mark. You've got to be tough, fit, and above all unsentimental. These guys are the past … '

Maybe so. But I was glad I'd found them. And I was glad I'd come here, to Collins' Piece. I turned the ignition key and inched the car out on to the main road and back towards the motorway. A two-hour drive lay ahead of me. Tomorrow the championship would be decided, and by the weekend, it would all be over – until next April, of course.

In Patrick Morrah's evocative chronicle about the game in all its Victorian and Edwardian splendour, *The Golden Age of Cricket*, he describes the final days of its pre-war bloom, before the guns began pounding and the mayhem commenced. It was generally agreed that the deciding factor in the decision to suspend county cricket was WG Grace's personal intervention. 'It is not fitting at a time like the present that able-bodied men should play day after day and pleasure-seekers look on,' he declared with magisterial authority. Jupiter had pronounced, and stumps were dutifully drawn.

In one of the final matches to be completed, a team of visiting Americans, the Merion cricket club of Philadelphia, arrived to play a Kent & Ground side at Tonbridge. In the fourth innings they required an improbable matter of 153 to win in less than an hour. Yet, in the way that Americans do, they nearly managed it. With the visitors requiring a mere two runs off the final two balls to achieve a glorious victory, the Kent & Ground captain ordered his bowler to roll both deliveries along the ground so they couldn't be hit.

As a metaphor for the loss of the age of innocence, you have to admit it takes some beating.

15

Corridor of Uncertainty

It was Neville Cardus who best summed up the uncertainties of the summer game. 'It is a capricious blend of elements, static and dynamic,' he once wrote. 'You can never take your eyes away from a cricket match for fear of missing a crisis.' But even his fertile imagination would have struggled to match the final day of my summer journey for its improbable finale.

I'd been anticipating spending the final day of the season back at home with a beer and some Doritos, watching the climax on Sky. So when the phone rang soon after 10am, I nearly didn't pick it up. Yet freelancers can't help it. However much you tell yourself it'll be someone ringing to offer you lower gas prices or deals on sets of patio furniture, whenever that bloody phone starts trilling you always convince yourself it'll be the call that changes your life forever.

Stephen Spielberg has read my piece about fly-tipping in the local paper and wants me to script-edit his latest film – Simon Russell Beale had ricked his ankle at the National – or Charles Colvile has just quit his job at Sky after an altercation with Paul Allott at the breakfast bar about who should have the last butter pat.

Sounds unlikely? An actress friend of mine who hadn't worked for years once confided in me she'd decided to give up showbusiness, so sick was she of the constant, spirit-sapping unemployment. Two hours later back in her flat at Camden Town, she told Kevin Costner over the phone to 'piss off, Simmo, and stop pulling my leg' after the Hollywood star called her to discuss a role in his next movie, having seen a clip of her in a three-year-old TV drama on the box. Two minutes later his secretary called back from LA to verify her employer's identity. Five days after that she was being screen-tested in Burbank. A decade and a half on and she's now one of our most bankable movie stars.

Sadly my call wasn't from Costner, or Spielberg, or Rupert Murdoch. It was my old mate Stuart, ex-actor turned small-time entrepreneur, and occasional conscript (at least, when we were really desperate) for the Harry Baldwins. What's more, he was crying for help.

After a largely catastrophic love life stretching back several decades, Stuart had finally found love in his early fifties after meeting a Polish girl on an internet dating website. They'd been living together for several months, and he'd even been over to Poland to meet her parents, an encounter so successful that he and his imminent bride were planning to honeymoon in Krakow in the New Year.

But that was before last night. While clearing out the top shelf in the wardrobe, he'd discovered a stack of love letters to his betrothed from some muscle-bound fitness trainer working in the nearby sports club, an establishment she attended two or three afternoons a week while he was out doing deliveries. Evidently the affair had been going on for many months, involving subterfuge and deception on a grand scale.

When he'd confronted Eva on her return from her Zumba class, she'd simply packed her bags and left without giving him either an explanation or forwarding address. He hadn't slept all night, he didn't know where she was, and was staring into the abyss. At least, I think that's what he told me: his narrative was frequently interrupted by huge keening sobs and wails of desolation. I don't think I'd ever heard such heartbreak conveyed by a human voice.

These are the times when you have to decide on the important things in life. What really matters when the chips are down – male friendships that have been nurtured over many years, or a footling sporting event?

'Well, the thing is, Stuart, it's just it's the last day of the championship ...'

Of course not. What sort of bloke do you think I am?

I aimed the remote at the TV set and pressed 'off'.

'Stuart, hang on in there, buddy. I'll be with you as soon as I can.'

His reply was a grateful sniff.

It was only once I'd replaced the receiver that I realised the problem. I still thought of Stuart as living in Isleworth, where he'd resided while still treading the boards, but now I remembered – since meeting Eva he'd moved out to some God-forsaken love-nest in the back of buggery – Wiltshire, I think. If only he'd phoned me the previous night when I was on my way back from Bristol I could have been with him in half an hour. Now I was going to have to virtually retrace yesterday's route. And there were roadworks on the M4. The best I could hope for was to make it home for the final session.

Keeping in touch with vital scores when you should be doing something else is a perennial problem for sports fans. In the old days before the invention of wireless, any England fans wishing to follow developments in the Test match would gather in front of giant scoreboards and spend all day watching the numbers being changed by men on stepladders. Nowadays you may never be more than a click of a mouse or a mobile phone call away from your particular field of dreams, and yet updates on the domestic championship are still something of a communications black hole: particularly if combined with a two-hour drive down the M4 and a knackered radio.

For some reason the example in my car had recently reverted to a series of presets tuned in by the vehicle's previous owner, an Iraqi gentleman who runs a delicatessen in West Hampstead. In the intervening weeks I'd nearly caused multiple pile-ups all over southern England as I attempted to get something recognisable in English: preferably Radio 4 or 5 Live, though by now I'd even settle for TalkSport. But the radio had remained stubbornly stuck on what appeared to be a series of Middle-Eastern hip-hop stations, and I no longer had the manual.

By the time I arrived at Stuart's it was past midday and I hadn't the faintest idea of progress in any of the deciding matches. It says everything about my friend's plight that when he came out to greet me at the door I briefly mistook him for Australian all-rounder Andrew Symonds. Misery and grief clung to him like a shroud. The curtains were drawn, there were lighted incense candles burning everywhere and the CD system was playing Celine Dion singing 'My Heart Will Go On' on a continuous loop. The moment we entered the kitchen he subsided afresh into heart-rending sobs, and it was some while before a cup of tea stemmed the flood. Watching a century by Chris Tavaré felt a bit like this.

But what to do? The psychology of women has never been my strong point, yet it was obvious Stuart was looking to me to lead him out of the abyss, or at the very least to offer a friendly arm round the shoulder and some words of masculine wisdom and encouragement. Doug Insole once described a captain's role as 'PR officer, agricultural consultant, psychiatrist, accountant, nursemaid and diplomat'. I was going to need all of them if I was to be of any use to my pal today.

I pulled up a chair and sat down beside him. 'So what exactly has happened? What did she say when you confronted her?' This was something of a redundant question since Eva only speaks Polish, but my queries seemed to comfort him and he was soon recollecting his misery in between halting sobs. After several minutes I flicked a glance at the kitchen clock on the wall behind his right ear. 12.30. Probably best not to ask if we could listen to the lunchtime sports summary. It was time to get my head down and dig in for my old mucker.

By 1pm Stuart had barely progressed his story beyond their first date, and I was forced to ask if he could pause his narrative while I nipped to the loo. There'd always been a much-loved old transistor beside his bathtub in Surrey, and with luck it would have survived the move, in which case I could catch the lunchtime scoreboard without even seriously delaying his narra- tive. To my relief the radio was exactly where I'd anticipated, but years of sitting in a warm damp environment had not been kind, and having endured years of damp fingers and industrial strength aftershave, it too was useless.

Back in the kitchen I made fresh tea while he ploughed on. Two o'clock came and went, then half past, and next time I checked the clock it was 3pm and approaching rush hour. It's not that I wasn't sympathetic to Stuart's plight – on the contrary, his heartbreak was palpable and dismaying, and I was anxious to do what little I could to help. But something had changed.

If you'd told me back in April that I would soon be demon-strating all the loathsome time-honoured behavioural traits of the average middle-aged male sports fan, namely avoiding real life in favour of catching the big match, I would have scoffed, but having spent the summer among county cricket and crick-eters, keeping check on the daily scores and charting the slings and arrows of outrageous fortune across the various competi-tions, I'd rediscovered a sense of personal investment in the outcome. This summer had quietly rekindled my passion for the odd, quirky and unpredictable progress of championship cricket, and having been there at The Oval in April for the start of hostil-ities, I now wanted more than anything to be there at the end, even if 'there' was only in front of my TV set. Particularly if, as I sensed, Somerset were about to sneak their first title.

Stuart, meanwhile, was now threatening to break open the photograph album. Something had to be done. Gradually my responses became more pointed. 'What do you mean?' and 'Are you sure you're not imagining all this?' progressed to 'Oh well, what's done is done,' and 'Never mind, you've got to look on the bright side.' The fact was, my friend was in paralysing shock, and only by recounting even the smallest detail of his doomed romance was he going to gain any closure from my visit. I promised myself I'd give him till 4pm and then tell him to pull himself together.

Then a chance came my way. A close neighbour who'd heard of Stuart's distress turned up with a bottle of Scotch, and with my host happy enough to go back to the beginning and exorcise his pain afresh, I snaffled the catch with both hands. Making an entirely bogus excuse about having to pick Julia up from the airport, I slunk away, abashed and ashamed. I might still make it back for the minimum twenty overs in the last hour.

But I was about to get my comeuppance. The traffic back was terrible, and I was still labouring through roadworks near Heathrow and listening to Shadia Mansour singing 'El Kofeyye Arabeyye' when I received a text. The message was from my old schoolmate Andy, the very boy with whom I'd played automatic cricket in his parents' bedroom and who'd accompanied me on my first trip to The Oval back in 1972. Now living near Yeovil, he'd transferred his allegiances from Sussex to Somerset, and his communication left me in little doubt as to today's outcome.

'What about that, eh?' it ran. 'Even Beefy and Viv didn't get them this far.' The inference was obvious. Somerset had done it at last. The eternal Cinderella of the county circuit, one of only three sides never to win a title, they'd obviously made it home at long last. I took my foot off the accelerator and moved to the inside lane. Oh well. Never mind. I was pleased for Andy, and for Marcus Trescothick too. Quite apart from the fact he was one of the most likeable and watchable protagonists in the modern game, he and his men had strained every sinew to gain some silverware this summer, and the triumph of this most bucolic of teams, with their rustic history and uncomplicated approach, seemed to strike a blow for any right-minded traditionalist. The only pity was that I'd missed their big moment.

I finally pulled up outside our house back in London at 4.53. Julia was out till seven, so I poured myself a beer, kicked off my shoes and switched on the telly. Yet instead of discovering Tresco waist-deep in pork chipolatas and Somerset president Vic Marks performing his Carmen Miranda impression on the players' balcony, I was greeted instead with the unnerving sight of Nottinghamshire captain Chris Read being showered in Veuve Clicquot by ecstatic teammates on the pitch at Old Trafford.

It turned out that even as I'd been poodling along the North Circular, this schizophrenic season had pulled off yet another cunning stunt. With time running out and Tresco already preparing his acceptance speech across at Chester-le-Street, Notts had belted the ball to all points of the compass, declared their innings, then taken three Lancashire wickets in the final few minutes of the season, to win the title by a single solitary point.

Afterwards, poor Tresco was interviewed on air. If possible he looked even more shell-shocked than Stuart. You had to feel profoundly sorry for him. Having already lost the T20 final at the Rose Bowl off the last ball back in August, he'd been pipped at the post in the one competition that really mattered. Worse still, he now had to pick up his distraught teammates and head down to Lord's for Saturday's Clydesdale Bank final, one in which Somerset were also featuring. God knows he'd already suffered enough well-documented nervous exhaustion for one lifetime – heaven help him if he lost Saturday's match as well.

I turned down the sound and raised a silent glass to Banger, his men and all other seventeen counties. What a finale! If I had to choose a domestic season to follow, I surely couldn't have picked a better one than this.

Eventually I switched over to the news. The BBC was show-ing live coverage of Pope Benedict, who had just arrived in Britain as part of a papal visit to the UK, albeit without one of his most trusted cardinals, who had suddenly pulled out of the official visit after being quoted as describing the UK as a 'third world country' (he'd obviously spent time at Chelmsford).

Nonetheless the scene at Bellahouston Park in Glasgow left no doubt as to the pontiff's continuing popularity. He was holding a crowd of some seventy thousand spectators wrapt simply by reading out a series of liturgical statements in Latin in a quavering tenor. When he finished, a surge of genuine and heartfelt applause swept through his audience. Many cheered. A few even seemed to be weeping. Perhaps that's where the domestic game was going wrong. If the ECCB could only persuade the pontiff to do the public-address announcements at Swansea, perhaps it would yet stave off the developers.

Yet even now the season had one final twist in its tale. Even as God's emissary was climbing back into his Popemobile, another individual with allegedly superhuman powers was also waving farewell. Freddie Flintoff's departure from the spotlight was not by way of trundling through the streets in a Perspex capsule, although it would have scarcely raised an eyebrow if he had. Instead, the announcement of his retirement from the game came via a tiny screw of paper handed to Charles Colvile back at Old Trafford by a blushing floor manager just as he was unclipping his radio mike for the last time.

The news of Freddie's departure hit the other channels about thirty seconds later. By the time I'd returned once more to the Beeb, any chance of either the pontiff or Chris Reed getting much of a look-in had already been shoved aside in favour of a medley of our hero's greatest moments.

I sat idly, surfing, up and down, up and down, from BBC to Sky to CNN and back again, watching again and again the same potted tributes to the great Freddie. All the favourites were there, from his one-armed embrace of Brett Lee in 2005 to his bleary-eyed stumble in Downing Street and his run-out of Ponting in 2009. Time could not weary him, nor custom stale his infinite variety. It was odd to think he would never again be seen on a cricket field. Even odder was the thought that, if so, I was the last man but one ever to bowl to him. Not a bad epitaph to put on my gravestone, even if it would cost a fortune in stonemason's bills.

At just after 7pm the key rattled in the lock. Julia entered to see Flintoff in his famous mid-pitch pose of self-crucifixion on *Channel 4 News*, a gesture even the Pope himself would have been hard pressed to pull off with a straight face.

'What's wrong with him?'

'It's Flintoff. He's retiring.'

'What do you mean, retiring? He looks all right to me.'

'That's archive footage. It's all over.'

'What is?'

'Freddie's career. And the season. All done and dusted. No more. End of.'

She started unbuttoning her coat. 'Good. Does that mean I can expect some help with the housework now?'

'Of course.'

'No more cricket?'

'No. That's your lot.'

'You mean it?'

'Of course.'

'Good … I'll get you some rubber gloves.'

16

A Fittin' Endin' ...

It was the first Sunday in March 2011, and the traditional pre-season get together of the Harry Baldwin Occasionals.

A lot had happened in the last six months. I'd been given the all clear by the hospital consultant. AJ Harris of Leicestershire had announced his retirement, following a career in which he'd taken 451 first-class wickets. 'I've been fortunate enough to play for eighteen seasons, during which I've played with and against some of the finest cricketers to have ever graced our beautiful game,' he'd said in his final press release. Nothing became him like the leaving of it.

More recently Somerset's Marcus Trescothick had been offered a million pounds if he could replicate Albert Trott's unique feat and hit a ball clean over the roof of the Lord's pavilion during the coming season – although during a recent Q and A with the great man, which I'd attended, he admitted that the main obstacle wouldn't be middling the ball so much as the fact that Somerset weren't scheduled to play there.

In all other respects it had been a stupendous winter for fans of the game, at least on this side of the globe. Back last July Freddie Flintoff himself had assured me personally over our prawn cocktails that England would win the Ashes, and so it had proved. Yet it had been the manner of the victory so much as the result itself that had warmed the long nights of snow and frozen pipes. Andrew Strauss had captained throughout with humour and good grace, a quality that only further accentuated the snarling posturing of his beleaguered opposite number, Ricky Ponting. Several of the squad had established themselves as players of true quality – Ian Bell, whose silky touch had once again had cricketing cognoscenti reaching for the superlatives, and Jimmy Anderson, whose swing and seam had recalled memories of Tate and Bedser in their pomp.

One player had stood out above all others: Alastair Cook. It had been many years since the name of Wally Hammond had been seen or heard in such profusion, yet Cook had reminded the current generation of his predecessor's true genius. During the series Cook scored a giddying 766 runs, a run tally only exceeded by the great Wally's 903 during his Olympian height of 1928/29.

If I seemed something of an authority on the subject, it was because I'd watched the entire series on Sky. Having finally signed up, I'd kept my subscription running, and had thus been able to savour our triumph in full. I'd even cracked open a bottle of bubbly when the final wicket had fallen at Sydney in the early hours of 7 January. Best of all, Julia had come down in her jim-jams to join me. Champagne never tasted better than this.

In the weeks and months since then, I'd found my thoughts returning again and again to the events of my previous summer. I'd set out roughly a year before on a haphazard and largely serendipitous journey to see if I could rediscover my old passion for the game I'd once loved: a journey that had started at The Oval with Hari Gupta showing me his scars and ended at Bristol with Jimmy Anderson offering to show me a whole lot more. But of course, like all good journeys, it had been continually blown off course. And it was the blown-off-course bits that had proved the most memorable.

My decision to avoid international cricket in favour of rekindling my love of the domestic version had proved a good one. A low-octane series against Bangladesh had been followed by a querulous and ultimately toxic contest against Pakistan, particularly once the allegations of match-fixing burst out from the front pages of the *News of the World*. If nothing else the winter had at least obliterated those doleful memories of a game mired in controversy and bad blood.

In truth, I'd initially approached my odyssey with some trepidation. It was Australia's answer to John Arlott, broadcaster Alan McGilvray, who had originally coined the phase that seemed to sum up so much of what troubled me now, when he'd entitled his 1985 autobiography, *The Game is Not the Same*. Back then he'd merely been lamenting the increasing prevalence of helmets, player dissent, bad sportsmanship and the one-day cricket. Goodness only knows what he'd have made of the game a quarter of a century further on.

It was a contemporary writer, Gideon Haigh, who had crystallised the greatest threat to the fabric of the sport in the first decade of the new century when he'd written, 'The fault is not in our superstars but in ourselves, in that we have succeeded in turning a game in which there is possibly more scope for self-expression than any other into another means of instilling mass conformity.' And, indeed, with cricket being played twenty-four hours non-stop from arsehole to breakfast-time, my suspicion when I'd started my journey had been that I'd find a slush of sterile uniformity, a game in which players were by and large identically built, identically contoured and identically programmed.

It had only required me to get up close and personal once more to discover the truth to be markedly different. I'd dipped my toe in virtually every form of the game from county championship to village green via public school cricket and T20, and, to para-phrase Mark Twain, reports of its death had been exaggerated. On the contrary, it was doing just fine.

Championship cricket may still be played to the proverbial one man and his dog, but that had been largely the case even back when I was growing up. Yet it was still chock-full of char-acters, eccentrics and individualists, if only you could get under the bloody helmets to see them. Players such as Cosgrove of Glamorgan, Rana of Sussex and big-bottomed Steffan Jones of Derbyshire were every bit as bespoke as the players I'd once thrilled to, and you only had to witness, as I did, the laughter round the tea table in the Chesterfield pavilion to know that modern players were capable of enjoying themselves every as bit as much as their flannelled forebears.

The other forms of the game, too, had provided some memorable moments. The forty-over format, one I'd assumed to be dead in the water, had provided the tensest contest of the entire summer, albeit in the fiercely old-fashioned setting of a Sunday afternoon at Scarborough with no frills and distractions to jar its impact. Perhaps therein lay the key to its survival.

And what of T20? Brash and garish it might be, but I was now a convert. What shortcomings it may possess as a satisfying spectacle were simply due to overkill. Matthew Hoggard and Durham captain Phil Mustard had been among several cricketers to plead with the administrators for less rather than more in the future, if only to allow spectators time to save up for the next entrance fee. It wasn't the game itself but the bottomless demands of the accountants and sponsors that most threatened its health and virility.

Yet for all that, I had to acknowledge, if only to myself, that it hadn't been the cricket that most lingered in the memory so much as the collection of oddballs and eccentrics with whom I'd sampled it. Helen and her racing tips, the occupants of Moaners' Corner, Randolph and his passion for Verdi, and Ashok, sitting in his curry house underneath his tinsel-clad photo of Tamim Iqbal. Rollo and Elspeth, Memory Man at Bristol, Arthur and his long-suffering wife, forever trailing around Yorkshire by herself on mystery coach trips while he sat glued to the cricket. God, I even missed Hairy Jack.

And therein had been the greatest benefit of my journey – the rediscovery of this tiny island in all its patchwork absurdity and glory. Whether sitting amongst the toffs at Lord's or the toughs at Swansea, I'd been reminded of what an odd, rackety and thoroughly unfathomable island we live on. The Barmy Army may have kidnapped the adjective for their own collective use, but ironically it was only when you got beyond their bray-ing chants and sterile responses and let the company of ordinary spectators wash over you that you realised the riches waiting to be discovered merely by leaning across and asking if you might look at your neighbour's scorecard. It had been many years since I'd had considered spending a holiday in England. The summer of 2010 had reminded me of all I was missing.

Best of all, I'd remembered just why I'd come to love the game. Like so many jaded, middle-aged fans, in recent years I'd fallen into the wearisome trap of thinking that the sport I'd grown up with had been the best vintage and the contemporary version was a pale imitation. But the fug of nostalgia, while lending a nice tint to proceedings, doesn't always offer the clearest view.

My favourite writer of the lot, the incomparable RC Robert-son-Glasgow, had in the 1920s deftly summed up the dangers of looking back in his poem 'The One-Way Critic'. In it he describes a day spent at a county cricket match, listening to a typically grumpy old codger grumbling about the good old days and how the game and the players involved in it have gone to the dogs. Eventually the author gives up trying to plead the merits of the modern protagonists to his intransigent companion, and instead settles back to watch the game in hand. The last two lines harpoon the dangers of 'in my day' thinking with quiet, deadly economy:

> *I ceas'd: and turned to Larwood's bounding run*
> *and Woolley's rapier flashing in the sun ...*

I arrived at the Cork & Bottle soon after 4pm and bounded up to the upstairs bar. The last time I'd attempted this ascent I'd needed a Stannah stairlift. Now I felt like Fred Astaire.

They were all there once more, gathered around the same mottled table in the same corner of the bar. Perhaps older and frailer, but still recognisably the same outfit as before: Chris Buckle, laying out the last season's averages, Les Sweeney, carefully double-checking the entries in the scorebook, and Steve Sarstedt, seeing how many bacon-flavour Rancheros he could balance on his index finger.

They were delighted to see me after a year's absence, but once pleasantries had been exchanged, the mood grew more sombre. It turned out that today's gathering was not so much a celebration as a crisis summit. The Baldwins had enjoyed, if that's the right word, a tough old season in 2010. Of the scheduled eighteen fixtures, three had been rained off, while the Baldwins themselves had had to scratch a further couple after mustering only half a team. There hadn't been a single victory.

'Match managing is certainly not for the faint-hearted,' admitted Chris. 'For instance, the nine players I managed to obtain for our match against Oxshott was as a result of no fewer than seventy-one phone calls.'

'Seventy-one? You don't know you're born,' interrupted Phil Coleridge. 'I was still making calls at the restaurant table during our wedding anniversary.' Both were trumped by Les Sweeney who weighed in with 114 separate queries for the match on August bank holiday: a statistic he was able to confirm as his phone bill had itemised billing.

The personal averages were equally sobering, with nearly all the batsmen hovering in late single figures. 'We did of course score three fifties and one century,' said Chris, 'but all but one were attained by opposition players who were lent to us on the morning of the match to enable us to compete. I was naturally very pleased for them, but it was a little galling to see the difference in class.'

The bowling made for similarly doleful reading. Our only new recruit, a university graduate who'd professed himself delighted to be playing with guys who didn't take things too seriously, had announced his resignation three games later by kicking over the stumps after we'd managed to drop five catches off his opening spell. Even our youth policy had collapsed when 40-year-old Lionel had announced in July he was taking the rest of the summer off to walk the Pilgrims' Way from Canterbury Cathedral to St Peter's Basilica in Rome. Although he strenuously denied it, the feeling was that his decision to embark on such a journey of ascetic self-denial had been brought on the dodgy LBW decision he'd received at Amersham.

Frustration gradually turned to contemplation. There comes a time in the arc of every social cricket team when facts have to be faced. The Baldwins been going nearly thirty years now, and as I looked at them now, in the wintry light of a Sunday evening, it showed. Sides such as ours usually begin as a confederation of thrusting young athletes before mellowing into canny middle-aged conviviality. That's how it should be. But if they hang around long enough, collective age and decrepitude inevitably set in.

A phrase of Ian Botham's kept coming back to me as I surveyed the tired, despairing faces of my teammates, scanning the statistics for some crumb of hope and optimism for the year ahead: 'Retirement wasn't difficult,' he'd said. 'I knew the time was right. I was no longer capable of achieving the standards I'd set myself and saw no light at the end of the tunnel.'

Twelve games. Twelve losses. Second-highest specialist batsman averaging seventeen. Sufficient ducks to start a poultry farm. Half the team crocked and those that can stand daren't risk bending to stop the ball in case they slip a disc. This wasn't how it was supposed to be.

'So what are we saying?' asked Les.

'I think we know what we're saying,' replied Chris, with tears already misting his spectacles. 'I know it's hard to accept, but there really doesn't seem to be any alternative. I'd give anything for it to be different, but I know several of you have already been talking about the possibility in private in recent weeks. We have to make some hard choices.' God, he was beginning to sound like Nick Clegg.

He removed his glasses and gently massaged the bridge of his nose. The weight of a March evening seemed suddenly unbearably crushing.

'OK. Let's not make this any more painful than it is already. We all know what we're talking about. Those in favour?'

A creeping forest of hands slowly went up. Eventually, mine, too, joined them.

'Then it's unanimously agreed. We drop two matches for

next season and see if we can carry on with only sixteen on the fixture list instead of the eighteen as before. I'll tell Saffron Walden we won't be returning, and we'll drop that lot down in Leatherhead. All agreed?'

There was a general murmur of optimism. Chris offered to buy a round. Les Sweeney went for a leak. Fresh supplies of crisps were ordered. The timeless rituals of pre-season AGMs everywhere swung into place once more, each small instance signifying that life would go on – at least for another season.

Funny. For a moment I'd thought the Baldwins had been voting ourselves into oblivion. Instead, we'd agreed to carry on regardless despite all the evidence to the contrary. Stupid? Perhaps. Misplaced? Probably. But such a mindset had kept both AJ Harris and those Chilean miners going long after lesser mortals might have given up and asked for the cyanide capsules. As if to prove my point, my teammates already looked twenty years younger again.

Back out in the street at the end of the meeting, Chris and I found ourselves alone once more.

'So how was it?' he asked.

'What?'

'Your summer of watching rather than playing?'

'Terrific. I enjoyed it. I met some interesting people and saw some wonderful games.'

'Sounds good. Anything else?'

'Yes, I revisited some places that were quite special to me. Unlocked some old memories. Slew a dragon or two.'

'Uh-huh?'

'And I was the last but one person in the entire world to bowl to Freddie Flintoff.'

'Wow. Respect!' Chris attempted a high-five, but a 52-year-old accountant with glasses and a Rotary club lapel badge was never going to quite carry it off. Nonetheless, I knew he was happy for me.

'Well, it's good to have you back,' he said as he opened the door of his Volvo. 'I've got a couple of surprises up my sleeve this summer. Guess where I've applied to try and get us a game? Hambledon! The cradle of cricket! I've written to their fixture secretary and I'm waiting to hear back. Can you imagine? You, going out to open the batting for the Baldwins at Hambledon!'

'Ah well, the trick is to get well forward.'

Chris studied me for a moment. 'If you say so,' he replied. 'Anyway, we'll be kicking off as usual against Burpham on April the ninth. I'll put you down, shall I? Come to think of it, why don't you come down the day before, have supper with the family, stay overnight. It'll be good to spend some time with you.'

'I can't, I'm afraid,' I replied. 'Surrey are playing Northants at The Oval. I'd like to catch the Saturday if I can. I've got some old friends there I'd like to catch up with. But I'll be down for the Sunday, don't worry.'

My route back home took me through the nearby area known as Portobello. A warren of jazzy little streets full of odd shops and antique markets, it's normally a lively place buzzing with commerce and eccentrics. But on a Sunday evening in March it was closed and shuttered. As I hurried along the pavement, an antiquarian bookshop caught my eye. The grille had been drawn across, but in the window, and lit by a single dusty spotlight, was *Cape Summer* by Alan Ross.

Ross had been another of my favourite cricket writers, as well as one of only a handful of great poets of the game. Educated at Haileybury and bullied mercilessly throughout his schooldays, he'd eventually found solace in cricket and risen to the dizzy heights of the varsity match and a single cap for Northamptonshire. But it's for his sporting prose that he's best remembered, above all for *Cape Summer*. I still had my copy in the loft somewhere.

Ross had captured the joy of watching cricket more intuitively than perhaps anyone else: 'In other sports,' he'd written, 'people have no time to think; a cricket match is a storehouse of thought, of thought occasioned by the game itself, by the beauty, wit or intelligence of one's companion: or simply a private unravelling of problems, personal, political, moral.'

Years after first reading this passage, I'd met the man himself. Once, down at Eastbourne in the late 1990s, while watching a day of Sussex versus – somebody or other, I can no longer recall who – I'd found myself sitting next to him by the boundary edge. Now in his last years he looked pale and gaunt and, indeed, although I only half suspected it at the time, didn't have much longer to live. But it was undoubtedly my literary hero.

After I'd sheepishly introduced myself, we fell into conversation. By chance our chosen spot on the boundary rope happened to be right next to a giant fibreglass egg, one of a set of four sponsored by a local poultry firm as a marketing gimmick. The promise from the firm was that any batsman successfully hitting one smack on the full would win a thousand pounds.

Sussex had trailed these bloody eggs back and forth across the county for nearly twenty years, from Hove to Hastings to Horsham and back; and now, as always, they were here, dotted round the boundary at regular intervals, spoiling the view and generally getting in everybody's way. In all the years they'd been in existence, they'd never once been hit. Indeed, the chances of such an occurrence were so remote that their presence had become something of what you might call a standing yolk among the Sussex faithful.

Yet halfway during my afternoon with Ross, our conversation had been interrupted when Sussex batsman Paul Parker smote a ball full tilt on to the egg directly next to where we were sitting. You could have heard the cheer in the next county. The memory of who scored what on that far-away summer's afternoon has long dissolved from my middle-aged memory bank. I remember nothing of the game at all. But two things from that day will stay with me forever.

The sound of the cheer when Paul Parker hit that fibreglass egg: and the sight of Alan Ross laughing until the tears ran down his face.